COUNTRY INNS
OF THE FAR WEST

COUNTRY INNS
OF THE FAR WEST

JACQUELINE KILLEEN
CHARLES C. MILLER
California

RACHEL BARD
Pacific Northwest

ROY KILLEEN
Illustrations

101 PRODUCTIONS
San Francisco

COVER DRAWING: Bed and Breakfast Inn, San Francisco, the West's first urban B&B. Drawing by Roy Killeen, color rendering by Sara Raffetto.

MAPS: Patricia Glover.

Some of the drawings in this book have been reproduced from the inns' brochures, with permission of the inns, and are credited to the following artists or sources: Bath Street Inn, James Zimmerman; Union Hotel, Scott Gorsline; Heritage Inn, Publicity Mill; Gosby House, Robert Wecker; San Antonio House, Charlotte Morton; San Benito House, Pavesich; The Spreckels Mansion, James Dowlen; Hermitage House, T. Anna Binkley; Gramma's Bed and Breakfast Inn, Steven Lustig; Fleming Jones Homestead, Ron Scofield; The Heirloom, Helen S. Lambert; Chalet Bernensis, Steve Doty; Larkmead Country Inn, Marilyn Indelicato; Whitegate Inn, Wesley Poole; Grape Leaf Inn, Mike Fitzpatrick; Jacksonville Inn, Jim Clotier; Columbia Gorge Hotel, Herbert E. Carlson; Frenchglen Hotel, State of Oregon; Starret House, The Drawing Board; North Beach Inn; College Inn, Diane Poole; Haus Rohrbach, Nance Kruger.

Printed and bound in the United States of America.
Distributed to the book trade in the United States
by Charles Scribner's Sons, New York, and in Canada
by John Wiley & Sons Canada Limited, Toronto.

Published by 101 Productions
834 Mission Street
San Francisco, California 94103

Library of Congress Catalog Card Number 81-86322

ISBN 0-89286-196-7

CONTENTS

INTRODUCTION

Our first edition of *Country Inns of the Far West*, published in 1977, recommended only forty-eight hostelries. Those were all we could find that met our standards of charm and comfort. Another twenty-six new or recently restored inns were added to the second edition of 1979. We thought the inn boom had peaked and were little prepared for the explosion that occurred within the next few years, especially of bed and breakfast places. In researching this third edition, we have personally visited over one hundred new inns, small hotels, B&Bs and other lodgings that were candidates for this book—and revisited and reevaluated many we had previously included. Our travels stretched from British Columbia to the Mexican border, and inland as far as Idaho. Many inns seemed appealing from their attractive brochures. But in some cases we have driven as much as several hundred miles, only to find accommodations that did not meet our criterion: Would we want to stay at this inn?

What is a country inn? We define it as a state of mind, a refuge of tranquility that can be found in an urban as well as a pastoral environment. "Country" inns can and do exist in cities—in San Francisco, for example, over a dozen have opened in the past five years.

Most dictionaries define an "inn" in prosaic terms as a public house that provides food and lodging. But a country inn in our sense of the word provides much more than an answer to hunger and fatigue. A visit to one of these inns may be a journey to the past. It may be your escape from pressure, from the humdrum weekly routine. Or it may be a comfortable sojourn in a spot set amid some of our nation's most spectacular scenic areas. Or your headquarters for outdoor adventure and recreation. Or just a place where you will be well fed and well treated and can sit in the garden and breathe fresh air.

One thing we can promise you: The country inns in this book are not stereotyped. The only thing they have in common is a commitment to quality, individuality and friendliness. Otherwise each goes its own way—which is definitely not the way of the standardized, computerized motels and hotels that dominate most travel guidebooks. And that, basically, is why we come to them: for a different experience. Looking for a change, a refreshment in our lives, we happily relinquish our king-size beds to cuddle in an old-fashioned four-poster. On arising we prefer the sound of the Pacific surf or the wind in the pines or the baaing of sheep to the morning news on television. We'll patiently wait our turn in the community bathroom because time no longer matters. We'll be glad to join our fellow guests for a family-style dinner at a long wood table.

This is not to say that the inns in this book are lacking in creature comforts. True, some are rustic and simple and may date back to the turn of the century. But many do have television, even color television, telephones, elegant dining rooms, king-size beds and a modern tiled bath for each room. And all, even the recently constructed ones, demonstrate a proper regard for the best traditions of innkeeping.

In some of the inns we checked, especially those in outlying areas, the proprietors were surprised that we had come so far just to visit them. They said writers of some other guidebooks had included them without setting foot on the premises, getting their information from brochures, questionnaires and/or telephone conversations. Other inn-keepers were relieved that we were not asking for a fee, as some guides do; nor did they have to join an association, pay dues or purchase books. To be recommended herein, an inn is obliged only to maintain the highest standards for its guests.

We hope you enjoy your journey through the hostelries of the far West as much as we have enjoyed researching it for you. We also hope that you will continue to tell us about new inns that you have discovered, as well as about any changes that have taken place in those we have recommended.

RULES OF THE INN

Reservations, Deposits and Rates Reservations are advised for all of the inns in this book, especially during peak travel periods. On holidays and weekends, they are often booked for months in advance. Most of the inns require a deposit of at least one night's lodging; many require a minimum stay of two nights on the weekends. Call or write in advance and ask about the current requirements, and current rates. Due to the enormous price fluctuations of these times, we no longer quote specific rates. Inexpensive would be about the same price as a good motel in the area; expensive would equate to a first-class hotel; and moderate would be somewhere in between.

Housekeeping In many of the smaller inns, guests share a community bathroom. Be sure to clean out your tub and washbasin, pick up your towels and leave the bathroom in immaculate condition for the next guest. In many of these small places, the chambermaid is actually the innkeeper; keep your room as tidy as possible.

Tipping In the larger inns, where you are presented your check at the end of each meal, tip as you would in any hotel or restaurant. In the smaller inns, where the owner does the cooking and serving, you are not required to tip. In fact most innkeepers will not accept tips and some would be insulted. If you wish to express your appreciation, send flowers or leave a bottle of wine as you would in a friend's home. You should, however, compensate the innkeeper's helpers. Some inns have a "kitty" and divide the tips among the workers; others expect you to tip individually. We recommend that, at the end of your stay, you ask the innkeeper for advice in handling this.

CALIFORNIA MISSION COUNTRY

Southern California
Along the Big Sur
To the Monterey Peninsula
And Half Moon Bay

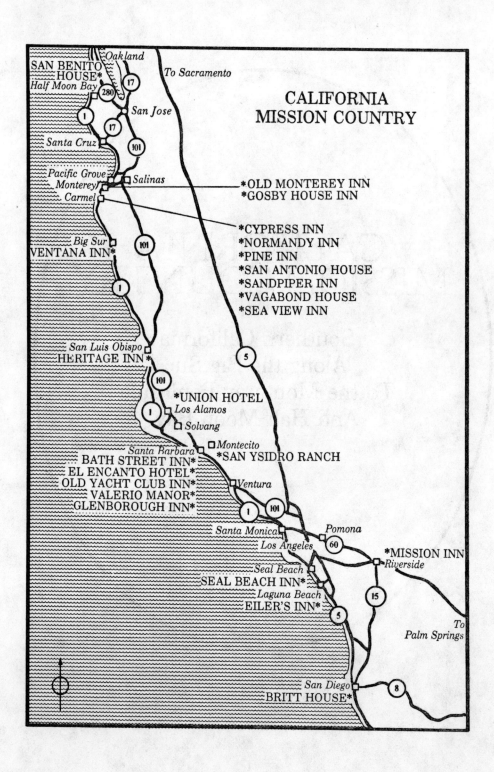

CALIFORNIA
MISSION COUNTRY

*OLD MONTEREY INN
*GOSBY HOUSE INN

*CYPRESS INN
*NORMANDY INN
*PINE INN
*SAN ANTONIO HOUSE
*SANDPIPER INN
*VAGABOND HOUSE
*SEA VIEW INN

Oakland
SAN BENITO HOUSE*
Half Moon Bay
San Jose
Santa Cruz
Pacific Grove
Monterey
Carmel
Salinas
To Sacramento
Big Sur
VENTANA INN *
San Luis Obispo
HERITAGE INN *
*UNION HOTEL
Los Alamos
Solvang
Santa Barbara
Montecito
*SAN YSIDRO RANCH
BATH STREET INN*
EL ENCANTO HOTEL*
OLD YACHT CLUB INN*
VALERIO MANOR*
GLENBOROUGH INN*
Ventura
Santa Monica
Los Angeles
Pomona
*MISSION INN
Riverside
Seal Beach
SEAL BEACH INN*
Laguna Beach
EILER'S INN*
To Palm Springs
San Diego
BRITT HOUSE*

MISSION INN
Riverside

The first innkeepers in the West were the Franciscan padres who came to California with Father Junipero Serra in 1769. They built a string of twenty-one missions from San Diego to Sonoma, spaced a day's journey apart, so that travelers could find food and lodging each night. The missions no longer take overnight guests, but the aura of those early days may still be experienced at Riverside's Mission Inn.

This magnificent example of Spanish-style architecture evolved from a thirteen-room adobe boardinghouse, built in 1876. In the 1880s the owners' son Frank Miller bought the building and embarked on an ambitious program to turn this modest hotel into one of the great resorts of the West. Over the next five decades he relentlessly added wing after wing, walkways, courtyards, fountains, bell towers, domes, galleries and chapels, all embellished with ornately carved wood and stone, stained glass, painted tiles, and religious statuary. Miller traveled widely, especially in Spain and Mexico, returning with treasures for his inn: signed Tiffany windows, valuable paintings, antique bells, carved Belgian pews, a Della Robbia wall shrine and an eighteenth-century gold-leafed altar from Mexico, around which he built a chapel dedicated to St. Francis. Eventually the hotel grew to 250 rooms surrounded by lush gardens. Its illustrious guests included Presidents William McKinley, Benjamin Harrison and William Howard Taft; Amelia Earhart, Henry Ford, John D. Rockefeller, Sarah Bernhardt and Lillian Russell. The Richard Nixons were married in the St. Francis Chapel as were the Humphrey Bogarts and the Ronald Reagans spent their honeymoon at the inn.

After Miller's death in 1935, the hotel was commercially viable until the 1950s, when a succession of owners allowed it to deteriorate; by 1976 this fabled inn was bankrupt and due to be demolished. Then

3

the city of Riverside rescued its most beloved landmark. The Riverside Redevelopment Agency purchased the inn and turned its management over to a nonprofit Mission Inn Foundation. Individual citizens and civic groups joined the effort to restore the hotel. By the end of 1981 most of the public rooms and fifty guest rooms or suites had been renovated.

Some rooms are quite simply, though comfortably, furnished, but the marble baseboards, massive carved wooden doors, and arched multipaned windows testify to the former grandeur of the place. Other rooms have been elaborately restored. One floor of the Cloister wing was redone as a Junior League project, with various individuals and organizations underwriting the cost of each room. One of the loveliest was revamped by the Kiwanis Club. This room has a high, beamed wood ceiling, tile floors, leaded windows of clear and stained glass, and intricately carved wooden doors and bed headboard. Wall niches contain antique artifacts, an archway sets off a small sitting area and a corridor leads to a tiny cubicle with stained-glass windows and a little writing desk.

Some of the inn's most luxurious rooms are located in a fourth-floor penthouse and open onto a tiled rooftop courtyard where plants surround a long reflecting pool. These have beamed ceilings some twenty-five feet high, fireplaces, antique furnishings and objects of art.

Many of the bedrooms, some with filigreed cast-iron balconies, face an interior court where a large fountain splashes and hummingbirds dart among the flowers, lemon trees, palms and magnolias. Meals are served here at umbrella-topped tables or in the adjoining tile-paneled dining room. The inn's cavernous music room, once the site of free organ concerts sponsored by Frank Miller, is now the setting for a popular dinner theater. Off the lobby are the beautiful gardens and a large swimming pool.

Orange groves surround the city of Riverside; California's first navel orange trees were planted here in 1873 from Brazilian cuttings. The city is also home of a University of California campus, several other colleges, and a number of museums devoted to collections of local history and anthropology, Indian culture and railroad memorabilia. But the chief attraction for visitors is the Mission Inn, where tours of its chapels and art galleries are conducted twice daily. The hordes of tourists and theatergoers are a detraction, as are the crafts sales that sometimes occupy the lobby, as is the somewhat impersonal management. But when you awaken to the tinkling of water in the fountains and the chime of the ancient bells, you can fantasize that you have really slept in an old California mission.

4

Mission Inn

MISSION INN, 3649 Seventh Street, Riverside, California 92501. Telephone: (714) 784-0300. Accommodations: twin, double, queen- and king-size beds; private baths with tub/shower; telephones; no television. Rates: inexpensive to expensive, no meals included. Open to the public for breakfast, lunch, dinner and Sunday brunch; full bar service. Children welcome. No pets. Cards: MC, VISA. Open all year.

Getting There: From Los Angeles take Highway 60 (Pomona Freeway) to Riverside. Take Rubidoux exit and go right on Mission Street, which becomes Seventh Street.

THE BRITT HOUSE
San Diego

After honeymooning through the inns of northern California, designer Robert Hostick and his wife Daun Martin decided that San Diego needed a similar place. In 1979 with another couple they leased a circa-1887 Queen Anne Victorian and after nine months of intensive remodeling opened the southland's first bed and breakfast inn. The three-story house with its circular tower and gabled roof was built by attorney Eugene Britt; he lived there only a few years before selling to newspaper publisher E. W. Scripps, whose family owned the house for many years.

The most dramatic feature of the Britt House is a monumental entrance hall with intricate paneled wainscoting and a stairway of oak. Three stained-glass windows rise from floor to ceiling, and a filigree of spoolwork arches over the entrance to the parlor, which contains a baby grand piano.

Robert Hostick designed the interiors, opting for country charm rather than authenticity. Each room is papered in a different pattern, but color themes of blue, burgundy, rust and eggplant appear in many variations. In the eight bedrooms, periods of furnishings are mixed with considerable grace. Marble-topped Eastlake dressers and old platform rockers mingle with wicker and rattan and comfortable queen-size beds with quilted spreads. Gilt-framed "family portraits" adorn the dressers, and Hostick's own bright contemporary collages and graphics hang on the walls. One room contains a carved headboard and couch, upholstered in brocade, both from King Ludwig's castle in Bavaria. Another is furnished with a bedroom set that belonged to Robert W. Waterman, governor of California from 1887 to 1891. The downstairs billiards room boasts a Civil War–vintage table, newly covered in rust felt.

Brightly colored rag dolls and stuffed animals recline around the bedrooms, and all have names. Harry the Hen inhabits the Music Room off the lower hall, and Ludvilla, a flamboyant ostrich, roosts on King Ludwig's bed. Bouquets of silk and fresh flowers, bowls of fruit and homemade cookies are placed in all the rooms. Two rooms have private balconies. A garden cottage has a kitchen and private bath.

Five community baths offer guests some intriguing choices of bathing. One has two "his and her" claw-legged tubs, equipped with bubble bath. Another has a sauna. All are stocked with emergency supplies of sundries travelers may have left at home: toothpaste, aspirin, needles and thread, sunburn lotion and the like.

Robert and Daun obviously have gone "the extra mile" in every detail of the Britt House, breakfast included. Daun bakes individual loaves of a different yeast bread every day—nine-grain, orange, carrot are a few—to serve on the bedroom trays along with fresh-squeezed orange juice, hard- or soft-cooked eggs and Viennese roast coffee. Wine is served in the evening, while guests peruse the large collection of menus from San Diego's many fine restaurants.

The Britt House is only two blocks from the famed Balboa Park and San Diego Zoo, and it's only a ten-minute walk to the beach and the harbor. Space does not permit a listing of this city's many tourist attractions, but among the most interesting are Old Town, a section of carefully preserved historic buildings and shops, and the Mission San Diego de Alcala, the first mission established by the Franciscan fathers in California.

BRITT HOUSE, 406 Maple Street, San Diego, California 92103. Telephone: (714) 234-2926. Accommodations: twin and queen-size beds; community baths with tub or shower, one with wheelchair access; no telephones; no television. Rates: moderate to expensive, breakfast included. No children under 12, except in cottage. No pets. Cards: MC, VISA. Open all year.

Getting There: From Los Angeles take Highway 405 or Highway 5 south to San Diego's Washington Street exit, proceed east to Fourth Street, turn right on Fourth to Maple. From Riverside, take Highway 15 to Highway 8; head west to Highway 5 and proceed south to Washington Street exit.

EILER'S INN
Laguna Beach

For many years a bearded figure in a bright-red jacket welcomed visitors to the artists' colony and resort of Laguna Beach. Each day Eiler Larsen stood on the corner of Coast Highway and Laguna Avenue, waving to all passersby. But he was no kook. Born in Denmark in 1890, he was an educated and cultured man who spoke six languages. His career as a "greeter" started while he was a messenger clerk on the New York Stock Exchange and spent his lunch hours waving to the passing limousines on Wall Street to cheer up "the dreary, drab world of high finance." Eiler developed his greeting skills during the Depression in Washington, D.C., and later headed west to San Francisco, Carmel and eventually Laguna. Here he supported himself by gardening, and was so loved by the citizens that in 1963 the city of Laguna Beach proclaimed him Official Greeter. Eiler died in 1975, but his memory lives on in the hearts of the millions he greeted over the years and in his new namesake, Eiler's Inn, located just up the Coast Highway from his favored corner.

Today innkeepers Kay Trepp and Jonna Iversen (the latter was born in the same town as Eiler) offer guests a welcome as warm as the Official Greeter's. They renovated a small thirty-year-old hotel, turning the lower store-fronts into a cozy game room and living room. Both are equipped with contemporary overstuffed couches covered in rich fabrics and lots of pillows, and an enormous supply of books and games. The living room has a corner fireplace with a Victorian mantel and a raised brick hearth that extends around one side of the room. A jigsaw puzzle is usually in progress.

The most charming feature of this inn, however, is an interior brick patio filled with potted orange trees, impatiens and fibrous begonias. The hotel, with its balconied second story, encloses three sides of the patio; a wooden fence covered with honeysuckle protects the fourth side. Round tables topped with potted flowers nestle around a pretty fountain. A buffet breakfast of coffeecake, fruit and hard-cooked eggs is set out here each morning; wine and cheese are served here in the evening, and on Saturday nights a classical guitarist entertains.

All the twelve bedrooms open to this secluded courtyard. Two also open to a large rear deck, which all the guests may use for sunning. From here you can view the Pacific; the beach is only a half-block away. The rooms are carpeted and appointed with English antiques, floral-patterned sheets and quilts, and fresh flowers. There is one suite with a living room, a fireplace, a kitchen and an ocean view.

The beaches and the many antique stores, crafts shops and art galleries are year-round attractions at Laguna. From mid-July until late August the famed Festival of Arts and Pageant of the Masters takes place. And only a short distance south is Mission San Juan Capistrano, founded by Father Junipero Serra seven years after his arrival in California and noted for the swallows that leave and return on precisely the same dates each year.

EILER'S INN, 741 South Coast Highway, Laguna Beach, California 92651. Telephone: (714) 494-3004. Accommodations: twin and queen-size beds; private baths with stall showers; no telephones; television in game room only. Rates: high moderate to expensive, breakfast included. Children not encouraged. No pets. Cards: MC, VISA. Open all year.

Getting There: From Los Angeles take Highway 5 or 405 south to Highway 133 and head west; turn left on Highway 1 (Coast Highway). From San Diego take Highway 5 north; just beyond San Clemente turn off on Highway 1 north to Laguna Beach.

SEAL BEACH INN
Seal Beach

During the 1920s Seal Beach was a popular playground for the wealthy residents of Hollywood and Pasadena. The town was the last stop on an electric railway that later extended to Newport Beach. But during Seal Beach's heyday, gambling palaces, wooden bathhouses and small hotels abounded. The only one of the hotels remaining is the Old Seal Beach Inn, a twenty-three-unit structure that was being operated as an unkempt motel when Jack and Marjorie Bettenhausen discovered it in 1977.

The Bettenhausens aspired to create an inn with an old-world atmosphere, reminiscent of those they had enjoyed in their European travels. To the nondescript motel-like exterior they added window boxes, shutters, carved archways and blue canopies over the doorways. They paved the parking lot with brick and planted flowering shrubs all around: roses, geraniums, jasmine, camellias, hibiscus and oleander. Ornate old street lamps from Long Beach now illuminate the courtyard at night.

To furnish the rooms Jack and Marjorie made cross-country treks,

9

returning with truckloads of antiques and bric-a-brac from Chicago, New Orleans and New York. The result is a busy and homey potpourri of periods: Early American and Victorian furnishings, bentwood love seats and overstuffed hideabeds, ruffled eyelet café curtains and lace tablecloths, accessories that range from collections of orange-crate labels to Art Nouveau pieces, from Renoir prints to a wicker hatstand with a 1930s-style floppy hat. Hollywood also gets into the act: A four-poster headboard from John Barrymore's bed occupies one room; a shower curtain with a nearly life-size painting of Esther Williams as a butterfly hangs in a bath; and a wood and stained-glass door from Universal Studios opens to the bridal suite that's bedecked with lace and rose satin.

The rooms range from tiny (about ten by twelve feet) to large, the latter with sitting areas and completely equipped kitchen bars. A penthouse suite has a flower-filled private deck, a large living room, a full kitchen with a breakfast nook, and two old-fashioned sleeping porches.

"The look of an inn is important," Marjorie believes, "but loving people and being hospitable are even more important." And she does these very well. Plenty of reading material is found in the downstairs library (as well as in the rooms), along with chess sets, Scrabble boards, puzzles and a decanter of sherry to sip by the fire. In the adjoining tea room a European-type breakfast is served of freshly baked croissants, orange juice and Viennese or French roast coffees. Both rooms open to a patio with another touch of Hollywood—a kidney-shaped swimming pool.

Marjorie's hospitality extends to helping her guests enjoy Seal Beach. The beach is only a block from the inn, with a pier, boat excursions, fishing and a windsurfing school. The Long Beach Marina and its Seaport Village are only five blocks away. And there are shops, boutiques and eighteen restaurants in the area.

SEAL BEACH INN, 212 Fifth Street, Seal Beach, California 90740. Telephone: (213) 493-2416. Accommodations: twin, double, queen- and king-size beds; private baths with tub/showers or stall showers; no telephones; color televisions. Rates: moderate, Continental breakfast included. Children welcome. No pets. Cards: AE, MC, VISA. Open all year.

Getting There: From Los Angeles take Highway 605 south to the beach; take Seal Beach Boulevard exit and turn left to Highway 1; turn right and head north; turn left on Fifth Street.

SANTA BARBARA

In 1786 the Spanish padres founded their tenth mission at the base of the Santa Ynez Mountains, which rise from the bay at Santa Barbara. After the 1812 earthquake, the mission was rebuilt and became known as Queen of the Missions for the beauty of its Moorish-Spanish architecture and the affluence of the surrounding ranches, orchards, gardens and vineyards. The resort city of Santa Barbara still retains the aura of its Spanish heritage. Red-tile–roofed buildings and old adobes, many enclosing inner patios, grace the palm-lined streets. There are splendid beaches, and sportfishing, plus botanical and zoological gardens. Excellent restaurants abound. The Santa Barbara Museum of Art houses a number of international collections; other museums focus on local history and natural history. And a visit to the mission, one of the most beautiful and well preserved in the state, recalls the days when the padres were this city's only innkeepers.

Getting There: From San Francisco or Los Angeles, Highway 101 leads directly to Santa Barbara, which is also serviced by United Airlines and Amtrak.

SAN YSIDRO RANCH
Montecito

Among the vast holdings of Mission Santa Barbara was San Ysidro, a citrus and cattle ranch high in the Santa Ynez Mountains, with views of the oak-studded hills sloping to the Pacific far below. After the missions were secularized, new owners built rustic stone and wooden cottages among the groves of orange trees, eucalyptuses and palms. By 1893, San Ysidro had become a guest ranch. The old adobe, built by the Franciscans in 1825, still stands. And guests dine today in a stone building once used as a citrus packing house.

San Ysidro's most illustrious era was in the 1930s and 1940s when Ronald Colman and State Senator Alvin Weingand jointly owned the ranch. The guest book from those years reads like a combination of *Burke's Peerage* and *Who's Who* in politics, literature and show business. Sir Winston Churchill wrote part of his memoirs in a house shaded by a large magnolia tree. Somerset Maugham produced several short stories in a cottage banked by geraniums. John Galsworthy sought seclusion here to work on the *Forsyte Saga*. David Niven, Merle

11

San Ysidro Ranch

Oberon and Rex Harrison found life at the ranch a respite from the glitter of Hollywood. Laurence Olivier and Vivien Leigh were married in the gardens. And later John F. Kennedy brought his bride to San Ysidro for their honeymoon in an ivy-covered stone cottage.

After Colman and Weingand, San Ysidro had a succession of owners. Through years of neglect, its facilities degenerated along with its reputation. The ranch was in deplorable condition by 1976 when it was rescued by Jim Lavenson, former president of the Plaza Hotel in New York City, and his wife, Susie.

After searching over a year for a hotel of his own, Lavenson had come west to bid on the Santa Barbara Biltmore, but ended up buying San Ysidro instead. "Everyone thought I was crazy and so did I. The buildings hadn't been painted for fifteen years," he guesses. Hardly a plant or a blade of grass was still alive. "There was one lawn mower and one vacuum cleaner and neither worked." Now the cottages gleam with white paint outside. Susie charmingly furnished them with her own antiques interspersed with bargains culled from sales and the Salvation Army.

Most of the cottages contain a living room and bedroom, with a wood-burning fireplace in each. Many have enclosed porches with views of the ocean or the wooded creek that runs through the property. Susie has splashed the rooms with color: bright upholstery and carpets, flowery quilted bedspreads, prints and paintings, bowls of fresh flowers, books. And the Lavensons say "welcome" in a very personal way: Each arriving guest finds his own name etched on a shingle by his cottage door.

Another custom instigated by Lavenson is the "honor bar." At a well-stocked table in the lounge of the main hacienda, guests mix their own drinks and write up their own chits. Among other comforts of the lounge are a large stone fireplace, a piano, game tables and a chessboard. Next door the dining room serves three meals a day, from hearty breakfasts to candlelit dinners.

Today San Ysidro's lovely gardens are abloom with marigolds, daisies, roses and geraniums, and the orchards are again bearing fruit. Lavenson has rebuilt the stables to shelter the fine quarter horses and Arabians that guests may ride over five hundred miles of mountain trails. The tennis court has been resurfaced and two new courts added. The heated swimming pool is surrounded by gardens and neatly tended lawns; some rooms have private Jacuzzis as well. And for evening entertainment, there's an excellent combo in the stone cellar of the dining house.

13

SAN YSIDRO RANCH, 900 San Ysidro Lane, Montecito, California 93108. Telephone: (805) 969-5046. Accommodations: twin, double and king-size beds; private baths with tub/shower; telephones in all rooms; no television. Rates: expensive to very expensive, no meals included; extra charges for tennis and horseback riding. Open to the public for breakfast, lunch and dinner; full bar service. Children welcome. Extra charge for pets and for boarding horses. Cards: AE, MC, VISA. Open all year.

Getting There: From Santa Barbara take Highway 101 south to Montecito; take San Ysidro Road east through Montecito Village to San Ysidro Lane.

EL ENCANTO HOTEL
Santa Barbara

High in the hills above Santa Barbara's old mission, this gracious Mediterranean-style hotel offers breathtaking views of the city, the Pacific Ocean and the Channel Islands. The main building was built in 1915 to provide student-faculty housing for the University of California campus that was originally located across the way. Over the years bungalows and stucco villas were built in the surrounding nine acres of lush tropical gardens. El Encanto has been operated as a hotel since the mid-1930s, but in recent years it had become quite shabby. When Eric and Ksenia Andreoli bought the place in 1977, weeds choked the gorgeous foliage, broken windows and torn screens bespoke neglect.

Andreoli, a former developer of franchises for Hilton, restored the hotel and redecorated it in French country style. An auberge in the south of France was his model. Window boxes filled with geraniums flank the canopied entryway. Beyond the etched-glass doors, in the public rooms, he has created a visual symphony, orchestrated with many different fabrics in shades of rust and blue, natural woods and an abundance of plants. A spacious lounge is filled with chairs of wicker and rattan cushioned in a variety of patterns. Fireplaces and love seats upholstered in floral prints grace the cozy living room and adjoining library. And in the dining room, flowered wallpaper harmonizes with provincial-patterned chinaware; ceiling fans slowly revolve overhead and large windows frame the dramatic view.

El Encanto's gardens are planted with bougainvillea, hibiscus, banana trees, pines and palms. Bird-of-paradise and petunias border the brick walkways that lead to the guest cottages. Some, but not all, of

14

these have been remodeled. The most lavish are one- or two-bedroom villas with fireplaces, kitchenettes and private balconies or patios, some with tiled fountains. In 1978 Andreoli constructed a two-story building of contemporary design that contains another twenty 2-room units. These have corner fireplaces, wet bars, and balconies or patios, but the bedrooms are smaller than in the older buildings. The least attractive accommodations here are the small bedrooms in a one-story motel-style building.

All guests may share in the use of the tennis courts and the swimming pool and in the pleasure of strolling in the beautiful grounds. Here you encounter joyful surprises: a swing set in a little lawn surrounded by a blaze of cyclamen and lilies, a grape arbor enclosing a lily-filled reflecting pool. Whether a guest at El Encanto or not, every visitor to Santa Barbara should at least come here for a drink at sunset. Seated on the patio under colorful umbrellas, with the tile-roofed town far below and the sea beyond, you would truly think you were on the French Riviera, rather than the coast of California.

EL ENCANTO HOTEL AND GARDEN VILLAS, 1900 Lasuen Road, Santa Barbara, California 93103. Telephone: (805) 965-5231. Accommodations: one- to three-room units; twin, double, queen-size and king-size beds; private baths, some with tub/shower, some with tub or shower only; some fireplaces; telephones; color television; villas have fireplaces, balconies or patios and kitchenettes. Rates: moderate to very expensive, no meals included. Open to the public for breakfast, lunch, dinner and Sunday brunch; full bar service. Children welcome. No pets. Cards: AE, MC, VISA. Open all year.

Getting There: From Highway 101, take Mission Exit east; when road ends at Laguna, turn left at the Mission, then turn right on Los Olivos; where road forks, take right fork, Alameda Padre Serra; from here follow signs to El Encanto.

OLD YACHT CLUB INN
Santa Barbara

The bed and breakfast phenomenon did not reach Santa Barbara until late in 1980. But within eight months four small inns opened and their owners banded together to form a guild to refer guests and to promote each other. No central reservation service exists, but if one inn is filled, the innkeeper can give you a general idea of availability of rooms elsewhere.

The Old Yacht Club was the first of Santa Barbara's B&Bs. The two-story bungalow was built in 1912, facing the beach, and for a while served as temporary headquarters for the Santa Barbara Yacht Club, which had washed out to sea in a storm. Thus the name, though nothing else is nautical here. The house was moved a block inland from the beach in the 1920s and is now decorated with homey, country-style furnishings. The large living room–dining area has a fireplace and a bookcase stocked with a set of the Harvard Classics. Big windows look out onto a wide front porch, lawn and gardens. Innkeeper Nancy Donaldson loves to cook and puts a lot of effort into the breakfasts. She usually serves an omelet (perhaps zucchini or spinach) or French toast, in addition to home-baked breads, and fruit and juice. She will also cook a five-course dinner (with advance notice) for her guests and/or the guests at the three other guild inns.

The four upstairs bedrooms are decorated primarily in warm shades of rose and gold, with plaid or print spreads and matching draperies edging the lace-curtained windows. Fresh flowers and decanters of sherry are set on the tables. In the two front rooms, French doors open to a private balcony where you can hear the ocean, though it's obscured from view. But the beach is only a block away.

OLD YACHT CLUB INN, 431 Corona Del Mar, Santa Barbara, California 93103. Telephone: (805) 962-1277. Accommodations: double and queen-size beds; two community baths with tub/shower and stall shower, sinks in bedrooms; no telephones; no television. Rates: moderate, breakfast included, dinner (with advance notice) extra. Children over 14 welcome. No pets. Cards: MC, VISA. Open all year.

Getting There: From Highway 101, take Cabrillo Boulevard exit (Milpas Street) to Cabrillo Boulevard; turn left to Corona del Mar, and turn left again.

THE GLENBOROUGH INN
Santa Barbara

Santa Barbara's three other new B&Bs are located within a few blocks of each other in a residential area close to the downtown shops, restaurants and museums, and an easy bike ride from the mission. Glenborough was the first of these inns to open. Innkeepers Jo Ann Bell and Pat Hardy have decorated the turn-of-the-century house in an old-fashioned style. The small, formal parlor has a velvet-upholstered settee pulled up to a Franklin stove. An old Victrola is stocked with records. Most of the four upstairs bedrooms are furnished with antiques: brass or oak or four-poster beds, patchwork or velvet quilts, marble-topped chests, wickerware and curtains of old textiles, crochet, knitting or lace. A collection of nineteenth-century watercolors on loan from a local gallery decorates the walls.

Jo Ann and Pat take pride in the small personal touches they provide: flowers, plants, and decanters of purified water in the rooms; beds turned down at night with a mint on the pillow; towels and soap changed twice daily. Each breakfast tray is set with a silver coffeepot, a lace mat, a linen napkin, homemade coffeecake or nut bread, a fruit plate and juice. You may have this in your room or out in the pretty rear garden. In back of the lawn, they've built a brick and redwood hot tub with a fence to insure complete privacy for individuals or couples who may want to bathe in the nude. And for a small extra charge they provide a "spa package" of fruit, cheese, and a "rubber ducky."

At this writing the Glenborough innkeepers are readying an 1880s cottage across the street as an annex. They have planned a Victorian decor with canopied beds. The cottage will contain two bedrooms and two suites with fireplaces and kitchenettes; occupants will be welcome to enjoy the spa and garden at the main inn and to join the other guests for wine in Glenborough's parlor each night.

THE GLENBOROUGH INN, 1327 Bath Street, Santa Barbara, California 93101. Telephone: (805) 966-0589. Inn accommodations: double and queen-size beds; two shared baths with tub/shower; no telephones; no television. Cottage accommodations: twin and queen-size beds; private baths; no telephones; no television. Rates: moderate to expensive, Continental breakfast included. Children over 12 welcome. No pets. Cards: MC, VISA. Open all year.

Getting There: Take Bath Street exit off Highway 101.

VALERIO MANOR
Santa Barbara

The gracious, homelike air of this inn belies its history. Valerio Manor was built in 1904 as the Blanchard-Gamble Boarding School for Girls, dedicated to the "proper upbringing" of young ladies. Later it quartered the boarders from the Santa Barbara Girls' School and at one time served as a sorority house when the University of California campus was located nearby. In fact it was operated as a women's boardinghouse until 1976. Joyce Simon and Rebecca Wamsley bought the building in 1980 for a bed and breakfast inn.

The five bedrooms have a handsome country-style ambience— lots of shutters, wicker and rattan chairs, plants and flowers, paintings and prints by local artists. Three of the rooms have wood-burning fireplaces; all have small sitting areas where a decanter of sherry is provided. But each is distinctively decorated with considerable charm. One has a southwestern motif with a bedspread of hopsacking and a Hopi Indian blanket on the wall. Another boasts a sun-splashed alcove with mullioned windows framing a giant camellia bush outdoors, its pink tones picked up in a floral quilted bedspread. This room was a private bath, two others have an adjoining bath and the other two share a stunning bathroom with a raised tile area resplendent with plants.

Breakfast is served in bed, or in the formal dining room, or in a plant-filled lanai or on the deck outside. Guests are encouraged to use the grand piano and guitar in the spacious living room, which also has a fireplace. French doors lead to a garden and lawn, where a croquet game is often in progress. Bicycles are available for a small fee to explore the sights of Santa Barbara.

VALERIO MANOR, 111 West Valerio Street, Santa Barbara, California 93101. Telephone: (805) 682-3199. Accommodations: twin, queen- and king-size beds; private bath with shower, semiprivate bath with tub, shared bath with tub/shower; no telephones; no television. Rates: moderate, Continental breakfast included. No children under five. No pets. No credit cards. Open all year.

Getting There: From Highway 101 take Chapala Street exit north; turn left on Valerio. Pick-up service from train or airport provided.

BATH STREET INN
Santa Barbara

The newest of Santa Barbara's quartet of B&Bs occupies the oldest
building: an 1885 three-story house with a gabled roof. Innkeepers
Susan Brown and Nancy Stover have kept the vintage charm of the
place, while rebuilding the rear to focus on the lovely gardens and views
of the Santa Ynez Mountains.

Some Victorian overtones remain in the attractive living room,
where wine is poured afternoons in front of a big fireplace; leaded glass
doors open to a shady side garden. From the breakfast room in back,
French doors lead to a deck and a brick patio that offer other
alternatives as a setting for your juice, coffee and croissants on sunny
mornings. Beyond the garden another covered patio serves as a
barbecue area. A rotisserie, hibachi, refrigerator and dishes are
furnished for guests who want to play backyard chef; they must provide
only their food. Susan and Nancy also plan to install a Jacuzzi here early
in 1982.

Books, decanters of port, and flowers are in all the bedrooms.
Three rooms occupy the second floor, and one of these has a small
sitting area and a flower-hung balcony. Two other bedrooms nestle
under the top-floor eaves, the beds set in alcoves draped with floral
patterns that match the spreads and window curtains. The third floor
also has a common room for use by all guests. It's equipped with love
seats, games and puzzles; nothing fancy, but as Susan says, "It's a place
where you can relax and put your feet on the table."

19

The Bath Street Inn should really be classified as a BBB&B: bed, breakfast, bath and bicycles. The baths here are very special, with basins set into Victorian dressers, and two have gigantic claw-footed tubs where you can soak with a view of the mountains after a bike tour of town. Bicycles are provided with the compliments of the house.

BATH STREET INN, 1720 Bath Street, Santa Barbara, California 93101. Telephone: (805) 682-9680. Accommodations: twin, double and king-size beds; one private bath with view tub, two shared baths, one with stall shower and one with view tub; no telephones; no television. Rates: moderate, Continental breakfast included. Children over 14 sometimes accepted midweek. No pets. No cards. Open all year.

Getting There: From Highway 101 take Bath Street exit.

UNION HOTEL
Los Alamos

In the sleepy little agricultural town of Los Alamos, Dick and Teri Langdon, with a dedicated staff, have recreated the spirit of 1880 in the Union Hotel. The original hotel was built of wood that year and served as a Wells Fargo stagecoach stop until it burned down in 1886. In the early 1900s the hotel was reconstructed in Indian adobe and renamed the Los Alamos Hotel. Then in the 1960s new owners modernized the place and removed whatever traces of antiquity were left

When Dick Langdon bought the hotel in 1972, he vowed to restore it as it was originally. With the help of master craftsman Jim Radhe, he dismantled twelve old barns and rebuilt the hotel's facade exactly as it appeared in an 1884 photograph. Inside they stripped decades of paint to reveal the original woodwork and brass. Rooms were papered with colorful Victorian prints.

Dick spent a year traveling the United States to find antiques. In the high-ceilinged downstairs parlor, a pair of two-centuries-old Egyptian burial urns found in Alabama flank an intricately chiseled fireplace mantel from a mansion in Pasadena. A coffee table was constructed from an oak-framed copper bathtub. There's an 1885 Singer sewing machine, chandeliers from Lee J. Cobb's home, and the hotel's original safe, blackened on one side from an early shooting. Swinging doors, from a bordello in New Orleans, lead into a saloon with a 150-year-old bar of solid African mahogany.

The large dining room contains furnishings and gaslights from a plantation in Mississippi. Tables are set with lace cloths and an array of old chinaware, no two dishes quite alike. Meals are family-style country cooking with some recipes derived from a nineteenth-century cookbook that Teri found: for dinner, tureens of soup, corn bread, platters of beef and country-baked chicken; for breakfast, eggs Benedict or bacon and eggs served with potatoes, cinnamon rolls, juice and coffee.

Upstairs, the fourteen rooms contain some beds that could be museum pieces: a two-hundred-year-old Australian brass and cast-iron bedstead with insets of cloisonne, and an original Murphy bed, concealed in a mahogany armoire. Vintage patchwork quilts and crocheted spreads serve as covers, and even the bedside Bibles are circa 1880. Langdon designates his rooms as dry rooms (sharing a bath) and wet rooms (private bath).

In and out of the hotel, Dick has created a flurry of old-time activity for his guests. An upstairs parlor houses a Brunswick pool table inlaid

21

with ivory. The yard is now an 1880s park, equipped with old-fashioned street lights and park benches, brick walkways, and (with a nod to the present) a swimming pool, and a Jacuzzi concealed under the floor of a Victorian gazebo. After dinner each night he throws a party for his guests in the saloon with complimentary wine and popcorn; innkeeper Doris Coen even tells ghost stories. And after breakfast each morning guests are shown the sights of Los Alamos in a 1918 touring car.

The area around Los Alamos has its own attractions. Many guests enjoy touring the eight local wineries or taking a picnic basket, prepared by the hotel, to nearby Zaca Lake. Solvang, a re-creation of a Danish village is not far away. And if the 1880s become too much, you can always slip back another century by visiting the area's two missions: La Purisima Concepcion and Santa Inez.

UNION HOTEL, 362 Bell Street (P.O. Box 616), Los Alamos, California 93440. Telephone: (805) 344-2744. Accommodations: twin, double and king-size beds; some private baths with tub/shower; community baths with tubs and showers; no television; no telephones. Rates: high moderate to expensive, breakfast included. Open to the public for dinner; full bar service. No children. No pets. No credit cards. Open all year, Friday, Saturday and Sunday only; also open Thanksgiving.

Getting There: Highway 101 passes through Los Alamos north of Santa Barbara.

HERITAGE INN
San Luis Obispo

"We like to think that history is repeating itself," say Rob and Kathy Strong when relating the history of their inn. The ten-bedroom house was built in 1901 by city constable Manuel Herrera for his large family. Later the building served as a lodging house, first for a group of professional men who called themselves the Bachelors Club and then for college students from nearby Cal Poly. The county purchased the house in 1974 and used it to house the YMCA and later county offices. In early 1981 when the county needed the land for a parking lot, the Strongs purchased the house at auction and set out to find a site for it. The Herrera family originally built the house near the center of San Luis Obispo on a corner where Highway 101 intersected with Highway 1. Its new location is at the freeway junction of the two highways, by coincidence on land purchased from members of the Herrera family.

Looking somewhat out of place among its neighboring buildings—modern motels—Heritage Inn offers the kind of hospitality that travelers experienced in an earlier era. While the motel guests wait in line for breakfast in the coffee shop across the street, visitors to Heritage House partake of a fresh fruit cup, homemade breads and hot chocolate or coffee in front of a cheery fire. While the motel guests tote cardboard ice buckets back to their rooms at cocktail hour, cheese, apples and local wines are offered at Heritage Inn beside yet another fireplace in the pretty blue and white parlor.

Eight bedrooms have been refurbished for guests, with antiques and canopied brass or wicker beds. Tile-hearthed fireplaces were added to four of them; two rooms have terraces and others have window seats with views of the surrounding mountains and the woods behind the inn. While the motel guests are fumbling for their light switches after a night out, those staying at the inn will find their beds turned down and a homemade cookie on the pillow with a note: "Sweet dreams."

On the bank of a creek that runs by the inn the Strongs have built a gazebo with picnic tables nearby. Bicycle paths lead through the wooded area. Picnic baskets (for an extra charge) and bicycles (at no charge) are provided by the inn. These are handy, too, for exploring the surrounding countryside. The town of San Luis Obispo has many quaint shops, the old mission and the mission plaza to see. At nearby Avila Beach and Morro Beach you'll find deep-sea fishing. Many local wineries are open for tours. And the fabled castle built by William Randolph Hearst for Marian Davies is only a thirty-minute drive up the coast at San Simeon.

HERITAGE INN, 978 Olive Street, San Luis Obispo, California 93401. Telephone: (805) 544-7440. Accommodations: double and queen-size beds; community baths with tubs, sinks in bedrooms; no telephones; no television. Rates: moderate, Continental breakfast included. No children under 16. No pets. No smoking within the inn. Cards: MC, VISA. Open all year.

Getting There: Take Morro Bay exit off Highway 101; head west across freeway and turn left on Olive Street.

VENTANA INN
Big Sur

Between San Simeon, where Hearst built his castle, and Monterey, the Santa Lucia Mountains rise precipitously above the incessantly pounding Pacific surf. Today Highway 1 traverses this rugged terrain across high bridges and along niches blasted out of the cliffs. The Spanish missionaries found this section of the coast impassable and detoured inland. But this very remoteness appealed to one of the first settlers, a Yankee sea captain with the unlikely name of Juan Bautista Roger Cooper who landed his cargoes at the mouth of Big Sur River to avoid paying customs duties to the Mexicans in Monterey. The struggles of the homesteaders who later tried to farm this land inspired the poetry of Robinson Jeffers. But it was another writer who shaped the destiny of Big Sur. Henry Miller moved here in 1944, seeking the serenity of the coastal mountains after his expatriate days in Paris. Other artists followed, and for the next decade or so Big Sur was a hardworking bohemian community.

Only recently has the traveler to Big Sur been able to sleep in style. In 1975, the Ventana Inn was built on a meadow twelve hundred feet above the Pacific. The contemporary architecture is spectacular, with soaring ceilings, giant beams, unexpected angles and planes. From every room there are views of the mountains, the meadow or the ocean far below. The rooms are paneled with knotty cedar and handsomely appointed with wicker furniture, hand-painted headboards and patchwork quilts from Nova Scotia. Some have Franklin stoves, or window seats tucked in alcoves. All have private balconies or patios and luxurious carpeted baths. There are also some two-story units with kitchenettes and living rooms.

A fire in the lobby helps remove the chill from the morning fogs that often shroud the Santa Lucia range. Here guests receive a light breakfast: freshly squeezed orange juice, breads and pastries from Ventana's own bakery, assorted fruits and coffee. Across the meadow on another hilltop is the Ventana's restaurant, which offers a diverse selection of lunch and dinner dishes.

There is a large swimming pool at Ventana, a sauna and a Jacuzzi. And there are hiking trails in the mountains above. Down the road is Nepenthe, a restaurant and bar of intriguing design built around a cabin that Orson Welles once bought for Rita Hayworth (although they never lived there). Today on a sunny afternoon the broad deck is crowded with locals and visitors sipping wine or beer, while enjoying the recorded classical music and a breathtaking view of the coast.

VENTANA INN, Big Sur, California 93920. Telephone: (408) 667-2331. Accommodations: queen-size beds or twin queens; private baths with tub/shower; television; telephones. Rates: very expensive, Continental breakfast included. Restaurant open to the public for lunch and dinner; full bar service. Small children discouraged. No pets. Cards: AE, DC, MC, VISA. Open all year.

Getting There: From San Francisco, follow directions to Monterey and take Highway 1 south. From Los Angeles, take Highway 101 to San Luis Obispo and Highway 1 north.

MONTEREY PENINSULA

In 1770 Father Junipero Serra founded Mission San Carlos in Monterey, the second in California's chain of missions. The following year he moved the mission to Carmel, and later returned here to spend his last years. The Spanish military expedition that Serra accompanied had established a presidio in Monterey. In 1775 Spain designated Monterey as the capital of California, and so it remained through the Mexican rule until the American flag was raised over the Customhouse in 1846.

Monterey had become a cultivated town, where the Spanish citizens and their families lived auspiciously in two-story adobe casas with roofs of red tile. Then the Yankees discovered the abundance of whales offshore and turned this sedate Spanish community into a bustling whaling port. Sardine fishing brought added prosperity; west of town, Cannery Row was built and later immortalized in the works of John Steinbeck. Today many of the old adobes are open to the public or house restaurants and shops. And after the sardines had all but disappeared, Cannery Row was converted into a complex of shops and dining places.

Steinbeck was not the only writer beguiled by this lovely peninsula. Robert Louis Stevenson lived in Monterey in 1879. Then after the turn of the century a group of writers and artists settled in Carmel. Edward Weston, Maynard Dixon, Ambrose Bierce, Don Blanding, Lincoln Steffens and Robinson Jeffers lived here over the years. Although Carmel is built in a potpourri of architectural styles—from Victorian and half-timbered cottage to neo-Spanish—new construction or remodeling is strictly controlled to preserve the woodsy, village-like quality of the picturesque streets.

Few places in the West offer such diverse recreational facilities as the Monterey Peninsula. There are eight public and four private golf courses. Sailboats may be chartered in Monterey Bay. Skin diving, scuba diving, fishing, tennis, polo matches—they're all here. Then there is the spectacular shoreline to explore from the cypress-bordered white sand dunes of Carmel to the rocky coves and hidden beaches of Lovers Point. Carmel is a shopper's paradise with a plethora of crafts, jewelry, clothing and antique stores. It's a sightseer's mecca, too, with choices that include reliving history at the old mission or viewing the palatial mansions along Pebble Beach's famed Seventeen-Mile Drive. The Monterey Peninsula probably has more restaurants per capita than any other area of the West. The two hundred or so dining places encompass almost every ethnic cuisine.

Getting There: From San Francisco take Highway 101 to the Monterey Peninsula cut-off, north of Salinas; in Castroville this joins Highway 1, which goes through Monterey to Carmel. For a longer and more scenic route from San Francisco, take Highway 280 to San Jose, Highway 17 through Los Gatos to Santa Cruz, and Highway 1 south to Monterey. From Los Angeles, take Highway 101 to Salinas and Highway 68 to Monterey; or for a more scenic but much longer drive, leave Highway 101 at San Luis Obispo and take Highway 1 through Morro Bay and the Big Sur to Carmel. There are direct flights daily to Monterey Airport from Los Angeles via United Airlines and Air Cal, and from San Francisco via Air Cal.

OLD MONTEREY INN
Monterey

When Ann and Gene Swett decided to open their elegant Tudor-style home for bed and breakfast, they vowed they would make it the perfect inn. And they have succeeded, down to every minute detail. Built in 1929 by Carmel Martin, a former mayer of Monterey, the half-timbered house sits on an oak-studded hillside surrounded by 1-1/2 acres of beautiful gardens. Begonias, fuschias, hydrangeas abound, along with twenty-eight varieties of roses. The wooded banks of a creek are rampant with ivy, ferns and rhododendrons.

The interior of the house (where the Swetts raised six children, now grown and gone) is decorated with impeccable taste. Some ideas were borrowed from other inns, such as the "swinging bed" suspended from the ceiling, à la Sutter Creek Inn, in one room. The covers on the goosedown comforters match the patterns of the sheets and pillowcases (two pillows—one firm and one soft—are provided for each person). Bedrooms are equipped with comfortable places to sit—wicker chairs or upholstered love seats or perhaps a chaise—and with books and magazines to read. Plants and well-chosen pieces of bric-a-brac make the house look homey but not cluttered. Bathrooms are well stocked with bubble bath and essentials you might have left at home, like toothpaste and razor blades. And off the hall is a large refrigerator filled with soft drinks and fruit juices, compliments of the house.

Woodburning fireplaces enhance some of the nine bedrooms. The most spectacular of these is the Library, which has floor-to-ceiling shelves of books, and a private balcony with a chaise. A king-size bed, covered in a jungle-motif fabric, occupies a niche with windows on all sides. There is no need for window shades here; the limbs of a massive gnarled oak provide all the privacy you need.

On the third floor, tucked under the eaves, are two other cozy rooms with fireplaces, half-timbered walls, and skylights in the slanted ceilings. Behind the inn is another fireplace unit: a two-room shuttered cottage dressed up in plaid and flowered patterns of lime and green. A sitting room with a dramatic skylight is furnished with wickerware; up a few steps is a cozy bedroom with a window seat.

In the evenings a fire also burns in the lovely high-ceilinged living room, where sherry is served with crackers and homemade cheese spreads. A table is set up for backgammon or dominoes. And to help you choose from the peninsula's many restaurants, there's a book in

27

Old Monterey Inn

which previous guests have written comments on their local dining experiences.

In the morning you may have a breakfast tray brought to your room, or you may join the other guests in the formally appointed dining room beside yet another fire, or you may take a tray out to one of the tables in the gardens. Breakfast starts with a glass of orange juice with banana slices floating on top, and a plate of melon followed by a basket of freshly baked muffins or cheese puffs or popovers.

As perfect as this inn is, Ann and Gene Swett continually improve it. They plan to turn the large front bedroom into a suite, and eventually every room will have a private bath.

OLD MONTEREY INN, 500 Martin Street, Monterey, California 93940. Telephone: (408) 375-8284. Accommodations: twin, queen-size and king-size beds; private or connecting baths with tub/shower or shower only; no telephones; no television. Rates: expensive to very expensive, Continental breakfast included. No children. No pets. No credit cards. Open all year.

Getting There: From the north, take Fremont Exit off Highway 1 to Abrego; turn left and proceed to El Dorado; turn right and proceed to Pacific; turn left, proceed one-half block and turn right on Martin.

GOSBY HOUSE INN
Pacific Grove

To the west of Monterey, just beyond Cannery Row, is the town of Pacific Grove. Here on a corner of the main street stands an imposing yellow Queen Anne Victorian, built by J. F. Gosby in 1887. In 1977 the mansion was restored as an inn by real estate developer William R. Patterson and banker Roger R. Post.

The Gosby House owners advocate clean air, and a "No Smoking in the Inn" sign at the entrance lets you know this. Inside, the living room is pretty as a picture. Above the white wainscoting, the walls are papered with brown and white floral print. Comfortable chairs are covered in rust and pale beige velour. Pots of yellow and white mums are set around the floor and on tables. A backgammon set, a magazine rack and an interesting collection of antique dolls complete the setting. A breakfast is served here of fruit juice, fresh fruit, Danish pastries and homemade breads.

The inn's seventeen bedrooms are decorated with antiques, marble-topped tables, handsome armoires, and ruffled curtains of unbleached muslin. One room, on the main floor, has a fireplace. All have marble-topped washbasins in the rooms; some have private baths. There are no numbers on the rooms; instead each is named for a prominent Monterey Peninsula figure from the turn of the century.

GOSBY HOUSE, 643 Lighthouse Avenue, Pacific Grove, California 93950. Telephone: (408) 375-1287. Accommodations: double, twin double and queen-size beds; private and shared baths with tub/shower or shower only; no telephones; no television. Rates: moderate, Continental breakfast included. Children under 12 discouraged. No pets. No smoking within the inn. No credit cards. Open all year.

Getting There: From Highway 1, take the Pebble Beach/17-Mile Drive turnoff. Turn right onto Highway 68, which leads to Pacific Grove. Turn left at Lighthouse Avenue and proceed three blocks to the inn.

PINE INN
Carmel

In 1902, the year after Queen Victoria's death, Pine Inn opened its doors, bringing all the gaudiness of the Victorian era to Carmel. The town was then a quiet refuge for artists and writers. But at the turn of the century Carmel had also been discovered by land developers who built Pine Inn to house prospective purchasers of lots, which cost $250 apiece! As the land boom prospered and Carmel grew, so did Pine Inn. The old Carmelo Hotel was moved from another location to serve as an annex; new wings were added haphazardly until the inn occupied most of a block by 1960. At that time Pine Inn was purchased by the McKee family who have carefully maintained its Victorian ambience.

Pine Inn is located on Ocean Avenue, Carmel's heavily trafficked thoroughfare. Yet a step inside is a step into the past. The original building houses the lobby and a bevy of dining rooms decorated with deep-red carpeting, flocked and flowered wallpapers, massive wooden sideboards, electrified gas lamps. There is also a cozy bar with stained-glass windows, marble-topped tables and a cast-iron fireplace—marvelous for a drink on a foggy day. A large brick patio was covered with a glass dome a few years back and converted into a gardenlike dining area.

The inn has forty-nine bedrooms, of which no two are alike. Those in the older part of the inn are small, but have the most historic charm. They are decorated in *fin de siècle* style with chintz wallpapers, white shutters and wainscotings, marble-topped wooden chests and brass bedsteads. In the newer additions, the rooms are larger and the furnishings are more modern and luxurious. An ornately furnished penthouse suite with fireplace opens to a private patio and will accommodate eight.

PINE INN, Ocean Avenue, P.O. Box 250, Carmel, California 93921. Telephone: (408) 624-3890. Accommodations: twin, double and king-size beds; private baths with tub/shower; telephones; color television. Rates: moderate to expensive, no meals included. Open to the public for breakfast, lunch and dinner; full bar service. Facilities for small conferences up to 50. Children welcome. No pets. Cards: AE, MC, VISA. Open all year.

CYPRESS INN
Carmel

The Spanish heritage of Carmel's missionary settlers is found in this quiet inn on a side street off Ocean Avenue. Though built in the early 1920s, the inn looks almost like a colonial mission itself, with a clay-tiled roof and a Spanish tower. To the right of a stately entrance hall, through an arched doorway, is a spacious living room with the look of a Mediterranean villa: white stucco walls, a high beamed ceiling, a large fireplace and wrought-iron chandeliers. Doors open into a tiled courtyard filled with colorful flowers: a lovely place to enjoy your coffee, juice and sweet rolls in the morning, but if fog prevails there is a small breakfast room on the side where ferns hang from a skylight.

The rooms are built around this secluded patio and no two are quite alike in decor or furnishings, though the Mediterranean wooden furnishings and white walls are found throughout. A few of the rooms have a view of the ocean. After many owners, Cypress Inn was acquired in 1975 by the owners of Pine Inn and is now beautifully maintained.

CYPRESS INN, Lincoln and Seventh (P.O. Box Y), Carmel, California 93921. Telephone: (408) 624-3871. Accommodations: twin, double twin, queen- and king-size beds; private baths, some tub/shower, some shower only; telephones; color television. Rates: moderate, Continental breakfast included. Children welcome. No pets. Cards: AE, MC, VISA. Open all year.

SANDPIPER INN
Carmel

Graeme and Irene Mackenzie, who bought the Sandpiper Inn in 1975, are no starry-eyed novices to the tasks of innkeeping. Rarely will you encounter a small inn managed so professionally. Born in Scotland, Mackenzie graduated from Lausanne Hotel School and did post-graduate work at Cornell University. He brings to Carmel over twenty years of experience in some of the finest hotels in Europe, Bermuda, Hong Kong, the United States and Canada.

The Sandpiper Inn, located on Carmel Point just fifty yards from the beach, has been in operation since 1929. The Mackenzies completely refurbished it, adding many antiques: a mixture of American country,

French and English pieces. Quilted flowered spreads cover the new king- and queen-size beds, and bowls of fresh flowers are on the tables. Some of the rooms have wood-burning fireplaces and many have views of Carmel Bay and Pebble Beach. The Mackenzies added full modern baths to all of the fifteen rooms and rebuilt two small cottages behind the inn.

George Washington never slept here, nor did any other American president, but Graeme Mackenzie jokingly points to a bed that President Ford slept in while staying at a home in Pebble Beach. There was no king-size bed in the guest room, but the Sandpiper graciously lent one of theirs for Ford's comfort.

The Mackenzies' guest book, however, does list the presidents of many corporations, along with an international clientele representing sixty-six countries. In the evening, around the stone fireplace in the spacious living room, you are likely to hear many languages. Graeme and Irene are both multilingual, which helps the foreign visitors feel at home. The cocktail hour is a convivial time here. Ice, glasses and mixes are provided; guests bring their own wine and liquor.

To one side of the living room is a cozy library with a writing desk and shelves stocked with books. At the end of the living room is a long table where a breakfast of orange juice, Danish pastries and coffee is served. Guests are invited to help themselves to chilled soft drinks in the kitchen refrigerator at any time.

Flower gardens surround the inn, with brick patios for sunning. Ten-speed bicycles are available for peddling along the cypress-studded drive that fronts Carmel's glorious beach. Graeme is happy to arrange tours of many of the excellent Monterey County wineries and to introduce guests to most of the famous golf and tennis clubs on the peninsula.

SANDPIPER INN, 2408 Bayview Avenue at Martin Way, Carmel, California 93923. Telephone: (408) 624-6433. Accommodations: queen- and king-size beds with an additional single bed in some rooms; private baths with tub/shower or shower only; no telephones; no television. Rates: moderate to expensive, Continental breakfast included. No children under 12. No pets. Credit cards: MC, VISA. Open all year.

Getting There: Take Ocean Avenue to Scenic Avenue and proceed south along the beach to the end; turn left at Martin Way.

VAGABOND HOUSE
Carmel

Don Blanding lived here in the 1940s, but no one is certain if his poem *Vagabond's House* was named for the inn, or if the inn was later named for the poem. Nevertheless Vagabond House is a poetic hideaway with rooms looking through treetops into a stone courtyard massed with rhododendrons, camellias, azaleas and roses. In the center, baskets of ferns, begonias and fuchsias hang from the branches of a large oak.

Vagabond House was originally built in 1941 for efficiency apartments when Carmel's population suddenly swelled from the influx of military personnel to Fort Ord. Later it became an inn. In 1974, Patsy and Chuck Watts, a young couple from southern California, purchased the inn after searching the state for just such a place. Four years later, in an astounding game of "musical inns," the Watts purchased the historic Benbow Inn in Garberville, and Benbow owners Dennis Levett and Jewell Brown took over the Vagabond House.

The rooms are large and charmingly furnished with Early American maple, pieces of wicker, quilted bedspreads, and antique pendulum clocks, books and flowers. All rooms have fireplaces and refrigerators; some have kitchenettes, a holdover from apartment-house days. There is a coffee-pot and fresh coffee in each room so guests may brew their own any time of the day. In the mornings fruit juice and Danish rolls are provided for a light breakfast in the patio—or, if you prefer, in your room. In the late afternoons a carafe of cream sherry is served.

Ms. Brown, who was a schoolteacher for thirty-five years, is resident manager at Vagabond House. For the past ten years, while teaching, she also managed Benbow. "I'm sorry I didn't get into innkeeping sooner," she says now. "It's a great business and I really like it."

VAGABOND HOUSE, Fourth and Dolores (P.O. Box 2747), Carmel, California 93921. Telephone: (408) 624-7738. Accommodations: twin doubles, queen- and king-size beds; private baths, some with tub/shower, some shower only; no telephones; color television. Rates: moderate to expensive, Continental breakfast included. No children under 12. No pets. Cards: MC, VISA. Open all year.

Getting There: From Ocean Avenue turn north on Dolores. Free pickup at Monterey Airport.

Vagabond House

SAN ANTONIO HOUSE
Carmel

This three-story shingled house was built in 1907 as a private residence, and during its early years served as a studio and weekend retreat for artists and writers from the San Francisco Bay Area. In the 1930s Lincoln Steffens lived next door and played host to a continuous flow of the literati of his day. In 1950, the handsome old house, set back from the street by a spacious lawn, became a guest house. In 1974 Michael Cloran, a young stockbroker from southern California, and his wife Joan came to Carmel for a weekend, bought the old house on impulse—"We wanted to change our lifestyle"—and stayed.

The Clorans live in the main floor of the house and rent the lower floor, top floor and a cottage behind as two- and three-room units. Privacy for their guests is their main concern. Each room has its own private entrance, patio and bath, as well as a coffeemaker and a refrigerator stocked with orange juice. San Antonio is for people who want the atmosphere of an inn without having to socialize.

Joan has decorated the rooms with vibrant colors and her own collection of European paintings and prints. One of the most delightful suites is called the Doll House: three little rooms under the gabled roof. Black wicker and wrought-iron furniture contrasts with the white board and batten walls, bright red and white print spreads and red corduroy

36

cushions. From mullioned windows there is a view of the ocean. Baby roses cascade over the outside stairs, while Martha Washingtons and geraniums bloom around the patio. A pleasant place to absorb the sun, the sound of the surf and the smell of the pines.

SAN ANTONIO HOUSE, San Antonio between Seventh and Ocean (P.O. Box 3683), Carmel, California 93921. Telephone: (408) 624-4334. Accommodations: twin beds and queen-size bed in each unit; private baths with tub/shower; no telephones, but rooms have television. Rates: moderate, coffee and juice included. Children welcome. Pets allowed. No credit cards. Open all year.

SEA VIEW INN
Carmel

The Sea View has been operated as an inn since the mid-1920s, but Marshall and Diane Hydorn, the present owners, think the three-story shingled house was probably built just after the turn of the century. Two of the early innkeepers here, the Misses Olive and Pearl Stout, advertised rooms for three dollars a night. Hydorn speculates that this included meals as well! Located three blocks from the ocean on a quiet residential street, the inn was obviously named for its view; however, over the years large pines have grown up around the house, allowing only a peek at the sea from upstairs rooms today.

The inn maintains the aura of Carmel in the twenties. The board and batten walls have been painted white, and the solid, comfortable furnishings of previous owners are mixed with the Hydorns' antiques. The homey living room has a large brick fireplace, shuttered windows and three tables where the Hydorns serve a morning spread of juices, dry cereals, English muffins and homemade coffeecake. Sherry and wine are offered in the evening.

The bedrooms have a country charm, with four-posters or wicker bedsteads, quilted spreads. A burled armoire in one room, a rocker in another, marble-topped dressers here and there, are interspersed with pieces of no discernable lineage. In some rooms a studio couch is cozily placed in an alcove; in others there are window seats by the dormered windows. Over the years this inn has developed a loyal clientele. Recently, to the Hydorns' delight, a couple who had honeymooned at Sea View returned for their fiftieth anniversary.

SEA VIEW INN, Camino Real at Eleventh (P.O. Box 4138), Carmel, California 93921. Telephone: (408) 624-8778. Accommodations: twin, queen- and king-size beds, some with additional studio couch; private or shared baths with tub/shower or shower only; no telephones; no television. Rates: inexpensive to moderate, breakfast included. Children over eight welcome. No pets. Cards: MC, VISA. Open all year.

Getting There: From Ocean Avenue, turn south on Camino Real.

NORMANDY INN
Carmel

On the south side of Ocean Avenue is a French Provincial complex of buildings designed and built by architect Robert Stanton and decorated by his wife Virginia, former party editor of *House Beautiful.* After graduating from UC Berkeley, Stanton worked for architect Wallace Neff on a number of Hollywood homes, including Douglas Fairbanks's Pickfair, and the Fredric March home, which inspired his interest in French Provincial design. Stanton moved to Carmel to practice architecture, and built the Normandy Inn in 1937. Over the years newer and larger units were added, and a group of cottages was built across the street. Today the Normandy has forty-eight units clustered around gardens and banked with pots of blooming flowers, and a kidney-shaped pool.

The older rooms have the atmosphere of a French country inn. Many have corner fireplaces adorned with painted tiles. Multipaned windows look out to the trees and gardens, or occasionally offer a glimpse of the ocean beyond. There are shuttered alcoves and beds tucked into niches in the wall. The newer units have more luxurious appointments such as king-size beds and large picture windows, but lack some of the charm of the older rooms. The cottages across the way are centered around a brick patio; there are fireplaces and kitchenettes in most of these.

In the mornings the Normandy serves guests juice, coffee and orange muffins in a quaint country dining room filled with pots of flowers. Here Virginia Stanton has installed her fine collection of antique Quimper plates from France.

NORMANDY INN, Ocean Avenue (P.O. Box 1706), Carmel, California 93921. Telephone: (408) 624-3825. Accommodations: twin, double

Normandy Inn

and king-size beds; private baths, some tub/shower, some shower only; telephones; television in newer rooms. Rates: moderate to expensive, Continental breakfast included. Children welcome. No pets. No credit cards. Open all year.

SAN BENITO HOUSE
Half Moon Bay

Some thirty miles south of downtown San Francisco, the coastal village of Half Moon Bay is surrounded by flower nurseries and fields of artichokes and pumpkins—a blaze of orange in the fall. Beaches and the fishing harbor of Princeton are nearby. The town's Main Street is lined with turn-of-the-century street lights and buildings. One of these structures is a small hotel built by Estanislaus Zabella, who married into the Miramontez family, holders of the original Spanish land grant. Known for years as the Mosconi Hotel, the name was changed in the 1930s to Dominic's. For years, despite the run-down condition of the place, huge bargain-priced, family-style Italian dinners attracted drivers from the city and the Peninsula.

Then in 1976, Carol Regan, a local schoolteacher, embarked on a three-year restoration project to turn the old hotel into a European-style inn. She chose the name San Benito after the original name of Half Moon Bay. Now the little hotel is resplendent with fresh paint and refinished redwood paneling and beams. The old corner saloon is outfitted with a mammoth bar, nineteenth-century decor and etched-glass swinging doors that lead to the dining room. Here butcher-block tables, covered with paisley cloths, are set with pretty china and bouquets of daisies, marigolds and whatever else is blooming in the large flower garden next to the inn. French doors open to a wide deck banked with more flowers.

Overnight guests at San Benito House are instructed to go into the kitchen to register. Here they are likely to find Carol at work making pâtés, pastries, desserts or bread. A serious student of cooking for years before she took over the inn, Carol has developed her talents lately by studying with such noted chefs as Roger Vergé in the south of France. The menus at San Benito tend toward country French, as well as her other favorite cuisine, northern Italian. The seafood of the area is emphasized, as is local produce; artichoke and pumpkin soups are among her specialties. And many of the vegetables come from her own gardens.

40

After checking in, guests are given a key to the front door. Inside, a hall and stairway, stunningly decorated in blue and white, lead to eight bedrooms, two suites and a sauna. These rooms contain a charming potpourri of furnishings: antique wooden chests, flowery comforters, some Italian lamps, paintings and artifacts from local flea markets, baskets of flowers, bric-a-brac or vases on wall brackets, a floor-to-ceiling headboard made from paneled double doors in one room, a rose-patterned canopy in another. Most of the rooms have private baths, decorated in great style with oil paintings, old chandeliers and bouquets of flowers, with stained-glass partitions behind the claw-legged tubs. The windows, bedecked with boxes of geraniums or impatiens, view the mountains, the ocean or the inn's garden.

The saloon, with its casual and friendly atmosphere, is a favorite gathering spot for overnight guests (who are offered a complimentary drink) and residents of the area. A quieter haven is the deck where a fire burns each night in a large stone pit. And even more privacy for sitting and sunning is found on a second-floor porch with an ocean view.

San Benito House serves a complimentary breakfast of homemade whole-wheat bread, fresh fruit compote, juice and coffee. On Sunday mornings, when the dining room is open to the public, overnight guests may order the full breakfast at a discounted price. Carol's creative cooking and constantly changing menu are incentives for taking all your meals at the inn. If you wish a change, there are several good seafood restaurants nearby. But on Sunday night in the summer and fall, you should plan to dine in: Carol stages a pit barbecue with live music out on the deck.

SAN BENITO HOUSE, Main Street at Mill (Route 1, Box 4A), Half Moon Bay, California 94019. Telephone: (415) 726-3425. Accommodations: double and king-size beds; private and shared bath with tubs; no telephones in most rooms, one has phone jack; television on request. Rates: inexpensive to moderate, Continental breakfast included. Open to the public for lunch, dinner and Sunday breakfast; full bar service. Children welcome. No pets. Cards: AE, MC, VISA. Open all year.

Getting There: From San Francisco take Highway 280 south to Highway 92 and head west; when you reach Main Street turn left. From Monterey, Highway 1 to San Francisco passes through Half Moon Bay.

SAN FRANCISCO BAY AREA

San Francisco
Berkeley
And Marin County

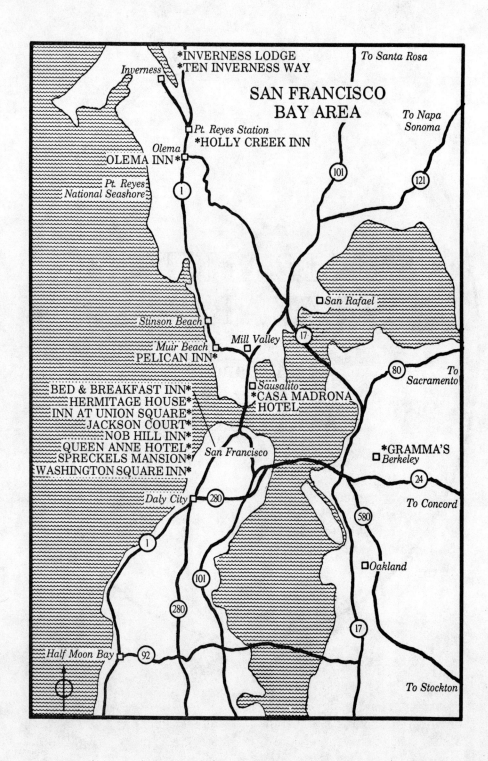

*INVERNESS LODGE
*TEN INVERNESS WAY

Inverness

SAN FRANCISCO
BAY AREA

To Santa Rosa

To Napa
Sonoma

Pt. Reyes Station
*HOLLY CREEK INN

Olema
OLEMA INN *

101

121

*Pt. Reyes
National Seashore*

1

□ *San Rafael*

Stinson Beach

Muir Beach
PELICAN INN *

Mill Valley

17

80

To
Sacramento

□ *Sausalito*

BED & BREAKFAST INN*
HERMITAGE HOUSE
INN AT UNION SQUARE*
JACKSON COURT
NOB HILL INN*
QUEEN ANNE HOTEL*
*SPRECKELS MANSION
WASHINGTON SQUARE INN*

*CASA MADRONA
HOTEL

*GRAMMA'S
□ *Berkeley*

San Francisco

24

Daly City

280

580

To Concord

1

101

□ *Oakland*

280

17

Half Moon Bay

92

To Stockton

SAN FRANCISCO

San Francisco is the needle's eye through which the threads of
California history have converged. Spanish missionaries first brought
Western culture here in 1776. But it was the fortunes in gold from the
Mother Lode in the 1850s and later the silver from the Comstock that
built the magnificent city by the Golden Gate. To her teeming port
came the European immigrants who planted California's fertile valleys
with grapes and returned their wines to San Francisco's splendid
tables. And from the redwood forests to the north came the lumber for
the houses that soon covered her hills and valleys. The fire of 1906
obliterated most of the Victorian houses east of Van Ness Avenue, but
many thousands of Victorians still impart a nineteenth-century aura to
the outlying neighborhoods. A 1976 survey of only nine districts
cataloged over thirteen thousand extant Victorian structures; Pacific
Heights and Cow Hollow were not even included.

Today San Francisco is a city of intimate neighborhoods, each with
a distinctive character that is usually missed by visitors who stay at the
downtown hotels. But now a number of small hostelries have opened in
the neighborhoods, many in Victorians. These offer the charm and
hospitality of a country inn, while being only ten or fifteen minutes from
the heart of San Francisco.

BED & BREAKFAST INN
San Francisco

San Francisco's first urban inn occupies two brightly painted Italianate
houses in a cul-de-sac off Union Street. Long before the bed and
breakfast craze swept San Francisco, Marily and Robert Kavanaugh
dreamed of opening a guest house patterned after England's B&Bs.
Finally in 1976 they found the perfect building, a former boardinghouse,

remodeled it with extraordinary flair, and decorated it with family heirlooms from England, combined with vividly colored contemporary accents. Two years later they purchased the house next door and added three other units.

The Bed and Breakfast Inn is a place for romance, and its *pièce de résistance* is a room in the second house called Celebration. Here a queen-size bed reposes in an alcove papered and curtained with a dainty blue and white Laura Ashley print. A love seat upholstered in blue velvet occupies a little sitting area. And beyond a divider containing pots of blooming flowers is a sunken double bathtub surrounded by brown-tinted mirrors. Downstairs is a suite named Mandalay that is decorated with grass cloth, rattan furniture, a Burmese-style ceiling fan, and sheer draperies emulating mosquito netting around the queen-size bed. On awakening, one would expect to see the dawn come up "like thunder outer China 'crost the Bay."

Next door the Victorian first restored by the Kavanaughs houses the breakfast area, a library and four bedrooms, each with a distinctive name and color theme inspired by boldly patterned quilts. Green Park and Kensington Garden open to a flower-filled deck behind the inn. A fifth unit on the top floor was formerly the Kavanaughs' living quarters. This penthouse suite has a living room, a dining area, a full kitchen and a latticed terrace filled with plants. A spiral staircase leads up to a bedroom loft that, like Celebration, is outfitted with a double bathtub. Mayfair, as the suite is called, is a favorite for honeymooners and is also popular for small business conferences.

Marily welcomes her guests with the warmth of an old friend. Upon your arrival you are offered sherry from a crystal decanter on a silver tray in the sitting/breakfast room. A Windsor table is set with Copeland china that belonged to Marily's grandmother. English country prints are on the wall. There's a white wicker settee with deep cushions covered in a floral print. Flowers and plants are everywhere; a spinning wheel is in the corner. Downstairs the cozy library contains a game table for backgammon, cards or puzzles, a color television and a leather-bound collection of the works of Dickens.

In all the rooms, Marily's gracious touches are found. A bouquet of fresh spring flowers on the nightstand. A bowl of fruit and selection of current magazines on a table. Beds turned down to reveal the pretty printed sheets and pillowcases. And on each pillow—a fortune cookie.

Breakfast is as important as the beds here. Marily serves juice, freshly ground coffee, hot croissants or occasionally "sticky buns" on her antique flowered chinaware. Some guests prefer to be served in the

The Bed and Breakfast Inn

breakfast room or outdoors on umbrella-covered tables in the flower-filled garden. But Marily prefers to pamper you with a breakfast tray in bed.

The Bed and Breakfast Inn is located in San Francisco's Cow Hollow district, named for the dairy farms that once covered the area. The neighborhood is a treasure trove of Victorian architecture, notably along Union Street where the colorfully painted old houses have been turned into fashionable shops, bars and restaurants. A bus line leads directly to downtown San Francisco.

THE BED AND BREAKFAST INN, 5 Charlton Court (off Union between Buchanan and Laguna), San Francisco, California 94123. Telephone: (415) 921-9784. Accommodations: twin, double, queen- and king-size beds; shared half-baths with tub/shower or shower only; private baths with shower or double tub; telephones and television in suites. Rates: moderate to very expensive, Continental breakfast included. Children discouraged. Pets discouraged. No credit cards. Open all year.

THE SPRECKELS MANSION
San Francisco

The Haight Ashbury district has become again a quiet residential neighborhood after enduring a turbulent notoriety in the 1960s as the blossoming place for San Francisco's flower children. This area on the northern slopes of Twin Peaks was countryside until the 1890s, when a flurry of building activity made it a popular suburb. Today some twelve hundred relics of Victorian architecture line its streets. One of these houses, a splendid example of the Colonial Revival style, was built in 1898 for Richard Spreckels, superintendent of the Western Sugar Refinery owned by his uncle, sugar baron Claus Spreckels.

The stately mansion, facing the heavily wooded Buena Vista Park, was well maintained as a single-family residence until 1979 when Jeffrey Ross and Jonathan Shannon turned it into a spectacular inn. "The house has had a way of adapting to the times and attracting artistic people," Ross observes. Ambrose Bierce and Jack London supposedly worked in the top-floor ballroom at one time. And during the 1960 s the producer for the Grateful Dead rock band owned the house and used the old ballroom as a recording studio.

Ross (an architect, interior designer and restorer of historic buildings) and Shannon (a designer of women's evening wear) did not intend to become innkeepers. When they heard the Spreckels house was threatened by a developer's scheme, they decided to save the building and possibly convert it into apartments. Then they saw the interior, with an amazing amount of its original embellishments intact: seven fireplaces, some with rare detailing such as a tortoise-shell tile hearth in the master bedroom; hand-painted Meissen chandeliers; museum-quality windows of leaded stained glass, many with Art Nouveau overtones; embossed wall coverings with gilt friezes; Corinthian columns in the hall and parlor. Ross and Shannon decided to preserve the residential character of the mansion by making it an inn.

They surmised that their guests would not feel comfortable in the stiff decor of the Victorian era and used their skills as designers to blend French and English turn-of-the-century antiques with pieces from other periods, including contemporary furnishings. All of the rooms have sitting areas with wing-back chairs, and throughout are fanciful touches. The bed in the spacious former parlor, for example, is set in a columned alcove with a canopy swooping up to the Corinthian capitals. Many of the bedrooms—and even the master bathroom— have fireplaces, and most look out either to Buena Vista Park or west over Golden Gate Park to the ocean. The gorgeous stained-glass windows obscure the views of the neighboring houses.

The third-floor ballroom is now a stunning two-bedroom suite, decorated with contemporary furniture and Oriental accessories. A gabled redwood ceiling rises some thirty feet over the living room, where sofas covered with navy-blue suede flank the large fireplace. Raised sitting areas in two large dormers provide panoramic views of the city, Golden Gate Park, the ocean and the Marin headlands. A tiled bar-kitchen at one end of this room and a commodious table at the other make this unit suitable for small conferences.

Next door to the mansion is a handsome Edwardian building that was built as a guest house around 1900. Ross and Shannon also acquired this as part of their inn. The pride of the music room, now a common salon for guests, is an extraordinary baby grand piano, built in Paris circa 1890, with every surface covered with Art Nouveau designs fashioned from inlaid woods.

The upstairs bedrooms are designed to inspire fantasies. Entering the very Edwardian English Rose, one would not be surprised to find Sherlock Holmes sitting in the black wing chair in front of the brick fireplace. In Sunset Suite, where a view of the ocean is framed by stained-glass panels, the decor is reminiscent of a room in the French countryside. Gypsy Hideaway has a view and a fireplace, and a paisley-

49

draped, -canopied and -covered bed that will make you think you've been abducted by a gypsy caravan. And the many skylights in Stargazers' Suite encourage flights of fancy to outer space; this suite also has a magnificent western view and an unusual beehive brick fireplace.

In the mornings trays of juice, croissants and coffee are brought to the rooms at Spreckels Mansion. In the evenings wine is served in the library of the main house. From here it's a pleasant stroll past rows of colorful Victorians to Haight Street, where the former hippie hangouts are being transformed into nice shops and restaurants.

THE SPRECKELS MANSION, 737 Buena Vista West, San Francisco 94117. Telephone: (415) 861-3008. Accommodations: queen-size beds; some shared baths, mostly private baths with tub and/or shower; telephones; no television. Rates: moderate to expensive, Continental breakfast included. Children sometimes accepted. No pets. Cards: AE, MC, VISA. Open all year.

JACKSON COURT
San Francisco

Pacific Heights is San Francisco's most exclusive residential district. Two inns in this area cater to guests who plan to stay a week or longer. The first to open was Jackson Court, located in a lovely old mansion that had disintegrated to a cheap rooming house before it was refurbished by interior designer Suzanne Brangham in 1978. You enter the inn through a plant-filled courtyard shared by an adjacent twin house. In the gracious living room with its dark ceiling beams and wooden wainscoting, a fire bids welcome under a monumental mantelpiece of carved Italian marble surrounded by cinnamon velvet love seats. Sherry is served here in the evening.

The hospitable feeling is emphasized by a "welcome home" sign on the wall of the staircase that leads to the upstairs bedrooms. These are light and spacious, painted in bright colors with contrasting trims and furnished with a blend of antiques and contemporary pieces, Oriental rugs on the hardwood floors, custom-made quilts on the beds. Several of the rooms have fireplaces and all have comfortable sitting areas, desks, color cable television and telephones with private lines. They were designed with a long stay in mind. Plants, flowers and books are scattered about.

Each of Jackson Court's three floors has a kitchen, one with a little brick fireplace. Juices, coffee or tea, croissants, muffins and jams are set out here each morning, and if you wish to cook yourself something more substantial at any time, you are free to do so if you provide the groceries. But if you want to dine out, the concierge will be happy to make your restaurant reservations, as well as obtaining your theater tickets and arranging your transportation.

The ownership of Jackson Court is through an unusual time-share program, whereby investors purchase as many weeks of residency as they wish in the inn. During the rest of the year the rooms are rented out. A Cadillac limousine is provided for the owners' use, but it's often available for hire by the guests as well.

JACKSON COURT, 2198 Jackson Street, San Francisco, California 94115. Telephone: (415) 929-7670. Accommodations: twin, double and queen-size beds; private baths with showers; private-line telephones; color cable television. Rates: moderate, Continental breakfast included. Reservations accepted only for a minimum of one week. Children sometimes accepted. No pets. Cards: MC, VISA. Open all year.

HERMITAGE HOUSE
San Francisco

This seventeen-room, four-story Greek Revival mansion is sited a block away from Pacific Heights's Lafayette Park in an area noted for its Victorians. The house was built at the turn of the century for Judge Charles Slack and was maintained as a single-family residence until the 1970s when it served as a drug rehabilitation center. In 1978 Ted and Marion Binkley bought the place for an inn. Their motivation was unusual: They had enjoyed meeting interesting people while staying at European inns and felt they could add another dimension to their lives by greeting visitors to San Francisco. As is nearby Jackson Court, Hermitage House is geared for guests of a week or longer, although exceptions are made if rooms are available.

The carved detailing in the redwood beams, pillars and stairway scrolls of the entrance hall is exceptionally fine, as are the carved mantel and the inlaid floors of the large living room with its graceful curved bay. A decanter of wine is set by the fireside here in the evenings. Marion has decorated a cozy breakfast room with mauve and white chintz wallpaper and matching cloths on little round tables. Magnificent leaded glass cabinets line the walls of this room and the adjoining formal dining room, where a buffet of juices, fruits, croissants and cold cereals is laid out each morning. As at Jackson Court, guests are invited to use the old-fashioned kitchen to prepare heartier breakfasts or other meals on the vintage 1900 Wedgewood stove.

Five of the bedrooms have working fireplaces, and wherever possible sitting areas and desks are provided. The bedrooms are cheerfully papered with chintz or floral patterns, beds are brass or four-postered or canopied, and each is stacked with as many as a dozen pillows of various patterns, sizes and shapes. Comfort is the byword here. The most unusual room is Judge Slack's former study under the eaves on the top floor. Paneled in redwood with a gabled ceiling, the room is lined with bookshelves and has a large stone fireplace. A desk has been placed in a dormered window with a southern view of the city towards Twin Peaks.

With private-line telephones and direct bus service to Nob Hill and downtown San Francisco, Hermitage House is an ideal head-quarters for people on the go. But it's also a place to relax. An upstairs refrigerator is filled with ice and cold drinks to take onto a little sundeck. Or you may laze in a chaise in the sunny western garden.

HERMITAGE HOUSE, 2224 Sacramento Street, San Francisco, California 94115. Telephone: (415) 921-5515. Accommodations: twin, double, queen- and king-size beds, studio couches in some rooms as well; private and shared baths with tub or shower; private-line telephones on request; television on request. Rates: moderate, breakfast included. Reservations for a week or longer given first preference. Children discouraged. No pets. Cards: MC, VISA. Open all year.

QUEEN ANNE HOTEL
San Francisco

In 1890 Senator James G. Fair used part of the fortune he had amassed from his Comstock silver holdings to erect a towered, turreted and gabled structure near Pacific Heights to house Miss Mary Lake's School for Young Girls. Gymnasiums, classrooms and dormitories for sixty-five boarders were provided. Fair spared no costs on the interior, installing stained-glass windows, English oak paneling and a monu-mental staircase of Spanish cedar. The school closed nine years later and an exclusive gentlemen's club, the Cosmos, moved into the four-story Queen Anne. In the 1920s the Episcopal Diocese purchased the building as a home for young working women: The Girl's Friendly Society Lodge. After World War II, new owners converted it to a residence club for men and women.

Queen Anne Hotel

Finally, in 1980, an investment group purchased the former girls' school, and after extensive renovation opened it as the Queen Anne Hotel. A newly installed elevator gives access to the forty-nine guest rooms on the upper floors. These rooms have been papered or painted and decorated with English antiques. Some bedrooms have fireplaces and wet bars. All have private baths with telephones!

Even though it's called a hotel, the Queen Anne observes the amenities of an inn. A Continental breakfast of juice, croissants and coffee is served in the bedroom or in the first-floor parlor and drawing room, where the original fireplace rises from floor to ceiling. Afternoon tea and sherry are also offered here. And in keeping with the European tradition, if you leave your shoes outside your door at night, they will be shined by the morning.

QUEEN ANNE HOTEL, 1590 Sutter Street, San Francisco, California 94109. Telephone: (415) 441-2828. Accommodations: queen-, double queen- and king-size beds; private baths with tub/shower; telephones; color television. Rates: moderate to expensive, Continental breakfast included. Children welcome. No pets. Cards: AE, CB, DC, MC, VISA. Open all year.

NOB HILL INN
San Francisco

Nob Hill's steep slopes made it virtually uninhabitable until the invention of the cable car in the 1870s. Then the city's nabobs—the Comstock and railroad millionaires—started building their palaces on California Street at the top of the hill. The only remaining testament to those extravagant times is the mansion of Bonanza King James C. Flood, which now houses the Pacific Union Club. The other homes were destroyed by the 1906 fire, and elegant hotels bearing the names of Huntington, Mark Hopkins and Stanford stand on their sites. The Fairmont Hotel, which did survive the fire, pays tribute to the memory of Flood's partner James G. Fair, who had lived down the hill at Pine and Jones. The Gothic-style Grace Episcopal Cathedral, with its bronze copies of Florence's Ghiberti doors, occupies the block where Charles Crocker had his mansion.

In this century Nob Hill gained another kind of notoriety when the famed madam Sally Stanford operated one of the poshest bordellos the city had ever known in a mansion on Pine Street. Supposedly she used a small hotel on the corner of Pine and Taylor for her overflow patrons. This building is now the locale of the Nob Hill Inn.

From the lobby an antique elevator with etched glass windows whisks guests to the three floors of rooms above. Each of the fifteen rooms has been individually decorated with nineteenth-century furnishings, but the third-floor rooms are preferable as they are lighter than the others. Fireplaces with tiled hearths and carved wooden mantels grace many of the rooms. Brass replicas of old-fashioned telephones are found in all. Some beds are wooden or brass four-posters, and all have interesting coverings, many draped or canopied. And each night the covers are turned back and a chocolate and a flower are placed on the pillows. Morning brings a Victorian wicker tray of fruits, croissants and coffee to the rooms. Or if you wish you can breakfast by the fire in the inn's parlor. Behind this is a wine cellar, its walls laden with California and European bottlings that guests may purchase. The crest of Nob Hill is only a block away from the charming hotel and Union Square is three blocks downhill.

NOB HILL INN, 1000 Pine Street, San Francisco, California 94108. Telephone: (415) 673-6080. Accommodations: single, double and queen-size beds, hideabeds in suites; private baths, some detached, with tub/shower or shower only; telephones; televisions on request. Rates: moderate to expensive, Continental breakfast included. Cards: AE, MC, VISA. Open all year.

WASHINGTON SQUARE INN
San Francisco

While the affluent citizens of San Francisco were building their palatial residences on Nob Hill and Pacific Heights, the working-class immigrants settled in North Beach. The city's ethnic mix is particularly mirrored in Washington Square, a small park at the base of Telegraph Hill. This square started out ignobly in the 1840s as the potato patch of Juana Briones, the Hill's first settler, and was later dubbed the "Spanish Lot." In 1849 the area around the park became known as "Little Chile," when the Gold Rush lured an influx of Chilean settlers here. Later came the Italians, who moored their fishing boats at the nearby wharves, and then the Chinese, whose homes and shops have spread into North Beach from neighboring Chinatown. Today in the early mornings office workers walk their dogs in Washington Square, while runners jog and

56

middle-aged Chinese faithfully perform their graceful tai chi exercises. Later in the day, elderly Italian gentlemen take over the park benches, reading *Italo-Americano*. At noontime, residents of Casa Costanzo, an Italian home for the aged on the south side of the square, observe the limousines lined up below, bringing affluent lunchers to the Fior d'Italia. Meanwhile, on the square's western perimeter, once the site of a Russian Orthodox church, the Washington Square Bar and Grill attracts a younger, sophisticated mix of literary types; and the Pagoda Theatre advertises Chinese-language movies. Chimes peal across the park from the imposing tower of SS. Peter and Paul Catholic Church on the square's northern boundary. And on the east side, with a view of the park and Russian Hill beyond, is the Washington Square Inn.

Until 1978 this two-story corner building housed a drugstore, medical offices and run-down apartments. After being condemned, the building was totally refurbished and charmingly decorated by Nan Rosenblatt, one of the new owners. An antique French desk and brass chandeliers accent the informal lobby where morning coffee and croissants are served beside an intricately carved fireplace. In the late afternoon, tea is offered, with cucumber sandwiches and shortbread cookies. Guests may also purchase a bottle of wine from the inn's cellar of California varietals and champagnes.

The inn's fifteen bedrooms are individually decorated with bright French florals and chinoiserie; each is coordinated around a different color. Antique armoires, dressers and tables are scattered about; most of the beds are draped with colorful canopies. Three of the rooms are large bedroom-sitting room combinations with hideabed couches that make them suitable for families of four. The others vary from spacious to small. The front rooms overlooking the square are, of course, the best. Here, from a seat by the bay window you may observe the colorful goings-on in the park.

Washington Square is midway between downtown San Francisco and Fisherman's Wharf—a short bus ride or a ten-minute walk from each. There is, however, much to see and do in the immediate vicinity. A block away is upper Grant Avenue—the center of the Beat movement of the 1950s and now the site of a conglomeration of crafts shops, antique stores, coffeehouses and so forth; a few blocks south, Grant leads into Chinatown. Strollers will delight in exploring the picturesque lanes hidden behind the main streets of Telegraph and Russian hills.

Since most of the pleasures of San Francisco are accessible by foot or by bus from Washington Square, you don't need an automobile; in fact parking is the nemesis of the area. If you wish to wander farther afield, the inn's manager will arrange a car rental or just about anything else to enhance your visit—theater tickets, a tour, a stenographer or a picnic.

WASHINGTON SQUARE INN, 1660 Stockton Street, San Francisco, California 94133. Telephone: (415) 981-4220. Accommodations: twin, double, queen-size and king-size beds; private and shared baths with tub or shower or tub/shower; telephones; televisions on request at no charge. Rates: moderate to expensive, Continental breakfast and tea included. Children welcome. No pets. Cards: AE, MC, VISA. Open all year.

THE INN AT UNION SQUARE
San Francisco

For those who want to stay in the heart of San Francisco, the Inn at Union Square offers a personalized alternative to the commercial hotels. One-half block from the Square and its elegant shops, the inn had been a sixty-room transient hotel, vacant for some years, when it was renovated in 1980 by interior designer Nan Rosenblatt, owner of the Washington Square Inn. She cut the number of guest units to twenty-nine, creating some two-room suites from the smaller rooms and a luxurious sixth-floor suite with a fireplace, wet bar, whirlpool bath and sauna.

The decor and service at Union Square is very similar to Washington Square. The bedrooms are furnished with English antiques; bright fabrics drape the beds and cover the goose-down pillows. Fresh flowers are set in the rooms. Each floor has a little lobby, with a fireplace, where an English tea is served in the afternoons, along with hors d'oeuvre. Bottles of wine may be purchased from the inn. A Continental breakfast—croissants, juice, fruit and coffee—is served by this fireside or in the rooms.

Also as at Washington Square, the Inn at Union Square has a concierge to take care of restaurant reservations, theater tickets and the like. Valet parking is available at the door.

THE INN AT UNION SQUARE, 440 Post Street, San Francisco, California 94102. Telephone: (415) 397-3510. Accommodations: twin, queen- and king-size beds; private baths with tub/shower; telephones; color television. Rates: expensive, Continental breakfast included. Children welcome. No pets. Cards: AE, MC, VISA. Open all year.

GRAMMA'S BED AND BREAKFAST INN
Berkeley

There is no real gramma here, but a large portrait of the owner's grandmother, Elizabeth Taber, hangs in the stairwell. She was an Irish immigrant who ran a boardinghouse in Boston. Steven and Kathy Lustig decided to dedicate their inn to her and to instigate some grandmotherly practices such as keeping a cookie jar freshly stocked at all times.

Gramma's is located in a splendid turn-of-the-century Tudor-style mansion, a five-minute walk away from Berkeley's UC campus. Constructed by builder J. A. Marshall as his residence, the house later served as a convalescent home before the Lustigs purchased it for an inn. Most of the original beautiful detailing of the lower floor remains intact, such as the intricately inlaid hardwood floors and foliated plaster friezes. In the living room a graceful bay of leaded clear glass windows looks out to the big trees that screen the inn from busy

Telegraph Avenue. Beige velveteen upholstered sofas are pulled up to the painted tile fireplace. In the rear is a second sitting room and a large breakfast area with enormous windows opening to a broad deck and bountiful gardens where a fountain bubbles away.

All of the nineteen bedrooms are papered with floral patterns and the brass or carved-wood bedsteads have homemade patchwork quilts, the work of a local quiltmaker. Rooms in the main house range from small to quite large, with sitting areas and window seats. One room has a private deck. The nicest accommodations, however, are in the reconstructed servants' quarters at the rear of the garden. These rooms all have tiled fireplaces, and windows on two sides.

For breakfast, Gramma's claims it serves the best granola in town, along with fresh fruits, home-baked breads and Italian roast coffee; on weekends quiche or bagels and lox are added to the fare. Sherry, wine and champagne are provided at an extra charge, but complimentary tea and coffee are available all day.

GRAMMA'S BED AND BREAKFAST INN, 2740 Telegraph Avenue, Berkeley, California 94705. Telephone: (415) 549-2145. Accommodations: twin, double, queen- and king-size beds; private baths with tub and/or shower; telephones; no television. Rates: moderate to expensive, breakfast included. No children under six. No pets. Cards: AE, CB, DC, MC, VISA.

Getting There: From San Francisco cross Bay Bridge and follow signs to Berkeley via Highway 80. Take Ashby Avenue exit east to Telegraph Avenue and turn left.

CASA MADRONA HOTEL
Sausalito

Across the Golden Gate Bridge from San Francisco, the residential community of Sausalito is built on steep wooded hillsides that rise above the bay. Antique shops, crafts galleries, restaurants, coffeehouses and often bumper-to-bumper lines of cars filled with tourists ring the colorful waterfront; a crowded yacht basin and a thriving houseboat community lie to the north. And clinging to a cliff overlooking the village, with magnificent views of the bay and San Francisco beyond, is one of the oldest buildings in Sausalito: the Casa Madrona Hotel.

When Vermont G. Barrett built this Victorian mansion for his family in 1885, it was acclaimed by the *Sausalito News* as "one of the finest . . . in Sausalito." The house miraculously survived an 1893 fire that destroyed much of the town. In 1902 it was sold by Barrett and converted into a guest house. Over the ensuing years, under various ownerships, Casa Madrona was operated as a hotel, reputedly as a bordello, and in the 1950s as a boardinghouse for the Beatnik generation. Then in 1959 the Deschamps family from France leased the property, turning the lower floor into an elegant French restaurant called Le Vivoir, and rehabilitating the upper floors into an unpretentious pension such as one might find on the back streets of Paris. This tranquil period ended in 1973 when heavy rains and mud slides threatened the building's foundations and its owner died. Casa Madrona was saved from condemnation by a group of local citizens who raised enough money for the foundation work. But the late owner's estate was in a bank trusteeship and the Deschamps were too uncertain of the future of their lease to invest in other needed repairs.

By 1978 the little hotel had sunk into a state of genteel shabbiness. But in the spring of that year, John Mays, a young lawyer with a penchant for restoring old buildings, bought the place and converted it into an inn of enormous charm and beauty. The restaurant, Le Vivoir, is still operated by the Deschamps family.

Each of the thirteen rooms is now decorated with a different theme, and most have spectacular bay views and private baths fitted with brass French hardware. One room even contains an old fireplace with a mahogany mantelpiece. It is difficult to say which is the loveliest: The Wicker Room provides a spacious springlike setting with a green and white ivy and fern motif, white wicker furniture and white shutters and a white cast-iron bedstead. The Bordello Room hints of Casa Madrona's shady past with red velvet, white lace and a rococo gilt mirror. The Regency Room boasts a canopied brass king-size bed, a velvet love seat and a handsome antique English desk. The Mariner Room is decorated in natural redwood and brick with a nautical touch. And the Bella Vista, decorated in French blue and beige, probably has the best view of them all. Mays has also renovated several vine-covered cottages next to the inn. These have their own living rooms and porches.

Casa Madrona has a comfortable sitting room with pink flowered paper above the white wainscoting. In the morning juice, fresh fruit and pastries are served here, and each evening Mays provides wine and cheese for hotel guests. And, snoozing by the fireplace in the sitting room or sunning on the broad veranda, is usually the hotel's permanent resident, Claudette—a fat, sleek cat who just arrived one day and apparently intends to stay forever, as most of Casa Madrona's guests would like to do.

CASA MADRONA, 156 Bulkley Avenue, Sausalito, California 94965. Telephone: (415) 332-0502. Accommodations: double, queen-size and king-size beds; nine rooms have private baths with shower or tub, four share community shower and half bath; cottages and sitting rooms can house four persons; television in some cottages. Rates: moderate to expensive, Continental breakfast, wine and cheese included. Children under 12 in cottages only. Pets in cottages only. Cards: AE, MC, VISA. Open all year.

Getting There: From San Francisco take Highway 101 north across Golden Gate Bridge. Take the Alexander Avenue exit and follow into center of town; turn left on Princess for one block; then turn right on Bulkley for three blocks.

PELICAN INN
Muir Beach

In Marin County, Highway 1 crosses the coastal range and plunges down the western slopes of Mount Tamalpais to Muir Beach. At the foot of this grade, encircled by coastal wilderness and bordered by the Pacific Ocean, is a very civilized bit of Old England. Pelican Inn is the creation of British-born Charles Felix, who is descended from four generations of pubkeepers in Surrey, England. According to Felix, the inn's name is derived from Sir Francis Drake's ship (originally called *Pelican* and later rechristened *Golden Hinde*), which was beached in Marin County "some four hundred years ago to claim California for Queen Elizabeth I and her descendants forever."

To help carry out this mandate, Felix purchased the Muir Beach property on the edge of the Golden Gate National Recreational Area and constructed a replica of a sixteenth-century English farmhouse. The white stucco building, crisscrossed with wooden beams, is surrounded by well-tended lawns, jasmine, and honeysuckle vines. Felix (a San Francisco advertising executive), his wife Brenda and two of their children have an apartment in the inn. The rest of the building houses six guest bedrooms, all with private baths, and a popular pub/restaurant.

Pelican Inn

On weekends the wood-paneled bar is jam-packed with drinkers, dart-throwers and would-be diners who order their food from a black-board, in true pub tradition. On Thursday through Sunday evenings a piano player adds to the conviviality. The adjoining dimly lit, low-ceilinged dining room is furnished with wooden tables and Felix's family antiques from Surrey. A huge inglenook (walk-in fireplace) of brick contains seats, a priest hole (hiding place) and a chamber for smoking hams. Outside, a flower-bedecked terrace accommodates the usual overflow of diners. As one would expect, the food is hearty pub fare: shepherd pies, Scotch eggs and the like. Breakfast, served downstairs or in the bedrooms with the morning paper, is big: juice, eggs and bangers (sausages), homemade breads.

In contrast to this hub of activity downstairs, the upstairs bedrooms are serene and romantic, with initials of honeymooners and other couples who have inhabited the rooms carved into the beamed ceilings. The unusually high beds are canopied with brocade and covered with quilted eyelet spreads. Oriental rugs, English antiques, pewter pots filled with fresh flowers and a decanter of cream sherry complete the decor. The leaded-pane windows (brought from England) offer vistas of the surrounding countryside, and some rooms have their own private balconies.

Felix admits that superstition is his great idiosyncrasy: "Witches and the little folk are all kept at bay." To keep the "evil eye" away, he buried bones and iron under the hearth. Pieces of holly on the doors protect the rooms from witches. And over each bed he has hung a stone with a hole in it "to insure no rickets in case of pregnancy."

THE PELICAN INN, Muir Beach, California 94965. Telephone: (415) 383-6000. Accommodations: queen-size beds; private baths with showers; no telephones; no television. Rates: moderate to expensive, full breakfast included. Open to the public for lunch and dinner. Rollaway bed provided for children at extra charge. No pets. Cards: MC, VISA. Open all year.

Getting There: From San Francisco take Highway 101 beyond Sausalito to the Mill Valley–Stinson Beach cut-off. From there take Highway 1 through Mill Valley (follow the signs to Stinson Beach) over the mountains to Muir Beach.

TOMALES BAY

The San Andreas Fault runs down the center of Tomales Bay, a long fingerlike inlet that separates Point Reyes Peninsula from the mainland. A railroad once ran along the east shore of the bay, bearing cargoes of lumber from the northern timberlands. Today Highway I follows its tracks, carrying carloads of Sunday drivers to the little seafood houses around the town of Marshall to feast on the bay's gastronomic gift to California: oysters. The west side of the bay shelters the village of Inverness, a popular weekend and summer resort. Beyond this is the Point Reyes National Seashore: 53,000 acres of coastal wilderness with magnificent hiking trails and beautiful beaches. Here a model village has been built, typical of those inhabited by the Miwok Indians who once dwelled on these shores. And here is the harbor that supposedly sheltered Sir Francis Drake's *Golden Hinde* during his expedition to the Pacific in 1579.

This area, far removed from suburban sprawl and freeway blight, is a mecca for nature lovers—and also for lovers of good food. Besides the oyster houses along the bay, there are a number of excellent restaurants.

Getting There: From San Francisco take Highway 101 north to the San Anselmo turn-off; continue on Sir Francis Drake Boulevard (Highway 17) through Fairfax to Olema and Inverness.

OLEMA INN
Olema

In the mid-nineteenth century Olema was a lively vacation spot and commercial center for the surrounding ranches and dairy farms. The town boasted three hotels and a racetrack and was even a candidate for the county seat. About all that's left is one of the century-old hotels, recently restored and rechristened the Olema Inn.

The site of Olema was once part of a 9,000-acre land grant given to Raphael Garcia, an illiterate Mexican soldier, for his service as commander of the San Rafael Mission guard. In 1876 Garcia's son Felix built a saloon on property inherited from his father, but three years later lost it to creditors. It was taken over by John Nelson, a Swede who ran the stagecoach from San Rafael to Olema. He added more rooms and named it Nelson's Hotel. At one time the hotel attracted visitors from throughout the state, including such celebrities as Jack London and John Steinbeck. It is even surmised that Teddy Roosevelt, while a guest of the Pacific Union Club in nearby Bear Valley, visited the hotel. Nelson's descendants operated the hotel until World War II, when it was turned into an army barracks. Then for the next three decades this lovely old American Colonial building was allowed to deteriorate, until 1973 when it was condemned and ordered demolished. But Gene Wedell, a Sausalito architect, heard of its plight and within weeks started plans for restoring the hotel as a historic landmark.

By 1980 renovation of the first floor was completed. A bar-library is outfitted with comfortable chairs and a selection of books. Beyond are two stately dining rooms, a popular rendezvous for Sunday brunch when live classical music is provided; dinner and lunch are served as well. There's also a terrace for al fresco dining. By 1981 three upstairs bedrooms and a breakfast–sitting room had been refurbished for overnight guests. The bedrooms have an old-fashioned country aura, with patterned comforters and brass bedsteads. A breakfast of cinnamon rolls, orange juice, quiche and freshly ground coffee is served in the sitting room.

OLEMA INN, 10,000 Sir Francis Drake Boulevard, Olema, California 94950. Telephone: (415) 663-8441. Accommodations: queen-size beds; one private bath, two rooms share bath, tub/showers; no telephones; no television. Rates: moderate, breakfast included. Open to the public for lunch, brunch and dinner. Children welcome. No pets. Cards: MC, VISA. Open all year.

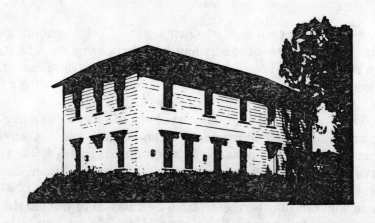

HOLLY TREE INN
Point Reyes Station

Down the road from Inverness, in a secluded nineteen acres of forest, is another new bed and breakfast house. This inn is named for the manicured holly trees that combine with English boxwood and lilac to form a hedge around the spacious lawn with its flower-covered stone wishing well. Owners Diane and Tom Balogh live downstairs in the two-story ranch house. Upstairs guests have their own large living room, papered in blue and white Laura Ashley prints, with comfortable overstuffed sofas and chairs upholstered in matching fabrics arranged around a brick fireplace. Another copper-hooded fireplace warms the adjoining dining room where a generous breakfast is served: fresh fruits and juices, quiche or cheese or eggs or waffles, home-baked breads such as poppyseed or banana-coconut, English jams, coffee and tea. These rooms open to a private deck sheltered by a flowery hillside. Four bedrooms, decorated with antiques, quilted bedspreads and ruffled curtains, offer views of the woodsy surroundings.

HOLLY TREE INN, 3 Silverhills Road (P.O. Box 642), Point Reyes Station, California 94956. Telephone: (415) 663-1554. Accommodations: twin, double and king-size beds; private and shared baths; no telephones; no television. Rates: moderate, breakfast included. Children welcome. No pets. No credit cards. Open all year.

Getting There: From Highway I, turn left on Sir Francis Drake Boulevard (marked "To Inverness"), take first left onto Bear Valley Road; take first right onto Silverhills Road and look for Holly Tree Inn sign.

INVERNESS LODGE
Inverness

Manka and Milan Prokupek came to California from Czechoslovakia by way of Holland and British Columbia, where they had a restaurant. In 1956 they opened Manka's Restaurant in Inverness Lodge, a rustic inn on a wooded hillside above Tomales Bay. Manka's rich Czech-Viennese dinners soon brought people from all over the San Francisco Bay Area to the village of Inverness. Many were delighted to discover that they could rent rooms here rather than drive back late to their homes.

The brown-shingled lodge, built at the turn of the century, contains four small pine-paneled rooms upstairs. They are comfortably appointed with maple furniture, quilted bedspreads, wing chairs and flowered curtains. Two of the rooms open to large, private sunny decks with chaises and boxes of primroses. There are four other rooms in a rustic red cottage behind the lodge; these share a patio edged with ivy, azaleas, camellias; from the back, windows look out to a forest of oaks and giant rhododendrons. Then there is a private cottage, set off by itself in a garden of calla lilies and nasturtiums. Inside there is a bright red Swedish stove set on a brick hearth, and two studio couches in a homey living area. A double bed is partitioned off in a sleeping area. And there is an equipped kitchen, too. Perfect for families.

Inverness Lodge is now managed by Milan Prokupek, Jr. and his wife, Judy, who does the cooking, though Manka herself still makes the luscious pastries. The dinners start with a visit to a lavish buffet of hors d'oeuvre: Danish cheeses, sausages, cold meats, fresh fruit, relishes, several salads and Norwegian herring. Then comes homemade soup and a choice from among eight Czech or Viennese entrées, ranging from roast duckling with caraway sauce and veal with paprika sauce to fresh oysters from Tomales Bay baked with anchovy butter. Complete breakfasts are served, too, with tempting choices such as French toast with cinnamon pears, or crêpes filled with raspberry preserves. The dining room is rather plain, but large windows offer views of the woods. It is the verdant setting that imparts a special magic to Inverness Lodge, rather than the rooms themselves.

INVERNESS LODGE, Callender Way and Argyle, Inverness, California 94937. Telephone: (415) 669-1034. Accommodations: double beds, some rooms with studio couch as well; private baths with tub only; one cottage with kitchen and bath with stall shower; no telephones; no television. Rates: inexpensive; no meals included. Open to the public for breakfast and dinner. Children welcome. No pets. Cards: AE, MC, VISA. Open all year except Tuesday and Wednesday; open Friday-Sunday only in the winter.

Inverness Lodge

TEN INVERNESS WAY
Inverness

A tranquil, homelike setting for those who want to get away from it all is provided in this spacious redwood-shingled house, built as a residence in 1904. Designer-contractor Stephen Kimball remodeled the building for a bed and breakfast inn in 1980, and his partner, Mary Davies, is resident innkeeper. A large fir-paneled living room, furnished with antiques and an Oriental rug, is a restful spot for reading during the day, but livelier in the evening when guests gather for sherry around the big stone fireplace—especially if there's someone who wants to play the player piano. Mary serves a full breakfast in the adjoining dining room cheered by a large Danish fireplace. There's always fruit, perhaps a half grapefruit, and goodies such as quiche, or banana pancakes with apricot sauce, or French toast made from homemade bread. Upstairs the five bedrooms, paneled with white carsiding, are furnished with handmade patchwork quilts and rag rugs. And there are always bowls of flowers cut from the gardens that surround the inn. It was rumored that a ghost once inhabited this house, but Stephen and Mary had the local Episcopal priest bless each room with holy water when the inn opened. Only good spirits live here now. As Mary says, "Peaceful is the word most often used to describe our place."

TEN INVERNESS WAY, 10 Inverness Way, Inverness, California 94937. Telephone: (415) 669-1648. Accommodations: twin and double beds; two community baths with shower, tub/shower; no telephones; no television. Rates: moderate, breakfast included. Children sometimes welcome. No pets. No credit cards. Closed Christmas and Monday night during winter months.

CALIFORNIA
NEVADA
MINING COUNTRY

The Mother Lode
Across the High Sierra
To the Comstock Lode

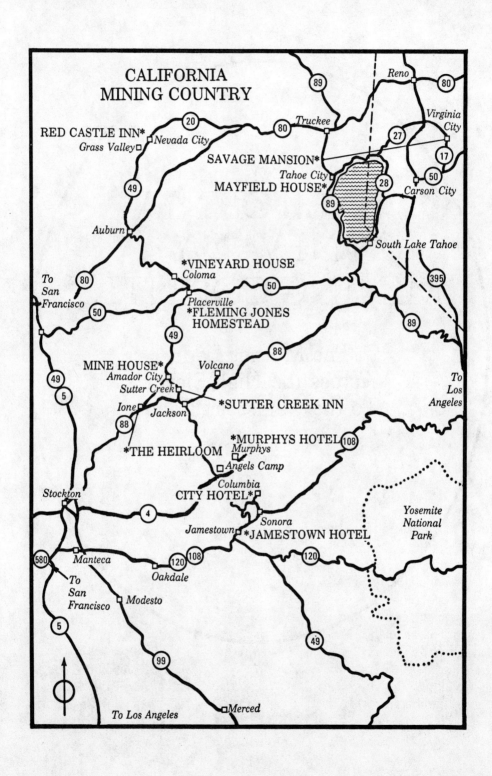

CALIFORNIA MINING COUNTRY

RED CASTLE INN*
Grass Valley □ □ Nevada City

SAVAGE MANSION*
Tahoe City
MAYFIELD HOUSE*

Reno
Truckee
Virginia City
Carson City

Auburn

*VINEYARD HOUSE
Coloma

South Lake Tahoe

To San Francisco

Placerville
*FLEMING JONES HOMESTEAD

MINE HOUSE*
Amador City
Sutter Creek
Ione
Jackson

Volcano

*SUTTER CREEK INN

*THE HEIRLOOM

*MURPHYS HOTEL
Murphys
Angels Camp

To Los Angeles

Stockton

Columbia
CITY HOTEL*

Yosemite National Park

Jamestown
Sonora
*JAMESTOWN HOTEL

Manteca
To San Francisco
Oakdale
Modesto

Merced
To Los Angeles

VINEYARD HOUSE
Coloma

In the 1840s the only riches to be found in the Sierra Nevada came from the mountains' timber. But on January 24, 1848, the destiny of California was forever changed. On that day James W. Marshall was deepening the tailrace of a sawmill he had built with John W. Sutter at Coloma on the south fork of the American River in the Sierra foothills. While at work, he noticed in the raceway some glittering specks. These turned out to be gold, and within months one of history's largest and most colorful gold rushes began. In the next decade some 100,000 prospectors would come to seek their fortunes in the Mother Lode.

A few years after Marshall's discovery, the town of Coloma had grown to over ten thousand inhabitants. But the prosperity of Coloma and of Marshall was short-lived. The gold of Coloma proved to be only a teaser for the vast wealth contained in the Sierra foothills to the north and south. Within a decade the ore here had been depleted and the miners went on to richer diggings. By 1868, only two hundred residents remained and among them was a bitter and impoverished James Marshall, who survived by occasionally working as a gardener.

Marshall died in 1885, a pauper. Five years later a large bronze monument was erected in his honor over the place of his burial and thousands of people flocked to Coloma for the dedication ceremonies. The highlight of these festivities was an elaborate ten-course banquet for two thousand guests at Vineyard House, the home of Robert Chalmers, an extravagant local vintner. Chalmers had built the house in 1878 as an elaborate residence for himself and his bride, a young widow, on vineyards she had inherited from her late husband, Martin Allhoff. Chalmers improved the original winery, built in 1866, and developed the vineyards to five hundred producing acres. The house had nineteen rooms with nine fireplaces, and he spent the then

73

exhorbitant sum of fifteen thousand dollars on furnishings. Later he had a special wing added for the Marshall Monument banquet.

In his later life Chalmers allegedly became insane and locked himself in the basement where he starved to death. (There is some evidence, however, that he actually died elsewhere.) After Chalmers's death, his ghost was rumored to haunt the house, which fell into disrepair. The vineyards withered away and the old winery crumbled into ruins.

The Vineyard House was being operated as a run-down hotel and restaurant when it was discovered by Gary Herrera, an Oakland restaurateur who wanted to escape the metropolitan rat race. In 1975, Gary bought the property in partnership with his brother and sister-in-law, Frank and Darlene Herrera, and a friend, David Van-Buskirk.

Thus began a gigantic, do-it-yourself restoration project. The four of them stripped floors and balustrades to the natural wood, papered walls, and hauled long-since forgotten pieces of period furniture down from the attic and refurbished them.

The dining rooms are filled with relics of yesteryear. In one, fire burns in a Franklin stove; genuine kerosene-burning lamps flicker on tables topped with brown and white checkered cloths. The dishes and flatware are a mishmash of patterns such as one might have inherited from a myriad of aunts. (Actually some of the chinaware came with the house, but much of it has come from doting customers who turn up with "grandma's dishes.")

The food is old-fashioned country cookery. Not always perfect, but always hearty and homemade. Pots of soup and big bowls of salad are set on the table and you serve yourself. The bread is freshly baked. Entrées include rib-sticking fare such as simmering chicken topped with a two-inch layer of dumplings and gravy. Vineyard House does not serve a complete breakfast, but coffee and homemade dessert breads are available for overnight guests.

Upstairs seven bedrooms have been renovated. "We will probably never be finished," Darlene observes. "There is always something to do." Each room is different, some with brass bedsteads, others with massive Victorian headboards. Homemade quilts top the beds.

The Vineyard House is very much a family operation, complete with a real grandma. Darlene Herrera's mother lives in the house and helps make the desserts. Her younger brother runs the gift shop. Her two sons are the "bellboys." And, as Darlene expresses it, "Everybody who comes here becomes automatic family."

VINEYARD HOUSE, P.O. Box 176, Coloma, California 95613. Telephone: (916) 622-2217. Accommodations: double and king-size beds; community bath with tile shower; no telephones; no television. Rates: inexpensive to moderate, Continental breakfast included. Open to the public for dinner; full bar service. Children over 16 welcome. No pets. Cards: AE, MC, VISA. Open all year except Mondays and Tuesdays from September to June.

Getting There: From San Francisco take Highway 80 to Sacramento, Highway 50 to Placerville, then Highway 49 north.

THE FLEMING JONES HOMESTEAD
Placerville

Just south of Coloma another gold camp was founded in 1848 and named Dry Diggin's because the miners had to tote the gravel that contained the ore to water for washing. Later, to keep the rowdy population in order, hangings became so commonplace that the town was dubbed Hangtown. But with respectability came the name Placerville. Towards the end of the century Fleming Jones, a dairy farmer from Wisconsin, came here to homestead a ninety-seven-acre tract of wooded foothills just east of Placerville. He liked to gamble and also acquired an interest in a saloon. After a particularly good night at the tables, he arrived home with twelve hundred dollars and told his wife, Florence, to go build herself a house. And she did. Descendants of the Jones family lived there until the late 1970s, and in 1980 the old farmhouse and eleven acres of the land were acquired by Janice Condit, an administrator at the University of California in Santa Barbara and a former State Department interpreter. She had decided to become an innkeeper.

Janice's inn mirrors her interests in cooking, antiques, farming and California wines. You enter through the farmhouse kitchen, rife with the aroma of freshly baked bread or simmering preserves of fruit from the pear, apple and fig trees in her orchards. A homey parlor is furnished with a Morris rocker, an overstuffed sofa and tables laden with magazines on farming, wine and Californiana. In the adjoining dining room guests gather for breakfast around a massive oak table with carved griffin feet. On gold-rimmed Haviland and Limoges china,

Janice serves an "expanded" Continental breakfast of fresh fruit, preserves from the farm, two or three kinds of homemade bread or muffins.

The Homestead presently has three guest rooms: one downstairs, and two upstairs that open onto a flower-filled porch with views of the rolling, wooded countryside. Rooms are furnished with cast-iron bedsteads (equipped with *new* mattresses, flowered quilts and matching sheets). Children's school desks, with vases of fresh flowers, serve as night tables. Janice plans to renovate the nearby bunkhouse to hold another two rooms for guests.

The area surrounding Placerville offers a number of diversions: tours of the old Gold Bug mine, visits to prize-winning wineries, walks in the woods to pick wild flowers or hunt for square nails. But a favorite pastime of Homestead guests is helping with the farm chores: feeding the chickens and collecting their eggs, helping to tend the vegetable gardens or harvest the fruit from the trees, petting Janice's Welsh pony and twenty-year-old burros. Other guests prefer just to loaf on the porch swing and admire the pastoral setting.

FLEMING JONES HOMESTEAD, 3170 Newtown Road, Placerville, California 95667. Telephone: (916) 626-5840. Accommodations: double beds; one private bath, one shared bath, tub/shower and shower; no telephones; no television. Rates: moderate, breakfast included. No children. No pets. No cards. Open all year.

Getting There: From Placerville, take Highway 50 east to the Newtown Road/Point View Drive exit. At the base of the off ramp, jog to the right to another stop sign and turn left onto Broadway, which runs parallel to the freeway and becomes Newtown Road. The Homestead is on the right just past a pond.

AMADOR COUNTY

Located in the heart of the Mother Lode, this is one of California's smallest counties in both size and population, yet its mines yielded more than half the gold that came out of the entire Sierra foothills. Gold may still be panned in the streams, and many of the old mines are open to the public. But today the commercial interests of the Amadoreans have turned from the mines to the vines. Amador County's Shenandoah Valley produces some of the state's most distinctive Zinfandel. And many of the wineries are open for touring and winetasting.

In Amador County, Highway 49 winds through oak-studded hillsides and the old mining towns of Amador City, Sutter Creek and Jackson. The brick or clapboard buildings, with their second-story balconies covering raised sidewalks, now house antique shops, art and craft galleries, saloons. A worthwhile side trip from Sutter Creek or Jackson is a visit to the picturesque mining town of Volcano, situated in a valley surrounded by pine-forested mountains above Highway 49.

It would be difficult to become bored in Amador County. Besides shopping, sightseeing, mine and wine touring, visiting historic museums, you may participate in a host of recreational activities. There are fishing and boating at nearby Lakes Amador, Pardee and Camanche, and rafting on the Mokelumne River. There are hunting, tennis, a nine-hole golf course, and even skiing in nearby Kirkwood Meadows. And on summer evenings the Claypipers Theater presents old-time melodrama. You can also eat well in Amador County. Jackson offers a number of family-style Italian restaurants, such as Buscaglia's, where the food is both hearty and above average.

Getting There: From San Francisco take Highway 580 east through Tracy to Manteca, Highway 5 north to Stockton and Highway 88 northeast to Jackson. Sutter Creek is four miles north of Jackson on Highway 49; Amador City is two miles north of Jackson. This part of the Mother Lode may also be reached by taking Highway 50 to Placerville and proceeding south on Highway 49.

THE MINE HOUSE
Amador City

Over $23 million in gold bullion was removed from the Keystone Consolidated Mines in Amador City before they were finally closed in 1942. The mining company's offices, grinding and assay rooms were located in a two-story brick building on a hillside across the highway from the mines. In 1954 the building, then abandoned and run-down, was purchased by Marguerite and Peter Daubenspeck, who came to California on a vacation, were charmed by Amador City and decided to stay. Originally the Daubenspecks intended to restore the old mine house for a residence; then they decided it would be an ideal inn.

After two years of renovation, the eight rooms were ready for guests. The Daubenspecks furnished the entire building with authentic period furniture, found within one hundred miles of Amador City. And the rooms are handsome, indeed. There are burled-walnut pieces,

78

Empire dressers, commodes topped with Italian marble, rockers, platform rockers, armoires, carved bedsteads, and under each bed an old-fashioned bed warmer. Many of the rooms contain old pitchers and wash basins set on commodes. But these are for show only. The Daubenspecks have added modern wood-paneled baths throughout.

The rooms of the Mine House are named after their original usage. Downstairs is the Mill Grinding Room, where the ore was brought to be ground; the supports that held the shafts for the grinding machinery are still on the ceiling. Next door is the Assay Room, where the ore was evaluated for its gold content. There is a Retort Room, where the ore was stored, and a Stores Room that once contained the mining supplies. All the interiors are of painted brick.

The upstairs rooms, however, are the most attractive, with thirteen-foot-high ceilings paneled in redwood. On one side, rooms open to a wide balcony overlooking the highway. On the other side they open to a covered patio dug out of the grassy hillside. These rooms originally housed the Keystone Consolidated Mining Company's offices and are appropriately named: Directors' Room, Bookkeeping Room, Keystone Room and Vault Room, which contains the safe in which the bullion was stored until the stagecoach transported it to San Francisco.

There is a swimming pool for guests at the Mine House. No meals are served, but each morning Peter Daubenspeck III, who now owns the inn, leaves a tray of orange juice and coffee by each door.

THE MINE HOUSE, P.O. Box 245, Amador City, California 95601. Telephone: (209) 267-5900. Accommodations: double and twin double beds; private baths with showers; no telephones; no television. Rates: inexpensive, orange juice and coffee included. Children welcome. No pets. No credit cards. Open all year.

SUTTER CREEK INN
Sutter Creek

"When I first saw this house, I fell in love. It was just like falling in love with a person," confesses Jane Way, vivacious proprietor of the Sutter Creek Inn. This instant love occurred back in 1966, while Jane was motoring through the Mother Lode with her children. The house was not occupied, but she sleuthed its history. When built in 1859 by a man named Keyes for his bride, this was the biggest house in town. Later it was the home of State Senator Voorhies, and in 1966 the house was still

79

Sutter Creek Inn

owned by his descendants—who refused to sell. For two months Jane Way persisted with phone calls. Finally, when she was about ready to give up, she was informed that the family had agreed to sell. And the Keyes-Voorhies House was rechristened Sutter Creek Inn.

Jane Way, a woman of enormous talent and energy, has changed far more than the name. She has dressed up every inch of the inn with a riot of color and charm. The gracious living room, painted a pale aqua, is comfortably furnished with large sofas upholstered in floral print, a hutch filled with antique china, a small piano and a grandfather clock. A chess set and a decanter of sherry by the fireplace are ready for the guests' enjoyment.

But the highlight of a stay at Sutter Creek Inn is breakfast in the country-kitchen/dining room. Walls, partially brick, partially paneled, are hung with copper colanders, an Oriental rug, a collection of guns. Two long, polished plank tables are gaily set with orange mats, gold-rimmed china and a pewter pitcher filled with dried flora. Shuttered windows look out to the lawn and gardens. Jane carries on an animated conversation with guests as she cooks, serves and pours a shot of brandy into the coffee. Her menu is ambitious: fresh fruit, perhaps berries, or peaches just picked from the inn's own trees. Jane might whip up pancakes with chopped nuts and apples, corn bread or a soufflé.

In the inn's early days, the only rooms rented were the small upstairs bedrooms, which are the least desirable today. The demand is for the outbuildings in the rear of the house—the woodshed, carriage house, storage shed and old laundry house, which Jane has extensively remodeled and furnished with flair.

Four of these have "swinging beds," actually suspended by cables from the ceiling. This was an idea she picked up in the tropics of Mexico where people often hang their beds to avoid crawling insects and lizards. But if you suffer from motion sickness, you won't need Dramamine; the beds may be stabilized easily.

No two of the rooms are alike, except that they are perfectly appointed down to the tiniest details: books, magazines, a deck of cards, a decanter of sherry. In one you might find a fireplace, in another a Franklin stove, in yet another a sunken bathtub. Some open out to private patios or porches, others into the lovely back garden. Some are furnished in solid Early American maple, others have canopied four-poster beds, still others contain brightly painted wickerware. Jane transforms whatever she finds around the countryside: an old drum topped with a wicker tray for a table, a miner's scale for a planter, a milk can for a lamp base, two water barrels for the base of a bathroom sink. All is visual joy.

Though there is much to see and do in the Sutter Creek area, Jane admits that most of her guests come primarily to relax, to get away from it all. But one diversion unique to this inn is a session of Jane's handwriting analysis, made with the warning: "This might change your life completely." So might a visit to Sutter Creek Inn.

SUTTER CREEK INN, 75 Main Street, Sutter Creek, California 95685. Telephone: (209) 267-5606. Accommodations: twin, double and queen-size beds; all private baths; no telephones; no television. Rates: moderate, breakfast included. Children discouraged; children under 15 not allowed. No pets. No credit cards. Open all year except first two weeks of January.

THE HEIRLOOM
Ione

The Ione Valley, west of Highway 49 in the lower foothills, was the supply center for the boom towns of Amador County during the gold rush. This valley had been settled in the early 1800s by a number of Virginians, most of whom left during the Civil War. One family among these settlers, the Stephenses, left a legacy of the Old South: a brick antebellum mansion adorned with classical columned porticos. This architectural heirloom was later purchased by Patrick Scully, a rancher who owned most of the surrounding valley. In 1980 Patricia Cross and Melisande Hubbs, two women whose children were grown, bought the Heirloom for an inn.

From a nondescript residential area you approach the Heirloom by a long driveway bordered by acacias, eucalyptuses and fruit trees, suddenly encountering a secret garden from another era. A giant gnarled wisteria, graceful magnolias, a brick terrace and a lush lawn nestle up to the gracious old house. From the veranda you enter a spacious sitting room appointed with a square piano, comfortable couches placed by the fireside, antiques, scattered Oriental rugs, tables equipped with decanters of sherry, dominoes and jigsaw puzzles. A breakfast of fresh fruit, crêpes and Louisana dark-roast coffee is served here, or on the patio or in one of the four upstairs bedrooms. These are decorated with irresistible charm, using family antiques from the innkeepers' former homes, brass bedsteads with flowered or patchwork

quilts, fresh flowers. Two of these rooms open to a broad balcony. One has a fireplace, along with its own private entrance, bath and balcony.

Although the sleepy town of Ione offers few diversions, it's only a short drive from Jackson and Sutter Creek and all the attractions of Amador County.

THE HEIRLOOM, 214 Shakeley Lane (P.O. Box 322), Ione, California 95640. Telephone: (209) 274-4468. Accommodations: twin, double, queen- and king-size beds; three rooms share bath, one private bath; no telephones; no television. Rates: inexpensive to moderate, breakfast included. No children under eight. No pets. No cards. Open all year.

Getting There: From San Francisco take Highway 580 and Highway 205 to Charter Way in Stockton. Take Charter Way to Highway 99, go north to Highway 88 and east to Highway 124, which leads to Ione. Turn left on Main Street, turn right on Preston and left on Shakeley Lane. From Highway 49, take Highway 124 or Highway 88 west.

MURPHYS HOTEL
Murphys

The historic mining town of Murphys was known in its heyday as Queen of the Sierra. It was not gold, however, but the discovery of the Calaveras Big Trees—a forest of giant sequoias in the mountains east of Murphys—that attracted some of the town's most illustrious guests. To accommodate them, in 1855 flour magnate J. L. Sperry built a luxury hotel, which after a fire and a succession of owners and names was finally christened Murphys Hotel and designated as a historic landmark on both the state and federal registers. Over the years the hotel hosted such disparate luminaries as Black Bart, Mark Twain, Count von Rothschild, John Jacob Astor and Horatio Alger, Jr. Ulysses S. Grant was another visitor, and the bed he slept in still occupies the Presidential Suite.

In the late 1970s a group of investors purchased and restored the hotel with the help of state funds, keeping most of the original furnishings in the nine guest rooms. No closets, televisions or private bathrooms detract from the authenticity of yesteryear, but for those who like these comforts, the new owners constructed a modern twenty-room motel next door. (If you want to be in the old hotel, be sure and specify when you make your reservations.) The downstairs parlor was refurbished with a pot-bellied stove, Oriental rugs and Victorian chairs. Adjacent is an old-time saloon, resplendent with hunting trophies, which offers live music on weekends; a large dining room is in the rear.

Besides hiking in the six thousand forested acres of Calaveras Big Trees, the area offers many attractions: river rafting, tennis, golf, horseback riding and exploring gold mining museums, natural caverns and caves. Historic Columbia is only a short drive away.

MURPHYS HOTEL, 457 Main Street (P.O. Box 329), California 95247. Telephone: (209) 728-3454. Accommodations: double, queen- and king-size beds; hotel rooms share bath; motel rooms have private bath; no telephones; television and air conditioning in motel rooms. Rates: inexpensive to moderate. Open to the public for breakfast, lunch and dinner. Children welcome. Smaller pets sometimes allowed. Cards: AE, MC, VISA. Open all year.

Getting There: From Placerville take Highway 49 south to Angels Camp, then head east on Highway 4 to Murphys and turn left on Main Street. From Stockton take Highway 4 east.

COLUMBIA AREA

Columbia was one of the most prosperous gold rush towns, with ore taken from its fabulously rich mines valued at over $80 million. Within three years after gold had been discovered in 1850 at Hildreth's Diggings, as it was then called, the town's population had grown to some twenty thousand and ranked as the second largest city in California. In those days Columbia boasted forty saloons, 150 gambling houses, eight hotels, four banks and two volunteer fire companies! Despite the firemen's efforts, most of the original frame structures were destroyed in two early fires and the town was almost completely rebuilt in brick.

The Columbians' paranoia about fire has benefited posterity. The durability of these brick buildings caused the state of California to purchase the town in 1945 and restore it as the Columbia Historic State Park. Today, except for an onslaught of tourists, the tree-shaded Main Street with its boardwalks and balconied buildings looks much the way it did in the 1860s. No automobiles are allowed in the town itself, but a stagecoach does lumber through offering visitors a ride. The old blacksmith shop, harness and saddle shop, carpenter shop and a Chinese herb store are in working condition. And the historic Fallon House Theater comes back to life for six weeks each summer as a repertory playhouse for University of the Pacific students.

Recreational activities in the area include tennis, fishing, hunting, swimming and waterskiing in nearby lakes, horseback riding, golf, and river trips down the Stanislaus. But the true attraction of Columbia remains its gold mine of early California history.

Getting There: From San Francisco, 580 to Tracy, 205 to Manteca; Highway 120 east past Knights Ferry to intersection of Highway 108; Highway 108 east to Sonora; Highway 49 north to Columbia.

CITY HOTEL
Columbia

One of the old brick buildings restored by the state in Columbia is the City Hotel, with its wrought-iron balcony overhanging the sidewalk of Main Street. Built in 1856 by George Morgan, the hotel was called the "What Cheer House" until it was ravaged by fire in 1867. Four years later it was rebuilt as the Morgan Hotel and three years later the name was changed to City Hotel.

In the 1940s the state of California acquired the City Hotel as part of Columbia Historic State Park, and after spending $800,000 on restorations and furnishings, opened its nine bedrooms, dining room and saloon to paying guests. The operation of the hotel is unique in California. The young chambermaids in their "granny caps," the waitresses in their long last-century dresses, the waiters and busboys in their black ties are not the college students off on a lark usually found at resort hotels. They are all serious students of the Hospitality Management Program at Columbia Junior College, which operates the hotel as an on-the-job training facility.

The bedrooms have been impeccably furnished with massive burled-wood Victorian bedsteads framing comfortable brand-new mattresses, brass coat racks, marble-topped bureaus. The rooms have half baths, no shower or tub, but the hotel thoughtfully provides each guest with a "bathroom caddy," a basket containing soap, washcloth, shower cap and even terry-cloth shower shoes. The trip down the hall to the shower is made as pleasant as possible here.

Upstairs there is also a homey old-fashioned parlor decorated with flocked paper, Oriental rugs and Victorian settees. There are a small library and games for the guests' use. A Continental breakfast is served here each morning.

Downstairs is the What Cheer Saloon and a gracious high-ceilinged dining room, a serene setting for the magnificently appointed tables set with cut-glass goblets, graceful wineglasses of varying sizes, flowered service plates, small brass hurricane lamps and even silver napkin rings on the sparkling white napery.

The food here is far removed from the mountain-country cooking you might expect to find in the Mother Lode. The City Hotel's kitchen is run by a first-rate chef from San Francisco, and his menu would come as no surprise in New York or Paris. But in Columbia? There are escargots and fresh bluepoint oysters baked with a sauce mornay among the appetizers. Kentucky limestone lettuce and hearts of palm

86

City Hotel

compose some of the salads. Shrimp bisque, French onion gratinée and vichyssoise compose the choice of soups. Then there is a choice of twenty elegant entrées: Chicken poached in wine with oranges and mushrooms, veal with apples and cream sauce, chateaubriand with a sauce béarnaise, and a loin of lamb stuffed with spinach are but a few. Dinners are à la carte, expensive, and worth it.

CITY HOTEL, P.O. Box 1870, Columbia, California 95310. Telephone: (209) 532-1479. Accommodations: twin, double and twin double beds; private half baths, community showers; no telephones; no television. Rates: moderate, Continental breakfast included. Open to the public for lunch, Sunday brunch and dinner; full bar service. Children welcome. No pets. Cards: MC, VISA. Conference facilities for 25 available. Open all year except Christmas and Christmas Eve Day.

JAMESTOWN HOTEL
Jamestown

Early in 1848 George James, a Philadelphia lawyer and veteran of the Mexican War, found a seventy-five-pound nugget in Woods Creek, south of Columbia. Prospectors rushed to the site and Jamestown, another thriving gold rush community, came into being. In 1859 the two-story Jamestown Hotel was built and served as a center for the boomtown's social life, later becoming a hostelry for travelers when Jamestown became a bustling railroad center. A fire, years of neglect, even a stint as a hospital marked the hotel's course during this century.

Then in the late 1970s, the Sierra Railroad, which is headquartered in Jamestown, bought the hotel and restored it to its original flavor. The balconied facade was rejuvenated, and the raised plank sidewalk that flanks the hotel's Main Street frontage was rebuilt. Inside, the eight guest rooms and suites were refurbished in the Victorian style: brass beds, patchwork quilts, floral papers, lace curtains, wicker settees and ornate coat racks. (No closets here.) Many of the rooms have tiny connecting sitting rooms and all are named after colorful gold rush characters like Black Bart, Jenny Lind and Calamity Jane. The community baths are resplendent with painted claw-leg tubs, toilets with overhead tanks and marble-topped basins supported by old treadle sewing machines. In the rear a bridge from a plant-filled solarium leads to a redwood deck.

In 1981 another change in ownership occured, resulting in the extensive remodeling of the downstairs area for a bar and restaurant. The hotel is scheduled to reopen in the spring of 1982. This will coincide with the opening in Jamestown of Rail Town, a historic park dedicated to railroad memorabilia. Along with the tours on the Sierra Railroad, the park should make this Mother Lode town a mecca for fans of the iron horse.

JAMESTOWN HOTEL, Main Street (P.O. Box 639), Jamestown, California 95327. Telephone: (209) 984-3902. Accommodations: twin, double and queen-size beds; shared baths with tubs; no telephones; no television. Rates: moderate. Children welcome. No pets. Open to the public for lunch and dinner; full bar service. Cards: AE, MC, VISA. Open all year.

RED CASTLE INN
Nevada City

At the peak of the gold rush Nevada City was the third largest town in California, with a population of twelve thousand. Today with only two thousand residents it's a much quieter place, except for a freeway that unfortunately cuts through its hilly streets. Despite a few misbegotten modern buildings, the town retains much of the character of an 1850s mining community, with picturesque gas lamps along the main street and many of the old buildings intact and restored. History buffs will find much of interest here. The American Victorian Museum, located in a former foundry, houses a collection of historical books, documents, photographs and old mining equipment. More history exhibits are mounted in the gingerbread-trimmed Firehouse No. 1 and at Ott's Assay Office, where the miners reportedly brought a booty of $27 million in ore over the years.

Five miles from Nevada City, in Grass Valley, California's richest mines once produced over $400 million in gold; a mining display with a thirty-one-foot waterwheel may still be viewed. Also open to the public are the homes of the infamous dancer Lola Montez and her young protégée, Lotta Crabtree, who later became nationally renowned as an actress. Four miles from Grass Valley is the semiabandoned town of Rough and Ready, which once tried to secede from the Union in protest of mining taxes. There are swimming and fishing in nearby lakes. The historic Red Castle Inn in Nevada City is a quaint and comfortable base for exploring the region of the northern mines.

Red Castle Inn

This heavily ornamented, four-story brick structure has been cited as one of the best examples of Gothic Revival in the West. The imposing house was built between 1858 and 1860 as a two-family residence by Judge John Williams, who crossed the plains in 1849 and became a prominent businessman, mine owner and civic leader in Nevada City. The judge's son and his family also occupied the house and, according to local lore, young Williams, a lawyer, used to serenade the townsfolk every Sunday afternoon from the top veranda of the Red Castle with impromptu recitals on the trumpet or cornet. Both Williamses, father and son, died before the turn of the century, and the judge's widow operated her home as a boardinghouse for a number of years. Then the house was sold and resold to a succession of owners, who allowed it to slowly decline.

In 1963 James Schaar restored the Red Castle and converted it into an inn. His wife managed it until 1978, when Jerry Ames, a former schoolteacher, and Chris Dickman, a department store display designer, bought the inn. They have redecorated most of the rooms with bright paint or floral wallpapers and an eclectic selection of furnishings. "We decided to make it comfortable rather than stiffly authentic," Jerry comments. They painted the walls of the small living room ochre and mixed some contemporary pieces—an overstuffed sofa—with a gilt-edged Victorian mirror, Oriental lamps and artifacts. Here and elsewhere in the inn the original pine plank floors and plaster ceiling moldings remain intact.

Seven bedrooms occupy three floors of the inn; all but two have private bathrooms in which old-fashioned wash basins remain, but new stall showers have been added. "I think quaintness should stop short of the bathroom," Jerry laughs. From the spacious, high-ceilinged rooms on the lower floor, lace-curtained French doors open out to the veranda. The middle floor contains "parlor suites," each composed of a tiny sitting room, with barely enough room for a love seat and a little cast-iron, wood-burning stove, and a bedroom almost entirely filled by a double bed. Two garret rooms on the top floor have Gothic windows and share a parlor, a bath and the balcony where Judge Williams's son conducted his concerts a century ago. From here and the lower verandas that surround the house, you look down on terraced, wooded gardens, and across to the picturesque town of Nevada City on the adjacent hillside.

In the mornings, when guests gather for coffee and home-baked breads in the parlor, Jerry likes to talk about the history of the house. "There really is not that much history, but like all old houses, it does have a ghost—supposedly the Williamses' governess—but I haven't

91

met her yet. Also in residence with Jerry and Chris are three cats, because, they explain, "Every Gothic building has to have a cat."

RED CASTLE INN, 109 Prospect, Nevada City, California 95959. rooms have private baths with shower, two rooms have connecting bath; no telephones; no television. Rates: moderate, Continental breakfast included. Children discouraged. No pets. No credit cards. Open all year.

Getting There: From San Francisco take Highway 80 through Sacramento to Auburn. Take Highway 49 north through Grass Valley to Broad Street exit in Nevada City; turn right to Sacramento Street, turn right again and proceed up hill to first road on the left; make a hard left turn onto Prospect Street.

MAYFIELD HOUSE
Tahoe City

High above the Mother Lode, cradled among the peaks of the Sierra Nevada, lies Lake Tahoe: one of the most beautiful lakes in the world and one of California's most popular year-round playgrounds. This two-hundred-square-mile body of blue water is ringed by sandy beaches and forests of pine, cedar, dogwood and aspen. Swimming, boating and waterskiing lure the summer visitors, while excellent skiing—Squaw Valley and Heavenly Valley, for example—attract the winter tourist. The lake is bisected by the California-Nevada border, and all year hordes of gamblers flock to the Nevada casinos, which also offer shows by big-name entertainers on a par with Las Vegas.

Far from the neon glitter of the casinos is the Mayfield House, on the edge of Tahoe City. This sturdy house was built of wood and stones among the pines in 1932 by Norman Mayfield, a contractor. A frequent guest was his good friend Julia Morgan, the architect responsible for the San Simeon castle of William Randolph Hearst. In 1980 Joanne Neft, a Tahoe travel agent, bought the house from Mayfield and converted it into an elegant little inn.

Joanne's impeccable taste and eye for detail pervade the inn, from the classical taped music in the living room to the restful rosy-beige and blue color scheme throughout, to thoughtful touches such as providing bathrobes for guests. The living room, with its dark-stained pine paneling, beamed ceiling and large stone fireplace, is furnished with Early American pine tables, chairs and love seats upholstered in blue, kerosene-fired hurricane lamps and an assortment of books and games. The adjoining breakfast room sports a corner hutch and some of the specimens of Joanne's African violet collection that abound throughout the house. Here a full breakfast is served on pretty blue and white flowered English china: homemade goodies such as Finnish pancakes or Portuguese toast with fruit sauce or cheese blintzes with berry sauce. Or, if you prefer, you may have your breakfast served in bed in one of the six guest rooms.

All rooms are appointed with fresh flowers, a selection of books, down pillows and comforters, and original watercolors by Margaret Carpenter. Mullioned windows offer views of the mountains, woods or the golf course across the road. But each room has its distinctive decor. One of the downstairs rooms, the former den of Norman Mayfield, is wood-paneled and decorated with brown, beige and rust plaid drapes. By contrast, the upstairs room where Julia Morgan stayed is all frills, with a blue and white papered gabled ceiling, a white chenille spread and a skirted dressing table. Mayfield's former bedroom asserts its masculinity with paneled walls, a quilted brown velvet spread on the king-size bed and a sitting area with a brown leather couch and chairs.

From Mayfield House it's only a short walk to the beach for summer guests. In winter, skiing at Squaw Valley is about a fifteen-minute drive, but several smaller ski resorts are even closer. The casinos of Tahoe's North Shore can be reached in about fifteen minutes. And good restaurants are plentiful in the area. Two of the best are the Petit Pier in Tahoe Vista and La Cheminée in Kings Beach.

MAYFIELD HOUSE, 236 Grove Street (P.O. Box 5999), Tahoe City, California 95730. Telephone: (916) 583-1001. Accommodations: twin, queen- and king-size beds; shared baths; no telephones; no television. Rates inexpensive to moderate, breakfast included. No children under ten. No pets. Cards: MC, VISA. Open all year.

Getting There: From San Francisco or Reno take Highway 80 to Truckee, turn south on Highway 89 to Tahoe City, turn north on Highway 28 to Grove Street, turn left.

THE SAVAGE MANSION
Virginia City

Gold was found first here on the side of Mount Davidson, but the discovery of silver in 1859 was the big bonanza of the Comstock Lode, one of the richest ore deposits in the world. Over $300 million in precious metals was excavated within twenty years from the deep mines that still lie under the streets of Virginia City. This silver helped to finance the Civil War and to build the city of San Francisco. It also made millionaires of those who exploited the mines: James G. Fair, George Hearst, James Mackay, William Ralston and William Sharon to name a few.

In the 1860s and 1870s, Virginia City was queen of the West, second largest city this side of the Rockies, the richest boom town in America. Palatial mansions studded her barren hills. Extravagant entertaining was the order of the day (heaps of oyster shells and wine bottles still lie around the town). Fortunes in silver passed over the lusty bars of the Bucket of Blood and 109 other saloons. The most glamorous performers of the day played to bejeweled audiences at Piper's Opera House. And in 1862, a twenty-seven-year-old adventurer-prospector started writing of these lively events for the *Territorial Enterprise* under the pseudonym of Mark Twain.

Today only about seven hundred people live in Virginia City and their bonanza is tourism. The main street is pure honky-tonk, with one-arm bandits in the old saloons reclaiming the lost silver. But around the town many of the old mansions stand freshly painted, proud of their new prosperity, and open for visitors who want to relive the colorful past.

One of the most splendid high-Victorian mansions built on these hilly streets is the Savage Mansion. The Savage Mining Company only unearthed some $20 million in silver from its mine—a pittance compared with Consolidated Virginia's big bonanza of $105 million. Yet the Savage Mine made a mark on history as the breakthrough point of the famous tunnel that Adolph Sutro built through Mount Davidson, at a cost of $6,500,000, to drain and ventilate the Comstock mines.

The three-storied Savage Mansion was built in 1870 to house the mining company's offices on the first floor and the superintendent's family on the upper levels. The house was magnificently furnished, even by the Comstock's opulent standards, and was used to entertain notables of the era. General Ulysses S. Grant was a guest for two days in 1879; Thomas Edison is rumored to have been another visitor.

The Savage Mansion

After the Comstock's silver was depleted, the Savage Mansion deteriorated along with the rest of Virginia City. By 1960 it was deserted and a veritable wreck, shingles missing from the mansard roof, paint almost totally peeled away, the foundation partly disintegrated. At this time it was purchased for a mere seventy-five hundred dollars by Elaine and Gerald Harwood, who had moved to Nevada from Redwood City. Restoration began and continued for nine years as the Harwoods duplicated the original detailing and reclaimed the mansion's furniture, which had been sold to a nearby museum.

Today the Savage Mansion is owned by Ann Louise Mertz and Bob and Irene Kugler, who moved to Virginia City from southern California seeking an active retirement project: "We didn't want to just play golf for the rest of our lives." They have continued the restoration to near-mint condition while living there and conducting tours of the building. The third-floor rooms can be rented by those who wish to savor the romance of the Comstock era. Among the four guest rooms is the one that was occupied by General Grant. The room is supposedly the way it was then, with floral wallpaper, a pot-bellied stove and an awesome bedstead that rises to ceiling height.

Guests share a bathroom that retains the plumbing of the 1880s: a toilet with overhead tank and a six-foot-long copper tub. In the morning, coffee and rolls are served in the Victorian kitchen.

SAVAGE MANSION, South D Street, Virginia City, Nevada 89440. Telephone: (702) 847-0574. Accommodations: double and twin double beds; community bath with tub/shower; no telephones; no television. Rates: moderate, Continental breakfast included. Children discouraged. No pets. Cards: MC, VISA. Open all year.

Getting There: From San Francisco take Highway 80 east to Reno, Highway 395 south to Highway 17 which leads south to Virginia City. From Lake Tahoe, take Highway 50 east through Carson City and Highway 17 north through Gold Hill to Virginia City. Nearest airport: Reno.

CALIFORNIA WINE COUNTRY

Sonoma, Napa Valley
And the Russian River Valley

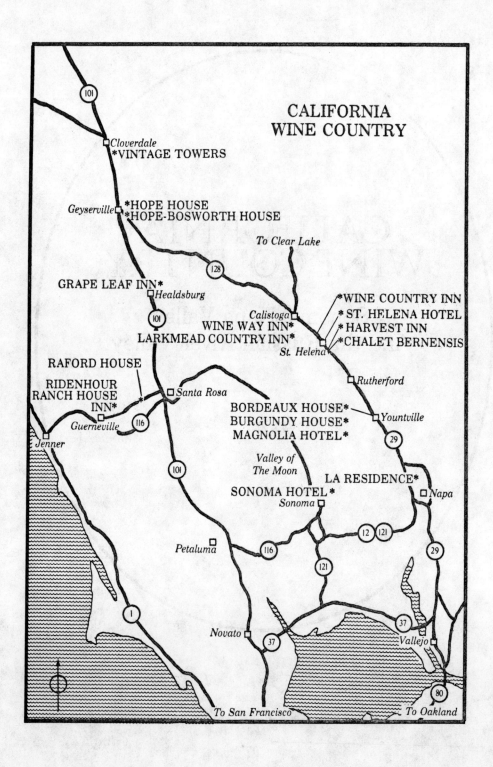

CALIFORNIA
WINE COUNTRY

101

☐Cloverdale
*VINTAGE TOWERS

Geyserville☐ *HOPE HOUSE
*HOPE-BOSWORTH HOUSE

To Clear Lake

128

GRAPE LEAF INN*
☐Healdsburg

101

Calistoga☐

WINE WAY INN*
LARKMEAD COUNTRY INN*

*WINE COUNTRY INN
*ST. HELENA HOTEL
*HARVEST INN
*CHALET BERNENSIS

St. Helena☐

RAFORD HOUSE

RIDENHOUR
RANCH HOUSE
INN*
☐Santa Rosa

☐Rutherford

☐
Guerneville
116

BORDEAUX HOUSE*
BURGUNDY HOUSE*
MAGNOLIA HOTEL*

Yountville☐

29

Jenner☐

101

Valley of
The Moon

LA RESIDENCE*

SONOMA HOTEL *
Sonoma☐

☐Napa

12 121

29

Petaluma☐

116

121

1

37

Novato☐
37

Vallejo☐

80

To San Francisco

To Oakland

SONOMA HOTEL
Sonoma

Sonoma's large tree-shaded plaza was laid out by General Mariano Guadalupe Vallejo in 1835 when he founded Pueblo de Sonoma as Mexico's most northerly outpost against hostile Indians. Twelve years earlier Mission San Francisco Solano de Sonoma had been built there as the northern tip of California's chain of missions. Vallejo built himself a two-story adobe *palacio* on the plaza where his regiment of Mexican soldiers marched daily. The peace was shattered on June 14, 1846, when a band of three dozen armed Americans, acting on their own authority, captured the town, imprisoned Vallejo, and proclaimed Sonoma capital of the Bear Flag Republic. The Bear Flag flew over the Sonoma plaza until the following month, when California became part of the United States.

At the northwest corner of the plaza is the Sonoma Hotel. No one knows for certain when the hotel was built, but the lower two stories are probably a century-old adobe. The third floor with its high gables was added at a later date circa 1880, when the building housed a dry goods store on the first level and a two-story meeting hall above. About 1920 it was purchased by the winemaking Sebastiani family, who converted the cavernous hall into two floors, partitioned these into seventeen rooms and rechristened it the Plaza Hotel. In 1974 John and Dorene Musilli bought the hotel and leased it to a group who ran it as the Waywith Inn for two years. When the Waywith group moved out, Dorene immediately began to redecorate the hotel with antiques. "There's not one reproduction in the place," she points out.

Sixteen of the rooms are furnished with French and English bedroom sets made at the turn of the century. In each room nearly all the pieces match—dresser, armoire, headboard, even chairs. Mattresses were custom-made to fit the odd-size beds, which were covered with

99

quilted flowered spreads. Ruffled organdy curtains and a watering can full of dried flowers and grasses add a homey note to each room.

The seventeenth room has been named the Vallejo Room in honor of the Italianate hand-carved burled walnut furniture that belonged to General Vallejo's sister and is on loan to the hotel from the Sonoma League for Historic Preservation. The bed looks fit for the general himself, with an eleven-foot-high backboard and a bedspread of scarlet velvet.

The Musillis stripped eight coats of paint off the wainscoting in the hotel lobby to reveal the natural dark fir. Here, in front of a large stone fireplace, guests are served a Continental breakfast of juice, croissants from a nearby French bakery, and a choice of teas, coffee or hot chocolate.

Sonoma's second important settler after General Vallejo was Colonel Agoston Haraszthy, a Hungarian nobleman who planted his Buena Vista vineyards here in the 1850s and started northern California's winemaking industry. Sonoma has ever since been an important viticultural center. The Buena Vista's old stone cellars are open to the public. Tours are also conducted at the Sebastiani Winery, Hacienda Cellars, and twenty-nine other wineries in the area.

Sonoma is rich in Californiana. The Sonoma State Historic Park maintains the mission, General Vallejo's home and the Toscano Hotel, which are open to visitors. The old barracks, which has headquartered three armies—the Mexicans, the Bear Flag rebels and the Americans—has also been restored. Near Sonoma is Valley of the Moon, last home of Jack London, now also preserved as a state park.

SONOMA HOTEL, 110 West Spain Street, Sonoma, California 95476. Telephone: (707) 996-2996. Accommodations: twin and double beds; some private baths with tub, community baths with showers; no telephones; no television. Rates: inexpensive to moderate, Continental breakfast included. Children welcome. No pets. Cards: AE, MC, VISA. Open all year.

Getting There: From San Francisco take Highway 101 north through San Rafael to Ignacio; there take Highway 37 east to Highway 21, which leads to Sonoma.

Sonoma Hotel

NAPA VALLEY

This lovely long valley, caressed by gentle mountains, is one of the world's most important wine-making regions. The Franciscan fathers from nearby Sonoma Mission started making wine here in the 1820s, but it was an inferior wine made from their Mission grapes. It was not until some thirty years later, in 1858, that Charles Krug produced the first European-type wine for which the valley is now known. After Colonel Agoston Haraszthy proved that the European *vinifera* grapes would thrive north of San Francisco Bay in his Buena Vista vineyards in Sonoma, immigrants from France, Italy and Germany flocked to the Napa Valley in the 1860s, planting cuttings from Haraszthy's stock.

This viniferous valley stretches north from the city of Napa, an early timber-shipping center and once even a mining town during a silver rush in 1858. The valley ends at the town of Calistoga, whose mineral spas have attracted the weary since Mormon settler Sam Brannan first discovered underground hot springs here in 1859. Towering above Calistoga is the forty-five-hundred-foot peak of Mount St. Helena, which Robert Louis Stevenson described as the "Mont Blanc of the Coast Range" after spending his honeymoon in a bunkhouse at the mountain's base in 1880.

One of the most interesting settlements in the valley is Yountville, named after the valley's first white settler, George Yount. In exchange for a favor to his friend, General Vallejo, the Mexican government granted Yount an eleven thousand–acre tract of land comprising most of the Napa Valley. The old Groezinger Winery in Yountville has been converted to a fascinating complex of shops, galleries and restaurants called Vintage 1870. Next door the train depot and railroad cars house yet more shops. And along the town's picturesque streets there are antique shops, restaurants—and a growing number of country inns.

North of Yountville is Rutherford Square, where outdoor musical productions are presented in the summer months. Just north of here is St. Helena, where a museum containing Robert Louis Stevenson memorabilia is housed in a stone hatchery. Beyond the town is an old bale mill with a waterwheel forty feet in diameter, and Freemark Abbey, another interesting complex of shops.

All through the valley, of course, are the wineries, most of which conduct tours of their cellars and tastings of their bottlings. This is unquestionably the most popular form of recreation in the valley. Space does not permit a description of all the wineries, but one stands out as spectacular over all the others. This is Sterling Vineyards, a recently built Moorish structure on a hilltop in the center of the valley between St. Helena and Calistoga. An aerial tramway whisks visitors to the winery over treetops. Inside, the wine-making operation is explained graphically, allowing visitors to tour the premises at their own pace. Afterwards, sipping wine in the late afternoon on the terrace as the mountains cast their shadows onto the vineyards below is an experience long remembered.

Other forms of recreation in the Napa Valley include aerial gliding around Calistoga, and swimming, fishing and boating at nearby Lake Berryessa. The valley also offers a diversity of dining experiences, in settings both elegant and casual: French haute cuisine, nouvelle cuisine and country cooking; Mexican, Italian and Chinese.

Getting There: From San Francisco take Highway 101 north through San Rafael to Ignacio; there take Highway 37 east to Highway 121 north to the intersection of Highway 12 which leads east to Napa. From Napa Highway 29 extends north through Yountville, Rutherford and St. Helena to Calistoga.

LA RESIDENCE
Napa

One of Napa Valley's early settlers was Harry C. Parker, a New Orleans river pilot who came to California during the 1849 gold rush. After working as a merchant in San Francisco and Stockton, he moved to Napa in 1865 to start farming. His home, just north of the town, was built in 1870 in the Gothic Revival style, fronted by a wide, columned porch and a balcony. Under a new Napa law that grants bed and breakfast permits as a measure to save historic buildings, the house became an inn in 1981.

Proprietor Barbara Littenberg has decorated La Residence in the style of a nineteenth-century country house, using antique armoires, sofas and queen-size replicas of brass and cast-iron beds covered with quilted eyelet or floral spreads and ruffled pillows. Marble or brick fireplaces enhance several of the seven bedrooms. Two large second-floor rooms have French doors leading to the balcony. The third-floor rooms are smaller, but cozy under the wallpapered eaves.

The cheerful breakfast area is furnished with small oak tables and a hutch where a morning buffet of fresh fruit, orange juice and croissants is laid out. Windows overlook a flower-filled brick patio and lawn. To one side is a hot tub. Guests also have use of a pretty parlor where wine and pâté is served in the evening.

LA RESIDENCE, 4066 St. Helena Highway North (Highway 29), Napa, California 94558. Telephone: (707) 253-0337. Accommodations: queen-size beds; private or shared baths with tub/shower; wheelchair access; no telephones; no television. Rates: high moderate to expensive, Continental breakfast included. No children. No pets. Cards: MC, VISA. Open all year.

Getting There: Take Highway 29 beyond Napa and past Salvador Road; turn right at Bon Appetit Restaurant, where a sign will direct you to the inn, which faces the highway.

MAGNOLIA HOTEL
Yountville

Built in 1873 with large stones from the Silverado Trail, this quaint three-story hotel has had a checkered history. Originally a traveler paid a dollar a night for a room, including a barn and feed for his horse. Those who could afford the luxury of rail travel were met at the Yountville depot by a surrey sent by the hotel. At one time the Magnolia was reputedly a brothel, and it is a known fact that the cellar was a center for bootlegging activities during Prohibition. Then for many years the hotel was boarded up, until Ray and Nancy Monte purchased it in 1968 and restored it to an inn of eminent charm and respectability. In 1977 the Magnolia was again sold, to Bruce Locken, former general manager of the Clift Hotel in San Francisco, and his wife Bonnie. They have continued the improvement process, adding four luxurious new rooms with decks and fireplaces in an adjoining building.

Furnishings of the hotel's eleven bedrooms are all from the Victorian era: marble-topped tables with crystal decanters of port, four-poster beds with crocheted or quilted spreads. Concessions to twentieth-century living have been made, however, with a few oversize beds and tiled baths. The two rooms on the top floor share a common sitting room, a unit popular with two couples traveling together.

Breakfast here, announced by the ringing of a gong at precisely nine o'clock, is an important event at the Magnolia. Guests gather around in the restaurant adjoining the hotel, introduce themselves and share wine-touring tips. Bruce, a skilled raconteur, moves around the table, telling anecdotes from several decades of hotelkeeping while replenishing the coffeepot and serving generous platters of food. The Lockens' system of devising the menu is unique: First-nighters are

Magnolia Hotel

served whole-wheat French toast with port syrup, second-nighters get shirred eggs, third-nighters receive a sherry and mushroom omelet, and so on, so that no one has the same breakfast two mornings in a row. On Friday and Saturday nights Bonnie takes over the kitchen in the restaurant, which is open to the public for dinner.

The Magnolia Hotel has several other attractions not offered by other inns in the Napa Valley. There is a large swimming pool surrounded by lawns. Here—or in your room if you like—Bruce will serve you a bottle purchased from his fine collection of Napa wines. And behind the hotel, set in an enclosed redwood deck, is a commodious Jacuzzi pool, which is lighted from under the water at night.

MAGNOLIA HOTEL, 6529 Yount Street, Yountville, California 94599. Telephone: (707) 944-2056. Accommodations: double, queen-size and king-size beds; private baths, some with tub/shower, some with shower only; no telephones; no television. Rates: moderate to expensive, breakfast included. Open to the public for dinner Friday and Saturday. No children under 16. No pets. No credit cards. Open all year.

BURGUNDY HOUSE
BORDEAUX HOUSE
Yountville

Architect Bob Keenan and his wife, Mary, became innkeepers almost by accident. Before the days of the bed and breakfast craze, they were quietly operating an antique shop in Yountville. The upper floor was furnished as bedrooms, and, much to the Keenans' surprise, customers started asking if they could rent the rooms overnight. For a while inn and shop cohabitated in Burgundy House. Most all the contents were for sale. One honeymoon couple even bought their bed, but now the furnishings are there to stay.

Charles Rouvegneau built Burgundy House in the 1870s to resemble the inns of the Saône, constructing twenty-two-inch-thick walls of fieldstone quarried from the Napa Valley hillsides. It was operated originally as a boardinghouse upstairs and a dirt-floored brandy distillery below. Over the years, the massive stone walls and hand-hewn posts and beams were plastered over or covered with dry wall; layers of linoleum covered the wood floors. The Keenans restored the building to reveal the original stone and wood construction. The five upstairs bedrooms are decorated with an assemblage of furnishings

Burgundy House

from many eras and many lands; two baths are shared by the guests. There is one bedroom downstairs, however, with a private bath and patio. Also downstairs are an attractive sitting room with a collection of unusual antique games, and a rear room with a fireplace where breakfast is served in the mornings and wine in the evenings.

In 1980 the Keenans opened Bordeaux House a few blocks away. A line from the esteemed Hugh Johnson's *World Atlas of Wine,* quoted in their brochure, aptly describes the difference between the two inns: "Aspects of Bordeaux appeal to the aesthete, as Burgundy appeals to the sensualist." Bordeaux House, a new brick structure designed by Bob Keenan, is as understated and contemporary as Burgundy House is frilly and old-fashioned—and it is much more luxurious. Decorated by designer Richard Tam, the rooms reflect the colors of the two great wines of Bordeaux, claret and sauterne. Each bed is set on a carpeted dais some two feet high with a carpeted headboard rising to the ceiling. Tables are white plexiglass or lucite squares. Walls are covered with grass cloth. Each of the six bedrooms has a fireplace and most have a private brick patio or balcony. A Continental breakfast is served in a common room or up the road at Burgundy House.

A somewhat rustic cottage next door to Bordeaux House with two guest rooms, and two cottages across the street from Burgundy House, are used to accommodate an overflow of guests. These rooms are not as attractive as those in the inns.

BURGUNDY HOUSE, 6711 Washington Street, Yountville, California 94599. Telephone: (707) 944-2855. Accommodations: double beds; some private baths; no telephones; no television. Rates: moderate to expensive, Continental breakfast included. Children in cottages only. No pets. Cards: MC, VISA. Open all year.

BORDEAUX HOUSE, 6600 Washington Street, Yountville, California 94599. Telephone: (707) 944-2855. Accommodations: queen-size beds; private baths with tub/shower; air-conditioned; no telephones; no television. Rates: expensive, Continental breakfast included. Children in cottages only. No pets. Cards: MC, VISA. Open all year.

CHALET BERNENSIS
St. Helena

In 1884 Swiss wine maker John Thoman built a handsome Victorian home for his family next door to his winery in St. Helena. Later the winery and the home were purchased by John Sutter (a relative of the John Sutter on whose land gold was first discovered in California). Today the Trinchero family owns the Sutter Home Winery, while Jack and Essie Doty operate the old Thoman mansion as an inn. When the Dotys first bought the place in 1973, they started an antique shop in the downstairs rooms and later rented the upstairs bedrooms. But as the innkeeping business began to boom in the late 1970s, the sale of antiques took second place, and the lower sitting room with a fireplace and a dining hall became pretty much for their guests' exclusive use. A breakfast of scones, muffins, fruit and juices is served here in the mornings; sherry, coffee and cookies are served in the evening.

The five upstairs bedrooms are small and cozy, furnished with antiques, floral papers, quilted spreads and Oriental rugs. Because old photographs of the Thoman-Sutter house showed a three-story water tower next door that no longer existed, in 1979 the Dotys constructed a replica of the tower containing four additional guest rooms. These have fireplaces with old mantels, and private baths.

Chalet Bernensis is surrounded by lovely grounds, planted with roses, palms and beds of ivy. It is a perfect place to picnic, and picnic tables are provided.

CHALET BERNENSIS, 225 St. Helena Highway (Highway 29), St. Helena, California 94574. Telephone: (707) 963-4423. Accommodations: double and queen-size beds; bedrooms in house share two baths, one with tub; private baths with tub or shower in water tower, also air conditioning; no telephones; no television. Rates: moderate, Continental breakfast included. No children. No pets. Smoking discouraged. Cards: MC, VISA. Open all year.

HARVEST INN
St. Helena

Next door to Chalet Bernensis are twenty acres of vineyards on which owner Richard Geyer has recently built a complex of cottages emulating Old English half-timber construction. Harvest Inn is for travelers who don't want to exchange their creature comforts for last-century quaintness: those who can't breakfast before checking with their brokers (there are telephones, even in the modern bathrooms), who can't get to sleep before catching the late news (televisions repose on top of antique trunks), and who like a cocktail before dinner (all rooms but one have wet bars with refrigerators). And the grounds contain a spa and a swimming pool.

The center of the inn is a two-story building that houses a large public room containing leather-covered couches, a big brick fireplace hung with copperware, a collection of old steins and a coffee bar where a Continental breakfast is set out each morning. Glass doors lead to a deck. Some of the inn's twenty-five guest rooms are located here; others are grouped in four separate cottages reached by walks through landscaped gardens.

The furnishings of the rooms are a mixture of old and new. In the larger rooms you'll find king-size beds with carved oak headboards, and contemporary couches covered in woven fabrics; electrified hurricane lamps serve as night lights. Eighteen of the rooms have brick fireplaces; four have private balconies or patios. All rooms have fresh flowers and bowls of fruit. Some have beautiful views of the surrounding vineyards.

HARVEST INN, One Main Street (Highway 29), St. Helena 94574. Telephone: (707) 963-9463. Accommodations: twin, queen- and king-

110

size beds; private baths with tub/showers; air conditioning; telephones; television. Rates: moderate to expensive, Continental breakfast included. Children welcome. Extra charge for pets. Cards: MC, VISA. Open all year except Christmas.

HOTEL ST. HELENA
St. Helena

In 1881, while the Beringers and Krugs were busy expanding their wineries, an elegant two-story hotel opened on St. Helena's Main Street. But as the wineries flourished, the hotel deteriorated, its rooms eventually little better than flophouses, its lower floor occupied by a branch of Montgomery Ward. Almost a century later Santa Barbara developer Carl Johnson bought the hotel and renovated it to a degree of luxury it probably never knew.

Downstairs, shops and a restaurant open onto a flower-filled arcade. Upstairs, a lounge and seventeen guest rooms have been skillfully decorated by Tom Brooks and Linda Daniels, who combined antiques with modern comforts. The hall is papered with a striped and floral pattern of burgundy, tan and brown—setting the color scheme for all the rooms. In the sitting room at the top of the stairs, love seats upholstered in burgundy velvet flank a fireplace; a beautiful old wooden sideboard is set with coffee, tea and fruit breads in the morning. The bedrooms are painted in colors of burgundy, mauve, chocolate brown, dark tan or pale gold; patterned quilted bedspreads and dust ruffles echo these hues. The larger rooms have headboards of brass or carved wood, armoires, lounge chairs and round, cloth-covered tables. The smaller rooms have painted iron headboards and ladderback chairs. Four rooms without private baths have bent-willow headboards and marble-topped commodes with baskets of fresh towels and soap. There's also a suite with a sitting room. All the rooms are richly carpeted; windows are shuttered in white throughout. At the rear of the hotel, overlooking the arcade, is a wide deck with chaises and tables: a restful spot to relax before or after a day of winery touring.

HOTEL ST. HELENA, 1309 Main Street (Highway 29), St. Helena, California 94574. Telephone: (707) 963-4388. Accommodations: twin and queen-size beds; 13 rooms have private baths with stall shower or tub/shower; four rooms share two baths; no telephones; no television. Rates: moderate to expensive, Continental breakfast included. No children. No pets. Cards: MC, VISA. Open all year.

WINE COUNTRY INN
St. Helena

Ned and Marge Smith had long dreamed of opening an inn in the wine country. For several years they spent vacations touring the inns of New England to get ideas and advice. One warning they heeded: "Don't restore an old building, build a new one. There will be fewer headaches and more comforts." The Wine Country Inn, though constructed in 1975, looks as though it has been sitting on its hillock surrounded by vineyards forever. That's the way they wanted it to look. The three-story stone and wood structure with dormered windows and a gabled tower is a composite of ideas borrowed from historic buildings in the valley. Several years later the Smiths added two smaller buildings nearby.

Comfort is the key word here. All rooms are carpeted and have modern baths. The furnishings are antique, from a potpourri of periods, but the old four-poster beds have been widened to queen-size and the brass-framed doubles elongated. The rooms are papered with a floral motif and each is different, but romantic in its own way. Fifteen of the rooms have freestanding fireplaces, seven have patios landscaped for privacy, and twelve have intimate balconies. Some have window seats in alcoves with views of the surrounding countryside.

On the ground floor of the main building is a large, homey common room, equipped with card tables and books on wine. Here in the mornings, at a long refectory table, a Continental breakfast is served of fresh fruits and juices, assorted hot breads and coffee. On warmer days this repast is served on a deck outside.

WINE COUNTRY INN, 1152 Lodi Lane, St. Helena, California 94574. Telephone: (707) 963-7077. Accommodations: twin, double and queen-size beds; private baths, some with tub/shower, some shower only; no telephones; no television. Rates: moderate to expensive, Continental breakfast included. No children under 12. No pets. Cards: MC, VISA. Open all year.

Getting There: From Napa take Highway 29 two miles past St. Helena and turn right on Lodi Lane.

Wine Country Inn

LARKMEAD COUNTRY INN
Calistoga

Lillie Coit is best known for her devotion to San Francisco's firemen and for the monument she had built for them on Telegraph Hill: Coit Tower. Few people connect her with wine history, but she owned the Larkmead Vineyards south of Calistoga in the 1880s. A later owner was Swiss-born Felix Salmina, who in 1918 built for his son and daughter-in-law a sprawling clapboard Victorian in the middle of his vineyards. The Hans Kornell winery, whose champagne cellars are next door, now owns the grape lands. Gene and Joan Garbarino bought the lovely old house for a second residence and then decided in 1979 to run it as a country inn.

Through fieldstone gates the driveway leads to a wisteria-covered loggia in the rear of the house. Up some stairs is the gracious living room appointed with a Persian carpet, antiques that the Garbarinos have collected in their European travels and a well-stocked library. A fire burns on the hearth evenings and mornings when guests gather for breakfast in the adjoining dining room. The table, which seats ten, is elegantly set with sterling silver and peony-patterned porcelain plates on which Joan artfully arranges grapes and slices of watermelon, oranges, pears, peaches and kiwis—whatever is in season. Then individual baskets of croissants, scones and French rolls are served with crocks of sweet butter, and freshly ground coffee.

114

European etchings and oil paintings grace the dining and living rooms, as well as the four bedrooms. These are named after various wines and command spectacular views of the vineyards. Chablis, dressed up in muted green tones, features an enclosed sun porch off the bedroom, while Beaujolais has private use of the open porch over the loggia. Chenin Blanc is feminine and flowery with draperies, wallpaper and a chaise covered in matching patterns. And Chardonnay has an Art Deco look, with old brass bedsteads that came from a Parisian hotel. Fresh flowers and a decanter of wine are placed in all the rooms.

The Larkmead Inn is surrounded by wide verandas and lawns shaded by sycamores, magnolias and cypress. It's a peaceful haven you will be reluctant to leave. But you don't have to go far for wine touring. Just walk next door to the winery, where Hans Kornell himself or members of his family will explain in detail the process of making bottle-fermented champagnes.

LARKMEAD COUNTRY INN, 1103 Larkmead Lane, Calistoga, California 94515. Telephone: (707) 942-5360. Accommodations: twin and double beds; private baths with stall showers; central air conditioning; no telephones; no television. Rates: moderate, Continental breakfast included. No children. No pets. Cards: MC, VISA. Open all year.

Getting There: Take Highway 29, and north of St. Helena turn right on Larkmead Lane.

WINE WAY INN
Calistoga

Once a sleepy, slightly run-down resort town, Calistoga is now a lively community with restored hotels, shops and restaurants lining its quaint main street. On the edge of town, at the base of a forested mountainside, is the Wine Way Inn. Built in 1915 as a private residence, the small house still retains a homey feeling, reinforced by the warm hospitality of innkeepers Allen and Dede Good who have owned the place since 1980. A glass of chilled white wine is offered to newly arrived guests who can sit and unwind on the huge overstuffed couch in front of the fireplace in the fir-paneled living-dining area. The rear wall here is entirely covered with cupboards, their leaded glass doors revealing a fine collection of silver, china and pewter. Round breakfast tables are covered with brown and blue checked cloths over blue underskirts, surrounded by ladderback chairs. Café curtains are at the windows.

The morning meal—a choice of three or four breads and pastries, plus orange juice and fruit—is served here or on the immense deck behind the house. Furnished with picnic tables and chaises, this is a great place to relax and stare at the mountain above. Now covered with redwoods and maples, the terraced slopes were once vineyards, the second oldest in the area.

Upstairs, the five bedrooms are small and pretty with gabled ceilings, antiques, and beds covered with heirloom patchwork quilts that range in age from seventy-five to a hundred years. In the rear a tiny cottage, once a carriage house, with half-timbered walls and a private porch, nestles among the trees.

WINE WAY INN, 1019 Foothill Boulevard (Highway 29), Calistoga, California 94515. Telephone: (707) 942-0680. Accommodations: twin, double and queen-size beds; three rooms and cottage have private baths with stall shower; two rooms share bath with tub/shower; no telephones; no television. Rates: moderate, Continental breakfast included. No children. No pets. Cards: MC, VISA. Open all year.

RUSSIAN RIVER VALLEY

From its origin in Mendocino County, the Russian River winds over two hundred miles through the lush vineyards of northern Sonoma County and through the redwood-forested coastal mountains to the Pacific. The first settlers here engaged in agriculture and lumber, but in the last quarter of the nineteenth century vineyards began to appear, from Guerneville in the south, where the Korbel cellars were established in 1886, to Cloverdale in the north, home of Italian Swiss Colony since 1887. Until very recently, however, most of the other wineries in this region produced mostly inexpensive wines. Then in the late 1960s, at the peak of California's wine boom, wine makers began to realize that the climate and soil of this area were capable of producing premium grapes to rival those of nearby Napa—particularly in the Alexander and Dry Creek valleys. Today twenty-seven wineries are bottling varietal wines from the vineyards alongside the Russian River, among them such prestigious names as Davis Bynum, Simi, Trentadue and Dry Creek. Many have tasting roms, winery tours, and picnic areas. (Specific information on these wineries, a map showing their locations, and schedules of forthcoming special events such as fairs, musicals, art shows and barrel tastings, can be obtained from The Russian River Wine Road, P.O. Box 127, Geyserville, California 95441.) The advent of the premium grape in the Russian River Valley was followed inevitably by the appearance of country inns in the river towns from Guerneville to Cloverdale.

Getting There: From San Francisco, Highway 101 passes through Healdsburg, Geyserville and Cloverdale. Guerneville is reached by taking River Road west, just north of Santa Rosa. From the Napa Valley, Highway 128 leads from Calistoga to Geyserville.

VINTAGE TOWERS
Cloverdale

At the turn of the century Simon Pinschower, a wealthy merchant, built himself a twenty-room Queen Anne towered Victorian on a quiet side street of Cloverdale. In 1913 two more towers were added. When Tom and Judy Haworth turned the stately old mansion into an inn in 1980, they named it after the three vintage towers: one round, one square and one octagonal These tower suites are now the choicest of the inn's seven charming guest rooms. And the pick of the lot is Calico Tower, where a spiral staircase winds up to a private balcony. Carousel Tower beguiles with bright colors, circus posters, Mickey Mouse prints, a children's merry-go-round horse in the corner, and a love seat, upholstered in a tiger print, made from a baby's crib. Wicker Tower lives up to its name with all wicker furniture: headboards on the bed, a love seat and chaise in the fern-bedecked tower area.

The spacious downstairs rooms promise a paradise for readers. Tom Haworth has been collecting books since his childhood, and his library contains fifteen hundred old volumes, most concerned with history. Music lovers will be happy here too. There are a piano and a "piano player," a device that is set on the keyboard to bang out tunes from Tom's large collection of player-piano rolls. Nearby an old-fashioned Victrola is stocked with several hundred records.

The wood-paneled dining room has a fireplace and windows looking out to the lawn and rose gardens. On weekends Judy serves a hearty breakfast here: perhaps a frittata, with fresh melon and blueberry muffins, or a poached egg on corned-beef hash with dill sauce. Weekdays she simplifies the menu to fruit compote with homemade rolls or muffins. On nice mornings guests may breakfast on the wide veranda, where wine is also served on balmy evenings. Across from the veranda is Tom's pride and joy: a gazebo he built himself, in which he occasionally stages concerts for guests and townspeople.

As if there weren't enough to do in the inn itself and in the surrounding wine country, Vintage Towers provides some very special diversions. Bicycles are available for exploring the town and countryside. And when time permits, Tom likes to take his guests white-water tubing or rafting on the Russian River or sailing in his boat on Lake Mendocino, some thirty-five minutes away.

VINTAGE TOWERS, 302 North Main Street, Cloverdale, California 95425. Telephone: (707) 894-4535. Accommodations: king-size and double beds; one private bath with tub, other baths with tub/showers shared by two rooms; no telephones; no television; air-conditioning. Rates: moderate; lower rates on week nights; breakfast included. No children under ten. No pets. No smoking within the inn. Cards: MC, VISA.

Getting There: From San Francisco take Highway 101 north to the first stop light in Cloverdale; turn right for one block; then turn left on Main Street.

HOPE HOUSE
HOPE-BOSWORTH HOUSE
Geyserville

For six years Bob and Rosalie Hope operated a resort in Guerneville while Rosalie pursued with a passion her hobby of collecting Victoriana. Then in 1980, when the Hopes moved up the Russian River to the tiny town of Geyserville, her avocation became an important asset in their new vocation: They converted two Victorian houses to inns and restored and furnished them with an authenticity rarely encountered in the current renovation craze.

Their first project was a 1904 Queen Anne cottage built from a pattern book by the Bosworth family, pioneers of the area. Rechristened Hope-Bosworth, the inn is papered with reproductions of Victorian wall coverings, but the furnishings in the cozy parlor, dining room and three upstairs bedrooms are genuine antiques from the era. The Hopes' daughter, Randi Hope Stevens, took over the management of this inn, while they moved across the street to tackle a bigger project with an even more zealous purism.

The Hope House is a stately century-old Italianate that stands on land once occupied by the Geyserville Hotel, a Wells Fargo stage stop. Here the wallpapers are magnificent custom-made replicas of *fin de*

Hope House

siècle patterns that Rosalie especially admired, complete with a frieze around the ceilings. The hall wainscoting is an original Lincrusta Walton pattern, unpainted and in mint condition. The pride of the high-ceilinged formal sitting room is a five-piece Eastlake walnut parlor set, with chairs upholstered in cranberry velvet. Pieces of cranberry glass, cut glass and crystal embellish the room. The dining room is distinguished by Tudor-style furnishings and a massive 1871 cast-iron chandelier with glass chimneys and its original shades.

In the rear of the first floor are two bedrooms with private baths, and a large enclosed porch with French doors opening to a back deck and a side garden. The four upstairs bedrooms contain some pieces of museum quality, such as an 1865 walnut and burl headboard and an 1850 child's crib. One room is entirely furnished with turn-of-the-century wickerware; another has an antique brass bedstead and an unusual chestnut dresser. Most of the bedspreads are old crocheted or handknit coverlets. Some six dozen vintage photos, prints and paintings cover the walls of the house, and everywhere you look are pieces from Rosalie's collections of Victorian bric-a-brac, plus old books and current publications on the era.

Homemade preserves and breads with fruit and juice start the day at both Hope houses. Sherry, port and Sonoma County wines are offered in the evening. With advance notice and a minimum party of six, The Hopes will also prepare a special dinner at the Hope House. But you need not worry about going hungry in Geyserville. Just down the road is Catelli's, a bastion of home-cooked, old-style Italian food. And nearby the Souverain Winery runs a beautiful restaurant set in the midst of their vineyards.

HOPE HOUSE, 21253 Geyserville Avenue, Geyserville, California 95441. Telephone: (707) 857-3945. Accommodations: double and queen-size beds; three rooms have private baths with shower or tub/shower, three rooms share two baths with shower or tub/shower; no telephones; no television. Rates: moderate, Continental breakfast included. No pets. No smoking within the inn. Cards: MC, VISA. Open all year.

HOPE-BOSWORTH HOUSE, 21238 Geyserville Avenue, Geyserville, California 95441. Telephone: (707) 857-3356. Accommodations: double and queen-size beds; three rooms share bath with tub/shower; no telephones; no television. Rates: inexpensive, Continental breakfast included. No pets. No smoking within the inn. Cards: MC, VISA. Open all year.

THE GRAPE LEAF INN
Healdsburg

In the heart of the Russian River wine country, Healdsburg is a quiet town, its side streets lined with trees and many Victorian houses. One of these, built in 1901, has just been made into an inn by airline stewardess Laura Salo. The four bedrooms are furnished with antiques she has collected in her travels—Austrian headboards, Oriental rugs, brass coat stands—and quilted spreads with matching sheets and skirts on the night tables. Bowls of flowers are on the dressers. Laura is also an art collector, and each room has at least one original signed print or painting.

The big living room in the rear is homey with a fireplace, lots of books, and a dining table covered with a hand-crocheted cloth by the café-curtained window. Guests may breakfast here, or out on the wide veranda that shades two sides of the house, or in a cheerful alcove off the country kitchen. The morning meal is ample and elegant, a typical menu consisting of freshly squeezed orange juice, two kinds of melon, zucchini frittata, peach coffeecake and champagne. In the evenings Laura offers a tasting of several local wines accompanied with crackers and cheese.

All the rooms in the inn are presently located on the first floor. The second floor of the house has stained-glass windows and three thousand square feet of space that was never finished; not even a stairway leads there. Laura plans eventually to build more guest rooms upstairs; an innkeeper's work is never completed.

THE GRAPE LEAF INN, 539 Johnson Street, Healdsburg, California 95448. Telephone: (707) 433-8140. Accommodations: twin, double and king-size beds; two rooms share adjoining bath with tub/shower; two rooms share a bath off kitchen with tub/shower and wheelchair access; no telephones; no television. Rates: moderate, full breakfast included. No children. No pets. Cards: MC, VISA. Open all year.

THE RAFORD HOUSE
Healdsburg

From Healdsburg the Russian River flows west through more vineyards and wooded mountains to the Pacific. Although this is wine country now, a century ago, much of this acreage was planted in hops. One of the major hop growers was Raford W. Peterson, who built in the 1880s a spacious house with broad verandas on the hillside overlooking his lands. Today the grounds are covered with grapevines and apple trees, and all that remains of the hop ranch are the Victorian farmhouse and the foundation of the hop kilns. In 1980 Alan Baitinger and Beth Foster bought the thirteen-room residence from the Peterson family and converted it into an inn.

Giant palms and gardens filled with roses and other flowers surround the building. Inside, a cheery fire burns on chilly mornings in the dining room, where guests are served a simple Continental breakfast at a long oak table. A big grandfather clock in the corner is a hint of the owners' hobby: Antique clocks of all sizes are found throughout the bedrooms, which are handsomely appointed with turn-of-the-century furnishings. Quaintness, however, ends with the beds (all new mattresses) and baths, which are as modern as tomorrow. Each room has its own distinctive decor and special features. Some have wood-burning fireplaces, others have private patios. Then there is a shared-bath suite of two bedrooms, one light and airy in champagne tones, the other one dressed up in deep burgundy hues with a brass bedstead. A little game room with garden view opens off this room. Raford House is certainly among the best of the many new inns.

RAFORD HOUSE, 10630 Wohler Road, Healdsburg, California 95448. Telephone: (707) 887-9573. Accommodations: double beds; most rooms have private baths with tub/shower; no telephones; no television; wheelchair access to one room. Rates moderate, Continental breakfast included. No small children. No pets. Cards: MC, VISA. Open all year except Christmas.

Getting There: From Highway 101 take the River Road exit three miles north of Santa Rosa and head west to Wohler Road.

RIDENHOUR RANCH HOUSE INN
Guerneville

As the Russian River nears Guerneville, its valley narrows and the redwoods become denser. Here, next to the Korbel vineyards, is another old ranch house restored as a charming inn. Its history dates back to 1856, when Louis William Ridenhour began to farm 940 acres of the fertile lands on both sides of the river. In 1906 his son, Louis E. Ridenhour, built his home of heart redwood on several acres of the ranch; his daughter Virginia and her husband, former Assistant Surgeon General Justin K. Fuller, continued to live there, enlarging and remodeling the house, until 1977. Martha and Bob Satterthwaite saw the house that year and knew it would be perfect for the inn they had dreamed of starting. After two years' work the Satterthwaites have created a gracious hostelry with the ambience of a private home, a quiet haven well away from the honky-tonk river resorts.

Fireplaces, Oriental rugs, comfortable furnishings and a profusion of greenery and African violets grace the large redwood-paneled living room and adjoining dining room. You can breakfast here, or in the cheerful family kitchen, or out on the patio: a light repast of freshly ground coffee, nut breads or muffins, fresh juices, cheeses and often hard-cooked eggs. The rest of the day guests are free to help

themselves to coffee or tea in the kitchen, or to pour a glass of wine from a bottle in the refrigerator. Decanters of sherry are also found in each room, along with bowls of fruit, fresh flowers and plants. The two spacious downstairs bedrooms have queen-size beds with Victorian headboards and quilted spreads. Each room has its private bath, and one has a little sitting room with a couch that folds into a bed. Upstairs three cozy little rooms with dormer windows nestle under the eaves, sharing a bath. These have an Early American look with hooked rugs and chenille spreads or handmade quilts. And the original touches of Martha Satterthwaite, a former interior designer, are here and there: straw hats on the wall of one room and in another a Japanese kite fashioned from calico fabric. And every room of this inn provides sylvan views of surrounding oaks and redwoods or the Korbel vineyards next door.

A stroll through these woods and through the gardens informally landscaped with daisies, zinnias, marigolds is a favorite pastime here. Other diversions include a redwood hot tub and a croquet court. The Korbel champagne cellars and secluded river beaches are a short walk away.

RIDENHOUR RANCH HOUSE, 12850 River Road, Guerneville, California 95446. Telephone: (707) 887-1033. Accommodations: queen-size and twin double beds; two rooms with private baths with tub/shower; three rooms share bath with shower; no telephone; no television; wheelchair access to one room. Rates: moderate, Continental breakfast included; midweek discount in off season. Children over ten welcome. No pets. Cards: MC, VISA.

CALIFORNIA NORTH COAST COUNTRY

The Redwood Empire

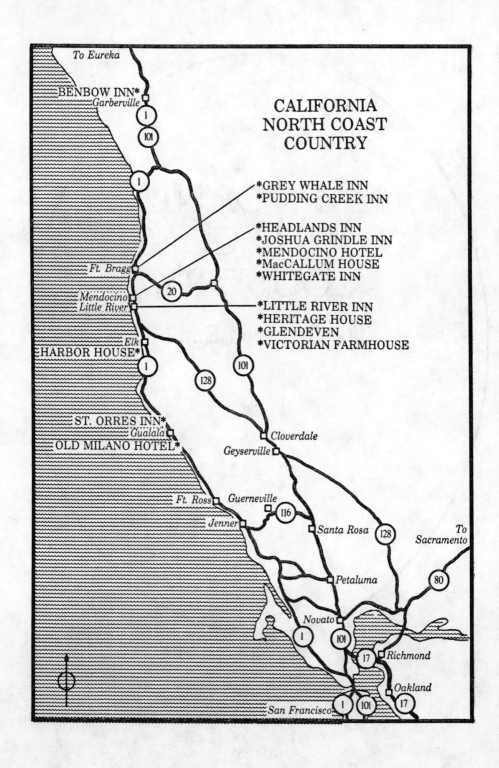

CALIFORNIA
NORTH COAST
COUNTRY

To Eureka

~BENBOW INN*
Garberville

1
101

1

*GREY WHALE INN
*PUDDING CREEK INN

*HEADLANDS INN
*JOSHUA GRINDLE INN
*MENDOCINO HOTEL
*MacCALLUM HOUSE
*WHITEGATE INN

Ft. Bragg
20

Mendocino
Little River

*LITTLE RIVER INN
*HERITAGE HOUSE
*GLENDEVEN
*VICTORIAN FARMHOUSE

Elk
HARBOR HOUSE*

1

128

101

ST. ORRES INN*
Gualala
OLD MILANO HOTEL*

Cloverdale
Geyserville

Ft. Ross
Guerneville
116

Jenner
Santa Rosa
128

To
Sacramento

Petaluma

80

Novato

1

101

17
Richmond

Oakland

San Francisco
1
101
17

NORTH COAST

North of Jenner, where the Russian River meets the Pacific, Highway 1 soars upwards, switchbacking through mountainous terrain, then stretches north along the craggy coast to Mendocino. This awesome drive through mostly isolated countryside takes you past the reconstruction of Fort Ross, the site of a Russian seal- and otter-trapping settlement in the early 1800s. It also takes you past numerous coves where weathered pilings and abandoned cemeteries are the only testimony to the once-thriving lumber towns that studded the coast in the last century. From the forested mountains that rise from the sea, millions of redwood trees were hewn to build the Victorians of San Francisco.

OLD MILANO HOTEL
Gualala

A midway stopping point on the rugged stagecoach road that linked the coastal lumber towns was Gualala. Here in 1905 an Italian family built the Old Milano Hotel, offering overnight rooms and refreshments in a large saloon to the stage passengers. But the demise of the logging boom reduced the hotel's business, and in 1922 new owners converted it into a lodge for anglers seeking the steelhead in nearby Gualala River.

In 1940 the highway was moved inland and the hotel was put out of business, becoming a residence. In the 1950s another set of owners with modern ideas sold off most of the surrounding land, installed large plate-glass windows, lowered the ceilings and tossed most of the Victorian furnishings into the gulch. When Bruce and Theadora McBroom discovered the place in 1977, there was not much left to remind one of the hotel's history.

Bruce is a photographer by profession; Thea is an artist and costume designer. Their home was Los Angeles, but for many years they spent their vacations on the north coast, eventually buying some acreage in Gualala for a campsite. When the Old Milano went up for sale again, they decided to become innkeepers.

The McBrooms restored the six upstairs guest rooms, installing new carpeting, wiring, plumbing, insulation and soundproofing. Furnishings are family antiques: big oak armoires, white-painted iron bedsteads, Victorian love seats, old handmade quilts and crocheted spreads. One of the two community baths has a tiled "his and her" shower with dual spigots and a tub big enough for two! Recently a downstairs suite was added, with a lace-hung eighteenth-century Angelica Kaufman bed, a sitting room and a private bath. Bowls of flowers from Thea's cutting garden and spectacular views of the Pacific pounding away at the cliffs and cove below add to the romantic setting. The most unusual quarters at Old Milano are in an old caboose next to the hotel. This unit is cozy and comfortable, with walls paneled in sandblasted wood, a red pot-bellied stove and a tiny galley. A ladder leads up to two brakemen's seats for admiring the view.

Thea papered the parlor walls with a fabric from London: a William Morris nature pattern circa 1860. The chairs are an Eastlake design, and the sofa is the first Riviera bed produced in 1906. The old saloon has been restored as another sitting area, with a huge stone fireplace, chintz-covered sofas, and plants and flowers. Tastings of Mendocino wines take place here in the afternoon. A patio in back is surrounded by flowers, including giant dahlias eight feet high. Walkways lead down to a gazebo with a hot tub on a point overlooking the surf, and picnic pavilions nestle in the hillside that descends to the beach.

Although Bruce's family was in the restaurant business for three generations, he is determined to serve only breakfast at the hotel. Served in bed, everything is homemade: bread baked in a wood-burning stove that came around the Horn in 1906, plum preserves and apple butter from the McBrooms' organically grown fruit. But you won't go hungry at dinnertime here. Just up the road at the St. Orres Inn is one of the north coast's finest restaurants.

OLD MILANO HOTEL, 38300 Highway 1, Gualala, California 95445. Telephone: (707) 884-3256. Accommodations: double and queen-size beds; shared baths with tub/shower in hotel, private baths and kitchenettes in cottage and caboose; no telephones; no television. Rates: moderate to expensive, Continental breakfast included. Infants in cottages only, otherwise no children. No pets. No credit cards. No smoking within the inn. Open April 1 to December 28.

Getting There: Take Highway 101 north to Petaluma; take Washington Street exit to road leading to Bodega Bay; then proceed north on Highway 1 to Gualala. The hotel is just beyond the town of Gualala.

ST. ORRES INN
Gualala

Midway up the coast between Jenner and Mendocino is an astounding piece of architectural sculpture: a miniature Russian palace rendered in hand-carved redwood, with onion-top turrets and stained-glass windows. A relic from the Russian settlers of over a century ago? No. St. Orres Inn is the creation of two young men from Marin County who painstakingly handcrafted every detail.

Eric Black and Richard Wasserman met at school in Mill Valley and worked together on several carpentry projects. Then they acquired a decrepit garage overlooking the Pacific on property once owned by the St. Orres family who homesteaded this area. For four years they scavenged wood from beaches and old barns, collected pieces of stained glass, sawed, hammered and sculptured their inn, which finally opened in early 1977.

Through a patio and trellis-covered terrace you enter a cozy parlor with oval windows, tapestries on the walls, furnishings of the last century. An oak door leads to a spectacular dining room over which the domed turret rises some fifty feet. From high above, light filters down from stained-glass clerestories while three tiers of mullioned windows provide glimpses of forest and sea through a cascade of hanging plants. Chocolate-brown carpeting, rust-colored tablecloths and primitive stoneware made by local potters complete the setting.

The French menu at St. Orres changes constantly, but a stand-out dish that's usually present is rack of lamb with a Dijon mustard crust; fresh local seafood is also featured. Mumm's champagne and Russian caviar are available as appetizers, and the desserts are decidedly sinful—try the chocolate decadence. In the morning a complimentary breakfast of fruit, juices, breads and coffee is served to overnight guests. Liquid sustenance is available all day from a new wine bar located next to a plant-filled solarium.

The most luxurious accommodations are in two new cottages, the Cottage and the Tree House. These have kitchenettes, carpeting throughout, wood-burning stove-fireplaces, queen-size beds and living areas with French doors leading to private decks. The Cottage will

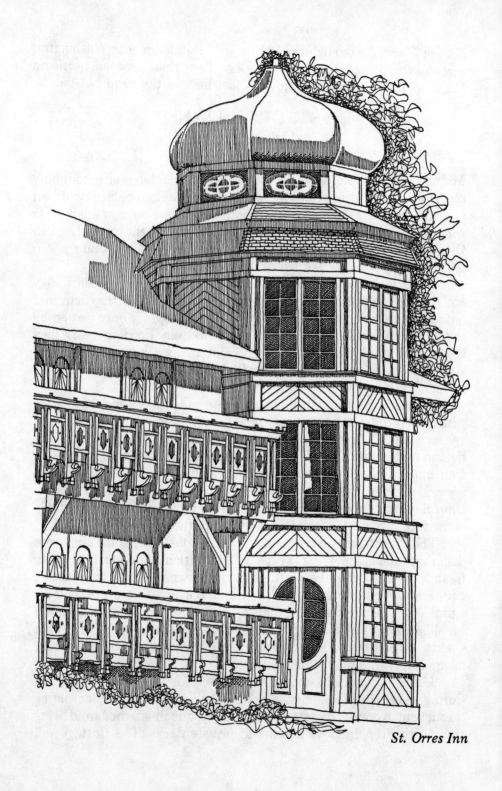

St. Orres Inn

house a family of four, as will the rustic Cabin, one of the original buildings on the property that has not been remodeled. The upstairs guest rooms in the inn itself are small and sparsely appointed with furnishings designed and built by Black and Wasserman. Guests share three community baths, labeled "his," "hers" and "ours"—the last has a large tiled tub and dual shower heads.

St. Orres Inn has its own private beach across the road. In season you can pick abalone from the rocks or fish for steelhead. On weekends there are flea markets and local arts/crafts festivals to be explored.

ST. ORRES INN, P.O. Box 523, Gualala, California 95445. Telephone: (707) 884-3303. Accommodations: double beds and community bath with shower in inn; double bed and private bath in cabin; double and queen-size beds, fireplaces and private baths in cottages; no telephones; no television. Rates: moderate in inn and cabin, expensive in cottages; Continental breakfast included. Open to public for dinner and Sunday brunch. Children welcome in cottages only; no children under six permitted in dining room. No pets. Cards: MC, VISA, for overnight guests only. Open all year.

HARBOR HOUSE
Elk

This stately house was built on the cliffs above Greenwood Landing by the Goodyear Redwood Lumber Company in 1916 to be used as an executive residence and for entertaining business guests. In those days the small port below was heavily trafficked by schooners coming for their rich cargoes of lumber from the nearby Albion forests. In fact the house itself is an enlarged replica of a redwood model house, designed by Louis Christian Mullgardt for the 1915 Panama-Pacific Exposition in San Francisco.

When the lumber boom came to an end in the 1930s, Harbor House was converted to an inn, which had become run-down in recent years. Since 1975 the inn has been owned and managed by Patricia Corcoran, a former schoolteacher. Her goal is "to recreate the Edwardian atmosphere which once permeated each redwood board."

The walls, vaulted ceiling and fireplace of the gracious living room are entirely paneled with hand-carved and hand-fitted redwood, still preserved by its original finish of polished hot beeswax. Furnishings are comfortable and eclectic: overstuffed chairs, a large Persian rug, a

131

Steinway piano, Chinese chests and tables, bookcases bulging with reading matter.

There are five spacious bedrooms in the house itself, four with fireplaces, and another four cottages built on the edge of the bluff next to the main building. With paint and flowered wallpapers, antiques, and four-poster beds, Trisha has restored these rooms to their original charm. Some of the cottage rooms have French cast-iron fireplaces set on brick hearths; some have private terraces overlooking the ocean. Harbor House offers the best of two worlds: Guests seeking comfort and companionship usually prefer the main house; those wishing privacy and romance opt for the cottages.

Trisha believes that home-cooked meals, leisurely served, are one of the traditional characteristics of country inns. She and her staff make all the soups, breads, salad dressings and desserts from scratch. Vegetables are from the inn's garden. Breakfast and dinner are served in a spacious dining room with a panoramic view of the Pacific and the large tunneled rocks in the harbor below. The morning meal includes juice, fruit and perhaps shirred eggs, omelets or eggs Benedict. At evening, the entrées may be broiled fresh salmon or veal or chicken or a French beef dish. An excellent selection of local wines is available.

Harbor House is only twenty minutes by car from Mendocino's shops and art galleries. But most guests choose to spend their time exploring the inn's private beach.

HARBOR HOUSE, P.O. Box 369, Elk, California 95432. Telephone: (707) 877-3203. Accommodations: twin, double and king-size beds; private baths with shower or tub/shower; no telephones; no television. Rates: moderate to expensive, full breakfast and dinner for two included; lower midweek rates in winter and early spring. No children. No pets. No credit cards. Open all year.

Getting There: Follow directions to Mendocino, but turn south on Highway 1 and drive six miles to Elk.

HERITAGE HOUSE
Little River

In this ivy-covered inn with its many cottages rambling over hillsides and meadows and gardens reaching down to a private beach, L. D. and Hazel Dennen strive to preserve the heritage of the Mendocino coast. Dennen's own roots are implanted in the history of the area. His grandfather, John Dennen, who had come from New England, built the inn's main building as a home for rancher Wilder Pullen in 1876. In the 1890s Pullen advertised that the 160-acre sheep and cattle ranch and the seven-room house were for sale; for the land, buildings and livestock he was asking seven thousand dollars. In the early 1930s neighbors started to eye the former Pullen house with suspicion: Baby Face Nelson was using the cove below the house for his bootleg operations and, before his arrest, had concluded one of his last deals inside the house. As recently as the early 1940s, Chinese immigrants were smuggled into the country here.

In 1949, L. D. Dennen bought the house his grandfather had built and turned it into an inn. Over the years, the Dennens have added cottages on the meadows below the original house, building some anew, moving others from elsewhere in the countryside. All have names such as Schoolhouse, which the Dennens built with lumber salvaged from the Greenwood School in Elk; the school's sign serves as a headboard and the children's desks as bedside tables. Firehouse, Barbershop, Ice Cream are some other names. Recently the Dennens converted an old water tower, brought down from Mendocino, into a two-story unit with a circular stairway leading from a living room to a balconied bedroom. There are sixty units altogether now, some with brick fireplaces or Franklin or pot-bellied stoves. All have private baths.

Some years back Dennen acquired an old apple storage house from a nearby farm for seventy-five dollars and rebuilt it next to the 1876 house as a bar. The comfortably furnished adjoining lounge with its walk-in fireplace commands magnificent views of the ocean. Even if you do not stay at Heritage House, you should at least drop by for a drink at sunset. The dining room, with its glass-domed ceiling, also has wonderful views and is open to the public. The menu changes nightly, but a typical dinner would be beef and barley soup, fresh pear and cheddar salad, a choice of chicken with sesame seeds or ginger-glazed corned beef, accompanied with buttered potatoes and freshly baked orange biscuits; for dessert, chocolate mousse. There is also an extensive selection of domestic and imported wines. Breakfasts are

BUILT 1877 AD

Heritage House

hearty, too, and are served on the deck on sunny days. A buffet of fruits, juices and cereals is followed by eggs Benedict (or any style), bacon, ham, sausage and dollar-size hotcakes. Heritage House operates on semi-American plan only; breakfast and dinner are included in the rates.

HERITAGE HOUSE, 5200 Highway 1, Little River, California, 95456. Telephone: (707) 937-5885. Accommodations: twin, double and king-size beds; private baths, some tub/shower, some shower only; no telephones; no television. Rates: moderate to expensive, breakfast and dinner included. Open to public for breakfast and dinner; full bar service. Children welcome. No pets. No credit cards. Open February through November.

THE VICTORIAN FARMHOUSE
Little River

Just up the coast from Heritage House, its builder John Dennen constructed a Victorian farmhouse in 1877 as a home for himself and his wife Emma Dora. When Tom and Jane Szilasi bought the building in 1981, they faced an enormous restoration task, even though the place had operated as a bed and breakfast for a year. They tore plastic paneling off the downstairs sitting room and installed wainscoting and wallpaper; the corner fireplace was faced with blue and white Delft tiles. The two upstairs rooms—named the Dennen and Emma Dora rooms—have views of the ocean or adjoining apple orchards, and share a Victorian sitting room that opens to a sheltered deck. Steps lead down to a terraced garden in which Tom has planted over two hundred daffodils. Private entrances from the garden lead to the two lower rooms: The Victorian room has its own sitting room, with a French wood-burning stove and a view of the orchard. The Garden Room has a window looking into a tiny garden that can be illuminated at night; one-way tinted glass allows the guests to admire the garden, but no one can look into the room. In the works is a stone-faced "caretaker's" cottage with two rooms, each with a fireplace.

The setting here is Victorian, but the comforts are contemporary. All rooms have queen- or king-size beds with dual-control electric blankets and white quilted spreads. By the window in each room is a tiny round table set with a white eyelet cloth, china plates and cups ready for the morning repast of juice, fruit muffins or bread.

THE VICTORIAN FARMHOUSE, Highway 1, (P.O. Box 357), Little River, California 95456. Telephone: (707) 937-0697. Accommodations: queen- and king-size beds; private baths with tub/shower; no telephones; no television. Rates: moderate, Continental breakfast included. No children under 16. No pets. No credit cards. Open all year.

LITTLE RIVER INN
Little River

In 1853 pioneer lumber and shipping tycoon Silas Coombs built an impressive New England–style mansion for his family on a hillside above Little River Cove, bringing much of the furnishings around the Horn from his native Maine. In 1929, as the lumber business diminished, the Coombs family turned the house into an inn, which has been expanded to fifty rooms and is run by Silas's great-grandson today.

The mansion, faithfully maintained in its original style, houses an antique-filled parlor and, upstairs under gabled roofs, four floral-papered bedrooms. There are also a cocktail lounge that affords excellent viewing of the annual migration of the California gray whale, and a large dining room. The old house is now the nucleus for a complex of garden cottages, a motel-style annex, and a challenging nine-hole golf course on 250 acres where Silas's orchard once stood.

Some of the garden cottages are two-bedroom units, wood paneled and furnished in Early American style. Six have fireplaces; all have sun decks, some private, and views of the gardens or ocean. The annex rooms all have sliding glass doors leading to a balcony with a beautiful view of the cove.

In the early days of the inn, the Coombs family served their guests abalone picked from the rocks in the cove below. Little River Inn still is noted up and down the coast for its rendition of the delicate shellfish, when available. Ling cod and sole from local waters, salmon in season, chicken, lamb and steaks are other highlights of the dinner menu, which also includes soup, salad, homemade rolls and cobbler.

LITTLE RIVER INN, Little River, California 95456. Telephone: (707) 937-5942. Accommodations: double, two doubles, two queen-size and king-size beds; private baths, some with tubs/showers; no telephones; no television. Rates: moderate to expensive, no meals included. Open to public for breakfast and dinner, full bar service. Children welcome. No pets. No credit cards. Open all year for lodging; bar and dining room closed in January.

Little River Inn

GLENDEVEN
Little River

Isaiah Stevens was one of a group of settlers from Maine who pioneered the Little River area south of Mendocino. He married Rebecca Coombs, whose family owned the house that later became Little River Inn, and in 1867 built her a farmhouse surrounded by a hundred acres of land on which he raised fine cattle and horses. Much of the land was later sold, some of it to create the town of Little River, but the Stevens family retained ownership of the house until the late 1930s. Then for some twenty years owners came and went and the old farmhouse fell into disrepair. In the 1950s, however, it was rescued by Warren and Dora Zimmer, who restored it for their home. Jan de Vries, then in college, visited there in 1962. Later he returned to Mendocino to teach, met and married Janet Bell, and moved to Portland. But the de Vrieses continued to long for the tranquility of the Mendocino coast. When the Zimmer house went up for sale, they bought it.

The grey and white farmhouse—flanked by cypress trees, lawns and flower gardens—looks over a headland meadow to the bay of Little River beyond. Inside the de Vrieses have blended antique furnishings with contemporary paintings and ceramics. In the spacious and airy living room, guests gather by the brick fireplace in the evening for a glass of wine. In the mornings Janet serves a breakfast of homebaked muffins, biscuits or coffeecake, fresh fruits and eggs. French doors lead out to a brick patio.

The seven guest rooms at Glendeven are charmingly furnished with Victorian walnut or painted cast-iron bedsteads, flowered quilts, marble-topped tables, dried and fresh flower arrangements and bright abstract paintings. On the main floor there are a room with a garden view and private bath and, off the patio, a two-room suite with fireplace and private bath. Four smaller rooms occupy the second floor, sharing two baths. But the most appealing of all is a large attic room with dormered windows called the Garret; here there are a queen-size Louis XIV bed, a private bath and a comfortable sitting area.

GLENDEVEN, 8221 North Highway 1, Little River, California 95456. Telephone: (707) 937-0083. Accommodations: queen-size and double beds; three private baths, two community baths, some with tub/shower, some with stall shower; no telephones; no television. Rates: moderate, Continental breakfast included. Children sometimes accepted. No pets. No credit cards. Open all year.

MENDOCINO–FORT BRAGG

Cabrillo discovered Cape Mendocino in 1542 and named it after Don Antonio de Mendoza, first viceroy of New Spain. But except for its name, nothing about the coastal village of Mendocino is Spanish. Situated on a bluff projecting into the Pacific, the town looks like a movie set of a New England village, reflecting the heritage of its founders. Except for fresh paint, time has not touched the Victorian clapboards, set among windmills, water towers and windswept cypress trees. Behind rise the redwood-covered mountains of the Coast Range.

It was this precious timber that attracted the early settlers to the Mendocino coast. Harry Meiggs, a San Francisco lumberman, brought the first sawmill to Mendocino from the East aboard the brig *Ontario* and the lumber boom began. Others harvested the seafood from these northern waters, and started a fishing industry that still flourishes in the nearby harbor of Noyo. In the late nineteenth century, some thirty-five hundred people lived in Mendocino, which then boasted eight hotels, seventeen saloons and as many bordellos.

Today the population is only eleven hundred, and includes many artists and craftspeople. The entire town has been declared a historic monument so that its character will be preserved. Along Main Street, which faces the sea, and along picturesque side streets, where hollyhocks rise over picket fences, there are seventeen art galleries and crafts shops. Within the area are tennis courts and a nine-hole golf course. The surrounding waters offer deep-sea and stream fishing, and canoeing.

Just north of Mendocino is Fort Bragg, a lumber town built on the site of a military post that was established in 1857. Fort Bragg is the departure point for the Skunk railroad, a scenic six-hour journey inland along the Noyo River, through forty miles of redwoods. Advance reservations may be made by writing California Western Railroad, P.O. Box 907B, Fort Bragg, California 95437.

Getting There: From San Francisco take Highway 101 north through Santa Rosa to Cloverdale; Highway 128 north to the coast where it joins Highway 1. Elk is a few miles south on Highway 1; Little River, Mendocino and Fort Bragg are located north on Highway 1. Driving time to Mendocino is about 3-1/2 hours.

MENDOCINO HOTEL
Mendocino

In 1878, one of the houses on Mendocino's Main Street was bought by San Franciscan Ben Bever; his family and furnishings later arrived by schooner. That fall the *Mendocino Beacon* broke the news that Ben Bever was building an addition to his house and starting a boardinghouse. "It shall be called the Temperance House and no liquor shall be served." Bever's brother Sam joined him in the enterprise, and the name was changed to Central House, later Central Hotel and finally Mendocino Hotel.

During the last five decades the hotel has changed hands frequently. Even though it was shabby, the hotel was still regarded fondly by locals as a meeting place. In 1973, San Diego businessman R. O. Peterson, founder of the Jack in the Box chain, bought the hotel and renovated it to a level of luxury that had not existed before. Even in its prime years, the hotel had been nothing fancy, just a comfortable hostelry for loggers and traveling salesmen. Peterson retained architect Wayne Williams and his wife Paula, an interior decorator, to invest the hotel with the elegance of the Victorian era. Polished dark woods and wainscotings, Oriental rugs and Tiffany-style glass were installed in the lobby and dining room. A spectacular dome of genuine Tiffany, found in Philadelphia, is suspended over the carved wooden bar. (Temperance most certainly is not the house rule today.)

Upstairs twenty-six bedrooms have been renovated to mint condition and decorated with bright flowered wallpapers, marble-topped dressers, Victorian chairs. Many rooms have views and balconies. A few have private baths, but lack of one is not so critical here. The community baths are modern and immaculate.

Hotel guests receive a complimentary breakfast of freshly squeezed orange juice, home-baked nut and fruit breads, and coffee. For dinner the hotel dining room is open to the public; lunch is served in an attractive, plant-filled greenhouse room that has been added.

MENDOCINO HOTEL, 45080 Main Street (P.O. Box 587), Mendocino, California 95460. Telephone: (707) 937-0511. Accommodations: twin, double and queen-size beds; some private baths, community baths with showers; no telephones; no television. Rates: inexpensive to moderate, Continental breakfast included. Open to public for lunch and dinner; full bar service. Children welcome. No pets. Cards: MC, VISA. Open all year.

HEADLANDS INN
Mendocino

Of the many north coast inns that have opened in the 1980s, Headlands is by far the loveliest. The three-story, nineteenth-century shingled house, surrounded by a picket fence and a flower-filled garden, commands unobstructed views of the Big River inlet and the tree-covered mountains beyond. Originally built in 1869 as a barber shop on Main Street, the house was expanded for use as a home by the barber's family, and later served as a saloon and as a hotel annex. In 1893 the building was moved to its present site and became a private residence. Over the years, however, time and neglect took their toll; by 1979, when a series of aspirant innkeepers began restoration, the building was completely dilapidated. Today, the former inhabitants would scarcely recognize the place.

Rich champagne-colored carpeting flows throughout the rooms, which are painted and papered in restful tones of beige and white and furnished with English and American antiques. Many rooms have wood-burning fireplaces, most have ocean views, and one has Dutch doors leading to a private deck. All are appointed with comfortable couches and chairs, queen- or king-size beds, magazines, plants and flowers—even in the spacious private baths. A second-floor common room contains games, books and a drafting table for would-be artists. Guests may breakfast here, but most prefer to enjoy in their rooms a tray of freshly baked breads and muffins, juice, coffee, the morning paper, and a fresh flower from the garden.

The present Headlands owners—Kathy Casper, Lynn Anderson and Pete Albrecht—took over the inn in 1980. Kathy and Lynn, both former teachers, had been next-door neighbors during a prolonged visit to England and became enthralled with the bed and breakfast idea. Back in the States, they pooled their talents as innkeepers: Kathy is an avid baker, Lynn a dedicated gardener, and Pete a skilled carpenter and handyman. They are also avoiding innkeeper's fatigue by splitting the managerial tasks: Cathy runs the inn half the year and Lynn takes over for the next six months.

HEADLANDS INN, 44950 Albion Street (P.O. Box 132), Mendocino, California 94560. Telephone: (707) 937-4431. Accommodations: queen- and king-size beds; private baths with tub/shower; some fireplaces; no telephones; no television. Rates: moderate, Continental breakfast included. No children. No pets. No credit cards.

MacCALLUM HOUSE
Mendocino

Lumber magnate William H. Kelley owned much of the town of Mendocino in the 1880s. So when his daughter Daisy married Alexander MacCallum in 1882, Kelley built the young couple a honeymoon house even finer than his own home. The three-story Victorian with gingerbread gables had a wide porch where the MacCallums could sit and watch the lumbermen float their logs down Big River into the Pacific. Daisy matured to become the matriarch of Mendocino, and much of the town's social life revolved around her home.

In 1974 San Francisco stockbroker William Norris and his wife Sue bought the house from the MacCallum family and transformed it into an inn. All of the handsome original furnishings were still intact: Tiffany lamps, Persian rugs, carved footstools, paintings and an enormous library of turn-of-the-century books.

The Norrises started out by refurbishing the bedrooms in the house itself, using flowered Victorian wallpapers and matching curtains. These rooms, however, are rather small and dark—especially those under the eaves in the attic—and the old-fashioned bathrooms are "down the hall." More comfort and privacy are offered by the outbuildings, which Sue has transformed one by one into sleeping quarters over the years.

The old greenhouse is now a rustic cottage with skylights and a free-standing Franklin stove. It shares an adjoining modern bath with the water tower, now a two-story unit. The old carriage house contains two rooms with stoves, and a shared bath. The redwood work shed has been furnished with rattan furniture, and the outhouse has been turned into a bathroom. Even the tiny gazebo, once the playhouse of the MacCallum children, is for rent and still contains its child-size chairs.

But by far the most luxurious quarters at MacCallum House are to be found in the Norrises' latest renovation project—the barn. The spacious upstairs unit has its own private deck with a view of the town and the ocean beyond. Under the high pitched ceiling, still sheathed with weathered barn siding, is a loft, and below is a charming sitting room with a massive stone fireplace. One of the bedrooms has a similar fireplace; the other has a spectacular view of the ocean. Off the sitting room is a large wet bar with a polished counter of burled walnut and a copper sink. The modern bath has an oversized shower and a skylight.

Downstairs in the barn is another one-bedroom apartment with a fully equipped kitchen and, again, fireplaces in both bedroom and living

MacCallum House

room. Massive double barn doors open to a deck. The lower floor of the barn also contains two smaller bedrooms with a connecting bath.

From the spring through the fall dinners are served in the book-lined dining room of the main house and cocktails are served in an adjacent bar. A Continental breakfast is served year round.

MacCALLUM HOUSE, Albion Street (P.O. Box 206), Mendocino, California 95460. Telephone: (707) 937-0289. Accommodations: double beds; community and connecting baths; some with tub/shower, some tub only, some shower only; private baths in barn; no telephones; no television. Rates: inexpensive to expensive, Continental breakfast included. Open to public for dinner April through December, weekends only February through March; full bar service. Children welcome. No pets. Cards: MC, VISA. Open all year.

JOSHUA GRINDLE INN
Mendocino

This lovely old home in Mendocino, like the MacCallum House, was built as a wedding gift—for Joshua Grindle and his bride in 1879 by her parents. Grindle had come to California from Maine to seek his fortune in lumber, but later went into banking. In 1977 Bill and Gwen Jacobson purchased the house for an inn.

The Jacobsons searched northern California for a likely piece of property. Then while vacationing at Heritage House they learned that the old Grindle house was for sale. The house was basically in good shape and, even more important, it had space for a private bath in every room. They added baths, carpeted and redecorated each room. The furnishings are Early American, in keeping with the town's New England heritage.

On the first floor one bedroom is papered with historic scenes of Philadelphia, boasts a handsome maple four-poster, and overlooks a patio shaded by a giant rhododendron tree. Another is decorated with pale yellow woodwork, a peony-patterned quilt on a queen-size bed, and comfortable chairs around a fireplace. An upstairs room has a nautical theme and a fine ocean view. Joshua Grindle's former bedroom, with its dormered windows, is large enough for three, with a queen-size bed and a studio couch. A recently completed saltbox cottage contains two rooms with Franklin fireplaces.

The gracious paneled living room houses a piano and an unusual fireplace decorated with hand-painted English tiles. A decanter of

144

sherry and a bowl of fruit are there for the guests' enjoyment. In the cheerful dining room an antique pine refectory table, a handsome old hutch and a grandmother's clock catch the eye. Here Gwen serves a full breakfast of homemade bread or coffeecake, fresh fruits, eggs, coffee and tea.

JOSHUA GRINDLE INN, 44800 Little Lake, Mendocino, California 95460. Telephone: (707) 937-4143. Accommodations: twin, double and queen-size beds; some fireplaces; private baths with tub/shower; no telephones; no television. Rates: moderate, full breakfast included. Children discouraged. No pets. No credit cards. Open all year.

WHITEGATE INN
Mendocino

Except for an eight-year stint as a hospital in the last century, this 100-year-old house was maintained as a private residence until 1980 when it succumbed to the bed and breakfast craze. The original crystal chandeliers still grace the parlor and former dining room (now a bedroom), and housed in the two-story inn are many authentic Victorian pieces dating back to the 1850s, including some stunning mirrored

145

armoires. Oriental rugs, plants and flowers are scattered throughout. For the guests' enjoyment the parlor contains an organ, books and wine. Weekend breakfasts feature cinnamon, apple or walnut waffles; the weekday menu is fruit with yogurt, nut breads and cream cheese. If you want an ocean view, request the upstairs front room.

WHITEGATE INN, 499 Howard Street (P.O. Box 150), Mendocino, California 95460. Telephone: (707) 937-4892. Accommodations: queen-size, double and twin beds; two rooms share bath with tub; two have private baths with stall showers; no telephones; no television. Rates: moderate, breakfast included. No children. No pets. No credit cards.

THE GREY WHALE INN
Fort Bragg

This grey and white building on Fort Bragg's Main Street functioned as a hospital from 1915 until 1974 when it was converted into a semiresidential hotel. In 1978 former San Franciscans John and Colette Bailey bought the place and started a massive remodeling program, adding carpeting, private baths, comfortable and attractive furnishings. Only a few clues remain to the inn's institutional past: an old examining table in the lobby, extra-wide doors, a window in the door of the former nursery and ramps leading up to the rear entrance. Today this gives easy access for wheelchairs; a spacious lower room has also been fully equipped for persons in wheelchairs. Some of the thirteen rooms have natural redwood ceilings or pecky cedar paneling; some have ocean views; others have kitchenettes and will accommodate a family of four; one has a fireplace; another an interior patio. Two glassed-in penthouse rooms have private decks and views of the ocean or mountains. Bright quilted spreads with matching linens cover all the beds.

In a small first-floor sitting room the Baileys have thoughtfully provided scrapbooks of information on local attractions, restaurants and other inns throughout California. Another lounge area on the second floor is equipped with plaid-upholstered love seats. In a little breakfast room, coffee, sweet breads and fruit are set out each morning for guests to help themselves.

GREY WHALE INN, 615 North Main Street, Fort Bragg, California 95437. Telephone: (707) 964-0640. Accommodations: twin, double, queen- and king-size beds; private baths; some kitchens; no telephones; no television; wheelchair access to one room. Rates: inexpensive to moderate, Continental breakfast included. Children welcome. No pets. Cards: MC, VISA. Open all year.

PUDDING CREEK INN
Fort Bragg

When Gene and Marilyn Gundersen bought two old houses, connected by a nursery, on Main Street in Fort Bragg, they knew little of the buildings' history. Later they were told that the houses were built by a Russian count in 1884, and that the old white lace dress they had found in one house belonged to the countess, the first wedding dress ever advertised in the Montgomery Ward catalog. After they converted the buildings to an inn in 1980, naming it after a nearby stream, the Gundersens displayed the dress in the lower parlor, along with a photograph of the titled pair and other memorabilia. Next to the parlor is a country store and behind that a cheerful old-fashioned kitchen with a wood-burning stove and several tables. Breakfast—homemade coffee-cake, fruit and juice—is served here as well as outdoors in the nursery, which is still a veritable jungle of hanging begonias, fuschias and ferns. Water splashes from a little fountain, and wine is served here in the evening.

At this writing, seven guest rooms had been redecorated with Early American and Victorian furnishings, flowered wallpapers, quilted spreads. By the spring of 1982, the Gundersens hope to have a dozen rooms ready, several with fireplaces and all with private baths. Each room has its individual touch: an antique spinning wheel in one, a school desk for a night stand in another, and a window box filled with pelargoniums in yet another.

PUDDING CREEK INN, 700 North Main Street, Fort Bragg, California 95437. Telephone: (707) 964-9529. Accommodations: twin, double, queen- and king-size beds; private baths with tub or shower; no telephones; no television. Rates: inexpensive, Continental breakfast included. Children over ten welcome. No pets. Cards: MC, VISA. Open all year.

BENBOW INN
Garberville

South of Garberville, Highway 101 follows the south fork of the Eel River as it flows through valleys edged with unusual red rock formations and groves of giant redwood trees. This is logging country, fishing country, rustic camping country. Then the valley widens, and at its head the Eel River snakes into a lake. There—lo and behold—stands a four-story English Tudor manor house.

The Benbow Inn, with its formal half-timbered construction and gabled roof, seemed even more incongruous in these forested mountains when the Benbow family built it in 1926. The Benbows, five sisters and four brothers with no prior hotel experience, dammed the river to create a lake and commissioned San Francisco architect Albert Farr to design the inn on its shores.

Today it's a step back to the 1920s as you enter the stately lobby with its high timbered ceiling, carved woodwork, Oriental rugs, massive sculptured stone fireplace and sturdy antique furniture. One would almost expect Scott Fitzgerald to step through the French doors onto the formal oak-shaded terrace to admire the statuary or observe a game of croquet in progress on the lawn beyond. Fitzgerald might not have slept here, but in the inn's heyday the Benbows did host the likes of John Barrymore, Charles Laughton, President Herbert Hoover and Mrs. Eleanor Roosevelt.

The Benbows sold the inn in 1952 and after a decade of decline it was purchased by retired advertising executive Albert Stadler, who restored the inn to its former grandeur, adding many antiques from his private collection. In 1974, Patsy and Chuck Watts, a young couple from southern California, tried to buy Benbow, but Stadler refused to sell. Later he changed his mind and contacted the Watts, but they had just purchased the Vagabond House in Carmel four days earlier. Instead he sold to Dennis Levett, who traded inns with the Watts four years later.

Patsy and Chuck have made significant changes at Benbow, adding numerous antiques and old clocks—a passion of theirs—to the public rooms, and old paintings and prints throughout. They are particularly proud of a beautiful table that holds the jigsaw puzzles that are one of the main evening entertainments at the inn. In the comfortable bar off the lobby, you can get as high on nostalgia as on spirits. The Wattses have kept the corner jukebox with its big-bands collection: Glenn Miller, Freddy Martin, Artie Shaw, Wayne King, etc.

Benbow Inn

In the large half-timbered dining room touches of the Watts regime may also be seen. Through the multipaned windows diners view the gardens blooming with rhododendrons, azaleas and camellias, which Patsy and Chuck have added along with some three dozen other varieties of plants. The Continental menu also has been upgraded with more seafood and Provimi veal. Chuck's favorites are duckling with apricot sauce and a chocolate mousse pie.

Upstairs, carved cherrywood wainscoting has been added to all the hallways, and all forty bedrooms have new carpeting, draperies and quilted bedspreads. The second- and third-story rooms are probably the nicest, all with views of the surrounding terrain from large windows or bays. Most are appointed with painted and gilded French furniture. A few contain some valuable and handsome pieces of Hepplewhite with intricate wood inlays. The fourth-floor rooms, originally reserved for servants, are quite cozy with dormer windows. Patsy and Chuck have recarpeted these and decorated them with wing chairs, prints and antiques. Most popular with families, however, are the two floors of rooms under the terrace. Though not as light and sunny as the upper rooms, they are interconnecting and open directly outside so the children can easily come and go.

Despite its remote location, Benbow offers a variety of recreational facilities. There are a nine-hole, par-thirty-six golf course, fishing, hunting and hiking trails. From mid-May through October, there are swimming from the inn's private beach, canoeing and paddle boating. Seven miles south of Benbow is Richardson Grove State Park, one of California's most important redwood preserves.

BENBOW INN, Garberville, California 95440. Telephone: (707) 923-2124. Accommodations: twin, double, queen- and king-size beds; most rooms have private baths, tub/shower or shower only; some share connecting baths or community baths down the hall; no telephones; no television except in lobby. Rates: moderate. Open to public for breakfast, lunch, dinner and Sunday brunch; full bar service. Children over three welcome. Dogs allowed. Credit cards: MC, VISA. Open April 1 to December 1, and December 18 through January 2.

Getting There: Benbow Inn is 200 miles north of San Francisco, two miles south of Garberville, on Highway 101. From the Mendocino coast, Benbow may be reached by Highway 1 to Leggett and then north on 101. The inn will send a car to Garberville airport for guests arriving by private plane.

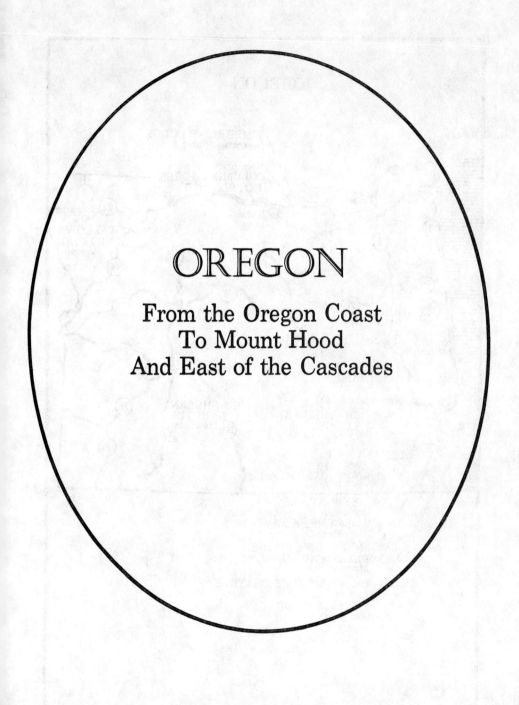

OREGON

From the Oregon Coast
To Mount Hood
And East of the Cascades

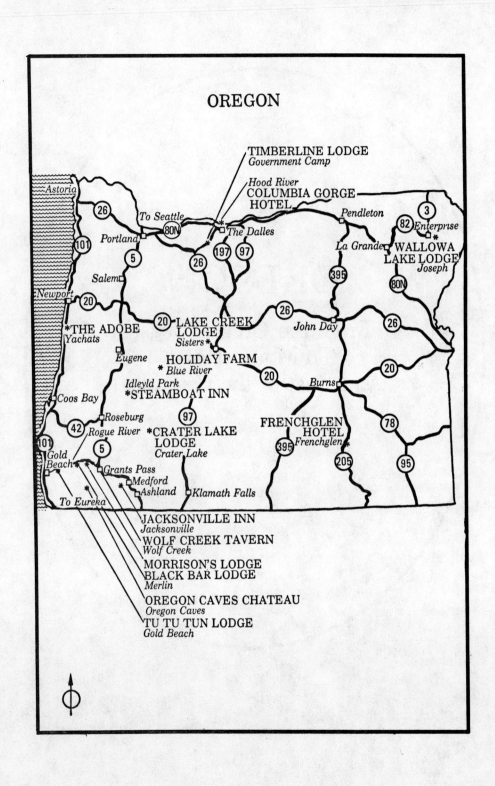

OREGON

TIMBERLINE LODGE
Government Camp

Hood River
COLUMBIA GORGE
HOTEL

Pendleton

Astoria

26

To Seattle
80N

The Dalles

3

82 *Enterprise*

Portland

5

26

197   97

La Grande

WALLOWA
LAKE LODGE
Joseph

Salem

Newport

20

20   LAKE CREEK
LODGE
Sisters

395

John Day

80N

26

26

THE ADOBE
Yachats

Eugene

HOLIDAY FARM
Blue River

20

Burns

20

Idleyld Park
STEAMBOAT INN

Coos Bay

Roseburg

42   *Rogue River*

97

FRENCHGLEN
HOTEL
Frenchglen

78

*Gold
Beach*

5

101

*CRATER LAKE
LODGE*
Crater Lake

395

205

95

Grants Pass

Medford
Ashland   *Klamath Falls*

To Eureka

JACKSONVILLE INN
Jacksonville
WOLF CREEK TAVERN
Wolf Creek

MORRISON'S LODGE
BLACK BAR LODGE
Merlin

OREGON CAVES CHATEAU
Oregon Caves
TU TU TUN LODGE
Gold Beach

THE ROGUE RIVER

The Rogue River in southwestern Oregon is famous for fish, raging white water, gold mining, Indian wars, awesome scenery, mail boats and Zane Grey. Eighty-four miles of its westernmost stretch have been declared a Wild and Scenic River, one of only ten rivers in the country so designated and protected.

The first distinct zone of the lower Rogue is between Grants Pass and the end of the road at Grave Creek. Here the river is visible from a good highway. Picnickers, photographers, and fishermen can get at it easily. Many kinds of boats ply this part of the river, which includes Hellgate Canyon.

Beyond Grave Creek are thirty-five miles of river where access is not so easy. The river is not only roadless but so rocky and treacherous as to be unsafe and indeed impossible for power boats. To ride this wild Rogue you may go it alone in a kayak, a flat-bottomed Rogue drift boat or a rubber raft, if you are experienced and have studied your adversary. Otherwise, a guided raft trip is the answer. Several dependable outfitters, including B. A. Hanten at Morrison's Lodge, will take parties on trips from a half-day to five days, for fishing or pure adventure. The Bureau of Land Management in Medford will provide a list of raft outfitters. Besides offering salmon, steelhead and white water, a raft trip on the river is an unparalleled chance for watching to see great blue herons busy at their fishing, and probably black bear too—also elk browsing on the hillside.

The longer raft trips give you the choice of roughing it (camping along the river) or stopping at rustic lodges. Since the number of people on the river at any one time is limited by law, reservations for these trips should be made well in advance.

Black Bar Lodge (see entry later) is a frequent overnight stop for rafters, and can be reached only by water. Marial Lodge, farther downstream and also usually reserved for rafting parties, has road access of a sort but is more often approached by water or trail.

Hiking is another rewarding way to experience the river. The forty-mile Rogue River Trail follows the north bank from Grave Creek to Illahe. The trail is not arduous, being mostly near river level, and has spectacular views as well as solitude, ample drinking water and a number of public camping areas. Some vantage points afford a fine view of rafters making their way through rapids or portaging.

Hikers who wish to stop at a lodge must arrange ahead. At Black Bar, for instance, they must halloo to the innkeeper to row across to get them, which he may be unlikely to do unless they have made reservations.

Rafters and hikers alike will want to visit Zane Grey's cabin, several rapids below Marial. It's on an old mining claim at Winkle Bar, where Grey often visited during the twenties to fish. The little cabin has been kept as it was in his day by the present owners of the land.

Several other lodges, on the lower reaches of the river, can be reached not only by river or trail, but also by jet boat from Gold Beach. (These are the fast and noisy descendants of the mail boats which, until not so long ago, were the only link between civilization and the settlers on the lower Rogue.) These lodges include Half Moon Bar Lodge, P.O. Box 1185, Gold Beach, Oregon 97444 and Paradise Lodge, radiophone 247-6249. Boating parties are lodged in these inns most nights during the season, but if you are traveling the river independently and reserve ahead, room can usually be made.

Getting There: From the east, turn off Interstate 5 at the Merlin exit, four miles north of Grants Pass. Continue on Galice Road through Merlin to Galice and your put-in point, which may be Almeda Bar or Grave Creek. From the Oregon coast, there is road access from Gold Beach (on Highway 101) to Agness and Illahe; jet boat excursions go to Agness and farther upriver to Paradise Lodge and Half Moon Bar Lodge. Air transportation to some lodges on the lower Rogue may be arranged through Jefferson Flight Center, Grants Pass. A single-lane road leads from Galice across the mountains to Agness, about 40 miles. It is open only from May to October and on weekdays motorists should be alert for logging trucks. This is the road the river outfitters use, and over which your car can be shuttled from your put-in point, so you will not have to be transported all the way back.

MORRISON'S LODGE
Merlin

Morrison's Lodge on the Rogue River, sixteen miles downstream from Grants Pass, is for people who love rivers in general and the Rogue in particular. The rustic log lodge and its cottages, half hidden by groves of evergreen and oak, attract not only fishermen, but also river rafters, gold panners, rockhounders, swimmers and those who take pleasure in the sight and sound of a river in the front yard.

The wide variety of guests who keep coming back indicates that innkeepers B.A. and Elaine Hanten must be doing something right, beginning with their purchase of the rather run-down lodge in 1964. It was built just after World War II by river guide and lumbermill worker Lloyd Morrison. He handpicked his materials—and the choice bird's-eye pine he used all through the lodge has become even more lustrous and beautiful with the patina of time. Mr. Morrison then gradually added cottages or moved little houses onto the property to accommodate his fisherman clientele. But after he sold the lodge, and during a couple of other ownerships, the buildings were somewhat neglected.

Then came the Hantens. They had decided it was time to leave Los Angeles and the aeronautics industry. Both had happy memories of working at Yellowstone Park, and Elaine, a home economics major, had always loved cooking. So they thought that running a ranch or a lodge might be the answer. They discovered Morrison's on their first research trip to Oregon, and that was that.

During the big flood of 1964, the rampaging Rogue wiped out all the cottages, which the Hantens had just begun to renovate, and water rose in the lodge to a point two feet above the mantel. The main building survived but they had to start from scratch on new accommodations, and that is why there is such a splendid set of cabins today. Determined to avoid another catastrophe, the Hantens built duplexes on stilts, and the cottages have stayed high and dry through several floods since the big one.

The big fishing season on this stretch of the Rogue is in the fall, with the best steelheading from mid-September through mid-November, after which the lodge closes until spring. Licensed guides pick fishermen up at the lodge, take them out on drift boats for the day and bring them back. Fishing gear is provided and licenses are available at the lodge. If you fish from the bank, though, you should bring your own equipment. The lodge has a smokehouse and will chill, freeze or smoke your fish—or cook it for your dinner.

Though Morrison's has traditionally been an angler's lodge, it is equally popular now with families, especially in the summer. A major attraction is rubber-rafting on the wild and scenic Rogue. B.A. (as Mr. Hanten is known) himself runs raft and jet boat trips, and calls in other outfitters as needed. White-water raft trips are from one, three or four days; jet boat trips run three times a day.

The lodge offers much to non-river rats, too. There are a tennis court, a putting green and a pool. And, since at the lodge the Rogue is quite calm and peaceful, there's river swimming. Hikers can drive to Grave Creek and the trailhead of the famous forty-mile Rogue River Trail, which follows the river through wilderness, joining the road at Illahe and proceeding to the river's mouth at Gold Beach.

Exploring up and down river from Morrison's is rewarding, too, with deserted gold mines and parks and picnic areas to discover. A few miles upstream is Hellgate Canyon, where the river gathers itself together and rushes through a narrow rocky cleft, one of the great sights in the West. In the other direction is tiny Galice, the last outpost of civilization before you enter the wild Rogue River country.

Guests usually congregate in the sitting room for cocktails before dinner, but are requested to bring their own materials, as the lodge has no liquor permit. This room is strictly for down-home-style relaxation: a thick red carpet, highbacked leather chairs, a capacious flowered-cretonne sofa, a grand piano in the corner and a roaring fire in the native stone fireplace on chilly days.

The adjacent dining room is just as comfortable. Particularly in the fall, dinners are planned for hungry, hardworking fishermen who look forward to a family-style repast. A typical October menu might start with a relish tray (including Elaine's noted homemade pickles, spiced figs and corn relish), then go on to crêpes, spinach salad, prime rib with Yorkshire pudding, broccoli soufflé and chocolate mousse.

Everywhere there is a lovely view of lawn and pines and river, whether from the main lodge's long veranda or from the balconies of the cottages. Four of the nine cottages are housekeeping units. All are snug and well built. The cottages have both fireplaces and gas heat, wall-to-wall carpeting, wood paneling and air conditioning. The housekeeping units have kitchenettes and little dining areas. Carports and boat storage space are under the cottages.

MORRISON'S LODGE, 8500 Galice Road, Merlin, Oregon 97532. Telephone: (503) 476-3825..Accommodations: twin beds; some rooms in lodge have private baths with showers, some community baths;

cottages have private baths and tub/showers; no telephones; no television except in lodge sitting room. Rates: moderate, breakfast and dinner included, May 1–September 15; three meals included, September 15–November 15; or no meals included (summer only). Meal Service: breakfast and dinner in summer; breakfast, lunch and dinner in fall. Children welcome. No pets. No credit cards. Open May 1 through November 15, at other times by special arrangement.

Getting There: By car, take Interstate 5 to the Merlin exit, about four miles north of Grants Pass; continue on Galice Road through Merlin to Morrison's Lodge, on your right 16 miles west of Grants Pass. By plane, take Airwest or United Airlines to Medford; arrange in advance for pickup by lodge. Or fly by private plane to Josephine County Airport, between Merlin and Grants Pass, and the lodge will meet you by prior arrangement. By bus, take Greyhound to Grants Pass; arrange in advance for pickup.

BLACK BAR LODGE
Merlin

This diamond-in-the-rough kind of lodge is the first stop on many Rogue River raft trips. It is not recommended for the faint of heart or the tender of foot. But the hospitality is genuine and hearty, and the accommodations are as welcome as a room at the Ritz after a damp and bumpy day on the river.

The lodge is invisible from the river. After you climb out of your raft (or kayak, or whatever nonmotorized vessel you arrived in), a jeep takes all the gear up a rocky track while guests trudge behind, getting their land legs back. Around the corner at the top of the rise is a rustic log house with a verdant lawn (where, of an evening, deer will browse).

Inside, the lodge is just like a big old family summer house that adapts comfortably to any number of friends and relations. The high-ceilinged living room has a balcony with a drying room (and there's an outdoor clothesline too), appreciated by travelers who arrive in a drenched condition. Meals are served at long tables in the dining room, which is open to the living room and within sight and sound of the kitchen. There is no bar, but guests who have succeeded in making room for bottles in their duffel bags will find ice and mixer available.

The lodge has been little altered since it began as a private home, nearly half a century ago. Bill and Sally Hull of Sunny Valley bought it in

1959 and fixed it up as their year-round house. In those days, they had to hike in from the end of the dirt road, eight miles away, with all supplies. Presently they began to accept guests, first for the fall fishing, then in the summer. Before they knew it they were operating a lodge. After the 1964 flood wiped out the landing strip, Bill built a jeep road to bring in the propane, groceries and other supplies he had been flying in. The road drops two thousand feet in 1-1/2 miles, and Bill Hull's jeep is the only vehicle with the guts and experience to tackle it.

Bill also built the seven cabins off to one side of the lodge. They're identical in plan but flexible in capacity, taking from two to four people each. Each cabin's front door opens on one room with one table, one stove, and one pair of twin or double beds. The partitioned rear section has a shower, washbowl and toilet. There are absolutely no frills, not even on the calico curtains.

Most guests don't mind the lack of luxury, being happy to be dry, warm and well fed. Meals are unbelievably hearty, with substantial main courses (roasts, chops, steaks, fried chicken, fish, etc.) and bowl after bowl of vegetables, potatoes, salads, relishes passing around the table and being constantly refilled. The freshness of the corn, gathered minutes before from the lodge garden, makes the whole trip worthwhile. Rolls, Sally's genuine sourdough biscuits, pies and pastries are fresh from the oven. All this comes with good talk, trading impressions of the day's rapids and adventures with voyagers from the other boats.

After such a meal, one is inclined to tumble into bed as soon as the lights go out, which is promptly at 10 pm when the diesel-fueled generator is turned off.

Breakfast, before everybody piles back into the boats, is as bountiful as dinner, with enough hotcakes, bacon, eggs, ham, biscuits, butter, jam, fruit and coffee to keep an armada of rafters going until lunch and then some. Lunches on these raft trips are provided by the outfitter for the first day out, then by each lodge for that day. But if you're staying over at Black Bar, the Hulls will see that you don't starve.

BLACK BAR LODGE, P.O. Box 510, Merlin, Oregon 97532. No telephone. One-bedroom cabins with twin and double beds; private baths with showers; no telephones; no television. Rates: by arrangement with raft outfitter; dinner, breakfast and packed lunch included. Children welcome. No pets. No credit cards. Open May to November.

Getting There: See Rogue River section. No road access. Black Bar Lodge is ten miles by water downstream from Grave Creek or 14 miles from Almeda Bar. (For a list of Rogue River guide services, including those offering lodge trips, write the Bureau of Land Management, 310 West Sixth Street, Medford, Oregon 97501.) By trail, Black Bar is opposite a side trail from the main Rogue River Trail, 9.6 miles from the trailhead at Grave Creek. Arrangements must be made in advance.

TU TÚ TUN LODGE
Gold Beach

Relatively off the beaten track, Tu Tú Tun Lodge (pronounced Tu *Tu* Tun), on the lower Rogue near Gold Beach, is a best-of-both-worlds transition point. Seven miles away is the beautiful but increasingly developed Oregon coast. A short distance upstream the real wilderness begins. Accessible by land or water, the inn has a respected place on the rather short list of distinctive Rogue River inns.

In the 1960s Ralph Priestley, a Marin County, California, architect, his wife and two friends teamed up to build a lodge on the Rogue—a river all had long known and loved. They opened Tu Tú Tun in 1970: a gracious, low-slung wood lodge on a grassy ledge between forest and river, with a separate two-story wing for sleeping rooms.

Now Tu Tú Tun is owned and managed by Dirk and Laurie Van Zante. These energetic young people have preserved the warmly hospitable character of the lodge and have become experts on local lore and on the area's Indian heritage. (Tu Tu Tun—"people by the river"—was the name of a subtribe of the Rogue Indians who had a village overlooking this same broad sweep of the river.)

Very likely you will be greeted by name when you arrive, and invited into the pleasant lounge. This room encourages relaxation both active and passive, with its settees drawn up around the huge stone fireplace, its library with a writing desk and well-stocked bookshelves, its billiard table and heirloom player piano, and, on the way to the dining room, a small bar.

An old school bell summons guests to dinner, which is served family style at big round tables. The menu might include fresh Chinook salmon and prime rib, home-baked breads and pastries.

The sixteen guest rooms are hardly what one would expect on the edge of the wilderness, with their wall-to-wall carpet, fresh flowers, easy chairs and good reading lamps. Old creels, nets and rods on the walls are reminders of the Rogue's fishing fame. The rooms are named for noted river points, each with its own story, such as Wake-up Riley Creek and Bear Riffle. Each room has a balcony or patio overlooking the river. There is additional accommodation for six people in the Garden House, situated in the apple orchard behind the inn. It was the original home on the property, and is a comfortable house with its own kitchen, dining room and living room with fireplace.

During the summer, family vacationers find Tu Tú Tun a convenient terminus or take-off point for a river excursion. Boats going from Gold Beach to Agness, or beyond into the wilderness portion of the river, will stop at the lodge dock by arrangement. (Dirk and Laurie will make reservations.) Or guests may moor their own boats here.

Since the days when the Tu Tu Tun Indians set fires along the river to mark the start of the salmon run, fishermen have sought the Rogue. There are spring Chinook from April to mid-June, summer steelhead from September through November, and fall Chinook in September and October. Dirk will book guests with experienced local guides, who provide boat, tackle and gear. Most guides have boats with tops and heaters to insure a comfortable trip for the less rugged. The lodge provides breakfast and lunch baskets. The catch may be cooked for breakfast or lunch at the lodge, with the remainder canned for future feasting.

For nonfisherfolk, there is plenty to do. There is a heated pool between the lodge terrace and the river. Get a taste of the wilderness by walking the Tu Tu Tuni Springs trail, which begins a few steps from the lodge and runs along a creek bordered by wild flowers and ferns. Also near at hand are horseback riding and hiking on the Lower Rogue Trail. A half-day's tramp leads one through ancient forests, along the Rogue in its many moods.

TU TÚ TUN LODGE, 96550 North Bank Road, Gold Beach, Oregon 97444. Telephone: (503) 247-6664. Accommodations: extra-long double beds in lodge rooms, twins in Garden House; private baths with tub/shower; no telephones; no television. Rates: moderate to expensive, no meals included. Open to the public for breakfast, lunch and dinner; full bar service. Children welcome. Pets, $3 per day. Cards: MC, VISA. Main lodge open May 1–November 1, Garden House open all year.

Getting There: By car, leave Highway 101 at the north end of the Rogue River Bridge at Gold Beach and turn east. Drive along the north bank of the river for seven miles to the lodge. By air, a private airport at Gold Beach is served by Pacific Air Service and Air Oregon. Arrange in advance for pickup at airport by Tu Tú Tun car.

WOLF CREEK TAVERN
Wolf Creek

In the 1870s it took a week to go by stagecoach from Sacramento to Portland, barring mishaps. One of the stops along the 710-mile route was the inn at Wolf Creek near Grants Pass in southern Oregon. Travelers, drivers and horses could be sure of a good meal and a restful night here. Today, Wolf Creek Tavern still dispenses hospitality in a style modeled on the great days of coaching.

The original tavern, built about 1870, was neat, white painted and well proportioned, fronted with an imposing "double piazza" in the Classical Revival style. On the main floor were the ladies' parlor and men's taproom, separated by a central hall. Sleeping rooms were on the second floor, as was a ballroom.

For some fifty years the tavern welcomed all, taking in its stride the passing of the stagecoach era and the arrival of the motor car. Another wing with more bedrooms was added by John Dougall in the twenties. But after the freeway bypassed Wolf Creek the tavern lost patronage. By the 1970s it had become run-down—in fact an eyesore.

In 1977 the state of Oregon bought the tavern and with help from enthusiastic citizen restorationists recreated an authentic, working

161

nineteenth-century inn. It reopened in 1979. Furnishings are appropriate to the ages of the two wings: from 1865–85 for the original portion, from 1915–30 for Dougall's addition. Some are genuine antiques, like the marble-topped washstands. Some are meticulous reproductions, like the soft-toned Pendleton wool rugs in the entry. Early craftsmanship has been preserved in three brick fireplaces and the paneled wainscoting, and reproduced in the "combed" finish of doors and casements.

Authenticity of bedroom furnishings means no gewgaws or unnecessary clutter. The only exception is the Parlour Chamber in the original wing, which is very Victorian. Rooms have high oak or brass or iron bedsteads, colorful candlewick or patchwork spreads and the original plank floors. Little stools are provided for aid in climbing into the high beds. All rooms have modern baths.

Local residents from Wolf Creek and the surrounding Rogue River country, as well as tourists and guests, have discovered how pleasant a meal or a meeting at the tavern can be. Hosts Vernon and Donna Wiard, who have managed the inn since its reopening, are genuinely proud of it and never tire of showing it off. The dining room offers a nice mixture of traditional items and cosmopolitan specialties. The homemade desserts lean toward the American: apple crisp, fruit and custard pies, a cream cheese pie with cherries. Oregon fruit and berry wines are a specialty.

Today's visitor joins an illustrious company, including Orson Welles, Clark Gable, Mary Pickford and those ubiquitous fishermen of Oregon rivers, Herbert Hoover and Jack London. It's fairly certain that the latter stayed here while completing his *Valley of the Moon.*

Wolf Creek itself is a tiny community, but worth exploring. The country store is a genuine example of that much-imitated genre. Ashland and the Shakespeare Festival are only a couple of hours away. Historic gold-rush–era Jacksonville is just down the pike. A fifteen-mile drive on a back road leads to the wild and scenic portion of the Rogue River.

WOLF CREEK TAVERN, P.O. Box 97, Wolf Creek, Oregon 97497. Telephone: (503) 866-2474. Accommodations: twin and double beds; all rooms with private bath with tub/shower (except one room for handicapped has shower only); no telephones; no television. Rates: inexpensive. Open to the public for Continental breakfast, lunch and dinner; Sunday brunch, 11 to 2; beer and wine only. Children welcome. No pets. No credit cards. Open all year.

Getting There: Take Wolf Creek exit from Interstate 5 (43 miles south of Roseburg, 18 miles north of Grants Pass).

JACKSONVILLE INN
Jacksonville

Jacksonville was born with the gold rush of 1851, and many of its original 1850s-vintage buildings still stand. The Jacksonville Inn is one of these veterans. Its brick facade is, except for the signs, the same as that of the store built in 1863 by Messrs. Ryan and Morgan. Later it housed a bank, a hardware store, professional offices and a furniture repair shop. It once had four floors, the upper two of wood, but these were lost somewhere along the way. The bricks were made in the Jacksonville kiln, one of the town's early industries.

Where most hotels would have a lobby, innkeepers Jerry and Linda Evans have a gift and wine shop. The restaurant, the brick-walled Dinner House, is in the basement, but this has not kept its fame from spreading. Food is excellent and presentation is stylish. The menu may offer prime rib, veal scaloppine, fresh salmon or petrale sole. Over five hundred wines are available.

The eight bedrooms are rather small but each has a private bath and all are charmingly furnished with antiques acquired in the area: brass bedsteads, oak highboys with beveled mirrors, Boston rockers and a few oak bedsteads with five-foot-high headboards. All rooms are air-conditioned.

You can start sampling nineteenth-century frontier architecture next door to the inn. The United States Hotel (now a historically recreated and functioning bank) was built in 1880. Rutherford B. Hayes was at the opening festivities. Nearby (almost everything is nearby in Jacksonville) is the handsome Pioneer Courthouse where more than a few horse thieves and claim jumpers met speedy justice. It's now a museum and houses valuable archives and artifacts. The Beekman Bank closed its doors back in 1915, but is now maintained for visitors, with much original equipment on display.

A walking tour will give you a chance to observe these and dozens of other historic sites and structures (homes, stores, churches) listed and described in a little brochure prepared by the Ashland Historic Preservation Committee.

The whole area abounds with events and attractions for the tourist. The annual Peter Britt Gardens Music and Arts Festival offers classical music for every taste for three weeks each August. Within driving range of Jacksonville are the Oregon Caves, a bit farther (seventy-seven miles) is lovely Crater Lake National Park, and twenty-one miles away is Ashland, site of the internationally known Shakespeare Festival. The Mount Ashland ski area is only thirty miles away, with skiing from Thanksgiving to May.

JACKSONVILLE INN, 175 East California Street, Jacksonville, Oregon 97530. Telephone: (503) 899-1900. Accommodations: twin, double and extra-long beds; private baths with showers; no telephones, no television. Rates: moderate, no meals included. Open to the public for dinner; full bar service. Children welcome. Pets discouraged. Cards: AE, MC, VISA. Open all year.

Getting There: From Portland, 290 miles south on Interstate 5 through Grants Pass to Medford, then seven miles west on 238. From Ashland, north on Interstate 5 to Medford and as above.

OREGON CAVES CHATEAU
Oregon Caves

Oregon Caves Chateau, with its weathered wood walls, shingled steep-pitched rooflines and rambling vertical architecture, looks as though it has been growing up out of its tree-lined canyon ever since the caves were discovered in 1874.

Actually, the Chateau has been there forty-nine years. And though the caves have always been the big attraction, over the decades the Chateau has engendered so much affection on the part of its guests that they keep coming back, to visit the caves or not. They like the remoteness (nineteen miles up a mountain road in the rugged Siskiyous), the perennial natural beauty and the simple, comfortable, unpretentious welcome the Chateau extends.

The lodge, designed by architect G. A. (Gust) Lium, must be unique, with six floors climbing up the canyon wall. The main entrance, leading into a spacious lobby, is on the fourth level. Here and throughout the Chateau almost every window reveals a different vista of the surrounding forest and the rocky, moss-covered ledges of the canyon. The main attraction in the lobby is a huge double fireplace in rough native marble, where you will nearly always find a cheerful fire. There are writing desks, card tables and inviting overstuffed chairs and sofas. A hundred-year-old grandfather clock ticks sedately against one wall. Cave tours are announced here so you may wait in comfort for your call.

A meal in the imposing dining room (one flight down) is a memorable experience. Huge wooden posts and beams are in scale with the grand proportions of the room. Nothing stands between you and forested slopes except big picture windows, and you almost feel you are dining in an enormous treehouse. A brook runs through the dining room, burbling along in its rock-lined, fern-bordered channel. There is an adjacent bar, screened by slabs of Port Orford cedar. The cafeteria is also on this floor. There are three floors of bedrooms. Those least changed from the original furnishings are at the top, with hand-carved oak bedsteads, exposed beams and startling close-up views of treetops. There are a few suites (with sitting room and bedroom) on the first floor. All rooms have private baths.

Besides accommodations in the big lodge, the Chateau has fourteen cabins. These are up the hill behind the dorms of the young people who work in the complex (dorm buildings also house the gift shop, soft-drink and snack bars and ticket counters for cave tours). The cabins are far more spartan, and less expensive, than lodge rooms, but are rather fun, obviously dating from the Chateau's earliest days. The siding is weathered bark. Interiors are bare and simple. All cabins have bath and electric heat.

As for the caves: They are spectacular and well worth the trip, even for those who think they are not cave enthusiasts. They were discovered in 1874 by Elijah Davidson, while hunting deer. In 1907 Joaquin Miller, the poet and conservationist, visited the caves, still inaccessible by road, and deplored the fact that early explorers had already defaced many of the chambers and had made off with choice formations. As a result of this publicity, President Taft made the caves a national monument in 1909. Since the road was built in 1922, and then the Chateau in 1932, visitors have come annually in increasing numbers.

A tour of the marble caves today takes you through dozens of mysterious chambers with weird, colorful and fantastic formations that suggestible viewers have named the Ghost Chamber, Paradise Lost, Dante's Inferno, the Joaquin Miller Chapel, and so on.

There is no organized recreation at the Chateau—no horseback riding or tennis or swimming pool. But there is plenty for the do-it-yourself outdoor enthusiast, including hiking trails and nature walks. The whole area is a bird watcher's paradise. A five-mile hike from the Chateau will take you to the top of Mount Elijah and a magnificent view of all southwest Oregon. (You may visit here year-round, tour the caves, and get snacks in the auxiliary lodge, but the Chateau is closed in winter.)

By car it is only a half-day's drive from Ashland and the Shakespeare Festival. The fascinating Kalmiopsis Nature Area is twenty-five miles away, back down Highway 46 to the Redwood Highway and north a few miles.

OREGON CAVES CHATEAU, Oregon Caves, Oregon 97523. Telephone: ask your local operator for Oregon Caves Toll Station No. 1 (area code 503). Accommodations: double and twin beds; private baths with tub or shower; no telephones; no television. Rates: moderate, no meals included. Open to the public for breakfast, lunch and dinner; coffee shop; full bar service. Children welcome. No pets. No credit cards. Chateau open mid-June through Labor Day; cave tours all year.

Getting There: By car from Crescent City, California, drive north 75 miles on Highway 199 (Redwood Highway); or from Grants Pass drive 50 miles south on Highway 199 to Cave Junction, then 19 miles on Highway 46 to Oregon Caves National Monument.

THE ADOBE
Yachats

The Oregon coast, so generously endowed with natural beauty, is remarkably lacking in country inns. Even the most pleasant motel suffers from being squeezed in with more of the same, along with some tasteless commercialism.

A couple of developments are welcome oases: Salishan Lodge at Gleneden Beach and the Inn at Otter Crest. Both are in superb seaside locations and have fine restaurants, but are large and impersonal.

An alternative, which has been around long enough now to become an institution, is the Adobe at Yachats, which calls itself a resort motel but functions more like an inn. It is in the right place—about halfway along the coast—and has become a favorite stopping-place for wise tourists.

The original builders really started from scratch. They made their own adobe bricks, in the time-honored way, and created a rambling, restful structure that has, especially in the bedrooms, much of the flavor of Early California. The older, beach-side sleeping rooms of the Adobe are attached in a row, as in a motel. Every one has a big picture window with a splendid view of lawn, rocks and sea. Walls are the original whitewashed adobe bricks—in the bathrooms too. Many rooms have fireplaces. (Annex rooms are much more modern.)

The approach from Highway 101, on a long blacktop drive lined with bent, windbeaten pines, brings you to a rather off-putting view of cars in carports. The lobby is a gift shop. But keep going. The ocean is the attraction here, and everything is oriented to it. The whole west side of the building is glassed. A wide passageway doubles as a lounge, with comfortable chairs and cocktail tables along the window wall, a spinet piano and a cherrywood desk.

The dining room is a semicircular room on the ocean side of the inn, and every table has a view of the sea. It is perhaps at its best on a partly cloudy evening, when the shades need not be drawn and the muted, pearly pink sunset is the star performer.

Before or after dinner—or both—you will certainly want to walk on the beach. Two small, perfect sandy coves are directly in front, but if you wish to explore farther you will have to scramble over the rocks. They're well furnished with barnacles, mountains of mussels, tidal pools, sea anemones, starfish, seagulls and cormorants. And for even more ocean, rock-hop out to the craggy points that jut into the sea and watch the waves crash against the rocks and shoot spray high into the air—

and over you. Whales are reportedly occasionally sighted here. But you may have more luck looking for agates; the gravelly sections of this beach are legendary among agate-hunters.

Besides beachcombing at the Adobe, there are surf fishing (for perch, rockfish and greenling) and smelt netting—smelt runs occur on the Adobe's own ocean doorstep every summer.

THE ADOBE, Yachats, Oregon 97498. Telephone: (503) 547-3141. Accommodations: king-size, double and twin beds; private baths, some with tub and shower, some shower only; telephones; television; rooms in annex have lanais. Rates: moderate, no meals included. Open to the public for breakfast and dinner; full bar service. Children welcome. Pets allowed (pets must be on leash on beach). Cards: MC, VISA. Open all year.

Getting There: Take Highway 101 to Yachats, which is eight miles south of Waldport and 26 miles north of Florence. Nearest airport: Eugene, 61 miles east of Florence, via Highway 126.

TIMBERLINE LODGE
Government Camp

Massive Timberline Lodge, six thousand feet up the south slope of Mount Hood, evokes the rebounding spirit that pulled the country through and out of the Depression of the thirties. Built as a WPA project in 1935 and dedicated by FDR in 1937, Timberline is constructed entirely of native Oregon materials.

Four hundred tons of stone went into the ninety-six-foot-tall central fireplace. The hexagonal pillars supporting the great beams in the main lobby are Ponderosa pines hand-hewn to a diameter of six feet. But don't get the idea that Timberline is merely big. It is also a beautiful, liveable gallery of craftsmanship and artistry, devoted to three themes: pioneer motifs, American Indian motifs and native Oregon wildlife and plant life. Fine examples are found throughout the lodge: carvings depicting native animals and pioneer history, handwoven rugs (some made of rags and scraps from old CCC uniforms), marquetry, metalwork, paintings, newel posts carved from telephone poles. An informative leaflet leads you through a self-guided tour of all these wonders.

Mount Hood is reported to be the second most climbed snow-capped peak in the world (after Fujiyama). Timberline is a natural starting point for hikes of any length. Only experienced mountain

climbers should try for the top without a guide. For those who would rather slide than tread, the lodge offers complete lift facilities for the year-round skiing the location offers. The Palmer chairlift, along with the older Mile chairlift, moves skiers, sightseers and photographers to the eighty-five-hundred-foot level. From there skiers can start the longest ski run in the country—eight miles down to Government Camp, another popular ski center on Mount Hood's slopes. There is also cross-country skiing.

Timberline's central "head-house" has three levels. The first-floor lobby is primarily used by skiers during the winter season. Off to its side is the Ski Grill, which serves informal meals. And around the corner from that is the Blue Ox Bar with its famous Paul Bunyan murals in glass.

The second floor has a comfortable lobby and the Cascadian Dining Room, where American and Continental dishes are served by candlelight. Several enormous fireplaces warm the first- and second-floor lobbies.

The balcony on the third level houses the hospitable Ramshead Bar, which has live entertainment on weekends. From large windows on either side of the bar you'll get magnificent views, either of the full scale of the mountain or, to the south, the high plateau stretching off from Trillium Lake to Mount Jefferson, forty-three miles away.

The rooms are in two wings leading out from the head-house. Some, including the Roosevelt Room with its historic mementoes, have fireplaces; all have views.

TIMBERLINE LODGE, Government Camp, Oregon 97028. Telephone: (503) 272-3311. Accommodations: twin, double and queen-size beds; private baths with tub and shower or shower only; some rooms with fireplaces; telephones; some televisions. Rates: moderate, no meals included. Open to the public for breakfast, lunch and dinner; full bar service. Children welcome. No pets. Cards: MC, VISA. Open all year.

Getting There: By car, from Portland, Highway 26 east; follow signs to Government Camp and Timberline (61 miles). From Hood River, 35 south, follow signs to Timberline (43 miles). Nearest airport: Portland. By bus, Trailways from Portland to Government Camp; arrange in advance for shuttle to Timberline.

LAKE CREEK LODGE
Sisters

The first-time visitor feels a sense of accomplishment on tracking down this little-publicized resort in the Oregon Cascades. There are no signs along the highway shouting "Only 10 miles to Lake Creek Lodge!" or telling you where to turn off Highway 20, the trans-Cascade route from Bend to western Oregon.

But once on the spot you understand the reticence: Most guests are regulars and need no guidance or urging to come back year after year to meet old friends and restore their souls in the carefree bucolic setting. Fathers and mothers who learned to swim and fish here as children are now bringing their own children to repeat the process.

The main lodge and a dozen cottages and houses are grouped around a lake, little more than a pond, formed by damming Lake Creek; the creek, a tributary of the Metolius River, runs behind and across a corner of the grounds. A lush lawn extends to the water's edge. Picnic tables and deck chairs are scattered about under the lofty Ponderosa

170

pines. Shuffleboard, badminton and horseshoe courts are unobtrusively handy; and near the pond children have their own little play area with swings and a slide that shoots them into the water. Lawn sitters and strollers may, on a clear day, gaze at some of Oregon's choicest peaks: North Sister, Three Fingered Jack, Mount Jefferson, Mount Washington. If they wish to deepen the acquaintance, access to the Pacific Crest Trail is only fifteen miles away. Or if they wish a bit of very mild close-at-hand activity, a walk behind the lodge and beside the creek is a summertime delight, through meadows dotted with forget-me-nots, buttercups, columbines and wild roses.

Other outdoor activities include trail riding, packing into the mountains, fishing or deer hunting trips. The Lake Creek Stables is just up the road. Cross-country skiing is fourteen miles away at Hoodoo Bowl.

Fishing attracts thousands to this area. Lake Creek Lodge is within the Deschutes National Forest, so fishermen will need a license. Fly fishermen have long respected the Metolius for its fighting rainbow; farther downstream there is bait fishing, and trolling and spin fishing may be undertaken on nearby lakes. At the lodge, the pond is kept stocked with rainbow trout, primarily for young apprentice fishermen.

But when the sun sets—or on those not infrequent days when it hides behind clouds—guests will find occupation indoors. And much of that occupation centers on the dining room, for Lake Creek Lodge is famous for its food. Dinner is a sociable occasion, with lively conversation and mingling of diners, since it is served buffet style. All breads and biscuits and pastries are homemade. So is the rich chocolate sauce served on the ice-cream cake. You may bring your own wine to the table; the lodge has no bar service. Although this is a family resort, the management recognizes that togetherness need go only so far; there is a separate children's dining room. Breakfast is another heartening and hearty meal, with thick, fluffy hotcakes, hot fresh rolls and a wide selection of eggs, breakfast meats and cereals.

The dining rooms and a broad deck (where meals are sometimes served) are to the right of the entry to the lodge. To the left is a comfortable and pleasantly cluttered lounge, with a fireplace, stacks of magazines and books, easy chairs and a billiard table.

Accommodations are in nonhousekeeping two-bedroom cottages, or in houses with kitchens and one to three bedrooms. All are beautifully kept and full of thoughtful touches. Lake Creek Lodge is in the heart of the pine country, so it's no surprise that paneling is knotty pine throughout, and most of the furniture is pine too. Interiors are attractive and well planned, with ample armoires, plenty of lamps, writing desks, bright floral-patterned curtains and blanket covers.

Some houses have fireplaces. Each cottage has a refrigerator on the front porch (tied shut to keep the raccoons out), and a basic survival kit in the closet: a tray with electric pot to heat water, and coffee, glasses, spoons, salt and openers.

Cottages and houses all have restful green views, electric heat and private baths with showers. Most date from the 1930s, when Roblay McMullin and her late husband built Lake Creek Lodge. Roblay's charming, antique-furnished house, just behind the main lodge, is a favorite gathering spot for her friends. She still serves as unofficial hostess for the whole establishment. The tenures of both manager Glenna Grace and cook Blanche Williams have bridged the transition from the longtime ownership of the McMullins to the 1974 purchase by a corporate group.

LAKE CREEK LODGE, Sisters, Oregon 97759. Telephone: (503) 595-6331. Accommodations: twin and double beds; private baths with showers; no telephones; no television; some houses have kitchens and dressing rooms. Rates: moderate, dinner included. Meal Service: breakfast and dinner, May 15 through October 15; no meal service in winter. Children welcome. Pets allowed, $1 per day charge. No credit cards. Open all year.

Getting There: By car, from Bend, drive 32 miles west on Highway 20 to the turnoff to Camp Sherman, then five miles on Camp Sherman Road. From Albany, drive east on Highway 20 to the Camp Sherman turnoff (87 miles). From Eugene, drive east on Highway 126 to Santiam Junction (78 miles), then 11 miles on Highway 20 to Camp Sherman turnoff. Nearest airport: Redmond. With advance notice, Lake Creek Lodge will meet guests at Sisters, Bend or Redmond.

HOLIDAY FARM
Blue River

It's not every lodge where you can cast your line into the river from your own front porch. But Holiday Farm is not your ordinary lodge. Though it's on the McKenzie River—one of Oregon's handful of world-famous fishing streams—it's as popular with vacationing families, hikers, horseback riders, golfers and nature observers as with pursuers of the fighting rainbow trout.

This easygoing, unpretentious little inn gives you all the privacy you want, in one of the nine self-sufficient cottages. And it offers you

172

companionship and society, when you feel the need, in its two restaurants, the Farmhouse and the Lodge.

The tradition of hospitality goes back to when the big white house now known as the Farmhouse was not only the center of a thriving farm, but also a stagecoach stop on the McKenzie River route from Eugene. That was in the 1870s. The post office for the little community of Rainbow (now only a dot on some maps) came along in 1906, and this became today's Lodge at Holiday Farm. The cottages were added a little later.

Vivienne Wright presides over the Holiday Farm complex (which embraces ninety acres, mostly woodland) with considerable aplomb, as she has done for some twenty years. Her eclectic interest in the history of her domain is evident at once when you enter the sun porch that runs across one side of the Farmhouse: It's crammed with old and not-so-old memorabilia and knickknacks, including some worthy antiques and gifts for sale. Newspaper clippings on the wall show and tell about noted guests at Holiday Farm, including Herbert Hoover. He was a frequent visitor and earnest fisherman in his post-presidential days.

In the Farmhouse, cocktails may be taken in the lounge with its fireplace and easy chairs. Dinner is served by candlelight in the small but inviting dining room. If you are lucky you will find McKenzie River rainbow trout on the menu. There are vegetables fresh from the farmhouse garden, and bread, rolls and pies fresh from the oven. Successful fishermen may ask the cook to prepare their day's catch.

Breakfast and lunch are served in the other Holiday Farm restaurant, the Lodge across the road. (The road is a little side loop through the trees, an offshoot of Highway 126.) Vivienne serves an ample breakfast in a big sunny room with cheery wallpaper and a fireplace, or on the balcony overlooking the rushing river. Breakfast's tempting offerings include omelets, chicken livers, blueberry pancakes and Vivienne's own strawberry jam and hot biscuits. On a fine day, nothing could be finer than to take breakfast or lunch on the Lodge balcony, practically on top of the river and with an unobstructed view of fishermen at their labors and wildlife going about its business. Next to this balcony is another choice viewpoint, the new deck. It was built without disturbing a huge maple that grows through a hole in the floor and is clad in moss and ferns and hung with baskets of fuchsia. Even in the midst of acres of forest, Vivienne Wright respects every tree.

There are a couple of suites in the lodge. Most of the cottages have full kitchens and come in a variety of styles and sizes, all on the river. The largest claims to be able to sleep twenty.

And it is indeed true that one may fish off the porch—or from the bank, or in a nearby stream or lake. The lodge will reserve guides and boats for river fishing. The trout season opens the last weekend in April. Spring Chinook salmon are taken from May until mid-July.

There are fine hiking trails, along the river and up into the mountains, and a championship golf course half a mile away. The famous scenic highway loop through the Cascades via 242 to Sisters and back by 126 (or vice versa) can be covered easily in a day. That allows time for short hikes to tall waterfalls, a picnic in the forest, and stops to photograph the Cascade peaks.

HOLIDAY FARM, Blue River, Oregon 97413. Telephone: (503) 822-3715. Accommodations: twin, hideabeds, doubles and one king; private baths with showers; kitchens or kitchenettes in cottages; no telephones; no television. Rates: moderate, American or European plan; special rates for groups. Open to the public for breakfast, lunch and dinner; full bar service. Children welcome. Pets not encouraged. No credit cards. Open mid-April to November.

Getting There: From Interstate 5, take 126 from Eugene through Springfield to Blue River (46 miles); look for signs to Rainbow and Holiday Farm. From 97, take 20 from Bend to Sisters (22 miles), then either 242 to junction with 126 (37 miles) and another eight miles on 126 to Rainbow; or 126 from Sisters to Rainbow (54 miles). Amtrak serves Eugene, and there is bus service from Eugene twice a day.

STEAMBOAT INN
Idleyld Park

The loyalty and affection felt for this little riverside inn are extraordinary, stretching back more than three decades. And since Jim and Sharon Van Loan took it over in 1975, a renewed emphasis on good food and warm hospitality has strengthened old ties and forged new ones.

The modest-looking establishment appeals primarily to people who come to fish for steelhead in the challenging North Umpqua. The whole rhythm of Steamboat is tuned to the fisherman's schedule, including the late great dinner after a long day on the river—a dinner calculated to augment a sense of well-being if luck has been good, to restore confidence if fish have been few.

But non-fishermen, and fishermen's families, love it here too. Steamboat is at the heart of Oregon's far-flung Douglas County

174

recreation land. There's swimming in Steamboat Creek or Canton Creek—the latter has fifty miles of swimming water, with deep pools for diving and shallow pools for children. There are backpacking and hiking trails all through the surrounding mountains. The one-mile climb on the Fall Creek Trail, a few minutes down the road, is a wilderness experience in miniature, complete with a misty waterfall. In winter, there's cross-country skiing at Diamond Lake, forty miles along Highway 138, on the way to Crater Lake.

The inn was built by Clarence Gordon, who owned and ran the respected North Umpqua Lodge just across the river, from the 1930s until he relocated and built Steamboat Inn in 1954. The Van Loans bought it after several years of acquaintance as guests. Jim was formerly a publisher's representative, Sharon a teacher; they have employed a vast fund of intelligent taste in the inn's refurbishment.

The main building, which from the highway looks like any rustic roadside eatery, houses the kitchen, dining room and back porch, from which a stone-flagged path leads through the garden to the cottages. There are six of these, with two under construction for completion by mid-1982. They share a common veranda overlooking the busy and burbling Umpqua. The cottages are simply furnished; the Van Loans are gradually introducing their own touches, such as wood paneling in the remodeled baths, and cheery comforters. But they have concentrated primarily so far on the most basic needs, such as complete reroofing for the whole complex. The cottages have pine-paneled walls, carpeted floors and plenty of storage space for fishing gear and clothes. The Van Loans have added built-in bunk beds, one per cottage, on the deck. The two new cabins will open to form a suite or a small conference center, with fireplace at one end and wet bar at the other.

The main lodge manages to fit a half-dozen functions into its one big room, with no sense of compression. There are a few shelves with basic grocery supplies, and racks with books on fishing and hiking in the area. Fly-fishing equipment especially suited to the devilishly difficult North Umpqua is displayed on the walls. So are framed pictures of smug fishermen with their catches. The big stone fireplace at one side has a jutting shelf holding a vase of field flowers. In fact, fresh flowers are everywhere—Sharon does not believe that people live by fishing alone.

As for the main business of this room: Sharon and Jim are clearly dedicated to providing food that is not only nourishing and plentiful, but that appeals to educated tastes. The Fisherman's Dinner (served nightly, about one-half hour after sundown) offers course after delicious course of a quality you are surprised to find in such an unassuming, out-of-the-way restaurant.

175

STEAMBOAT INN, Box 36, Toketee Route, Idleyld Park, Oregon 97447. Telephone: (503) 496-3495 or 498-2411. Accommodations: double beds; cabins have private baths with showers; no telephones; no television. Rates: moderate, no meals included. Open to the public for breakfast, lunch and dinner until 6:30; Fisherman's Dinner one-half hour after sundown in summer, 7 pm in winter; wine and beer only. Children welcome. Pets discouraged, $4 fee. Cards: AE, MC, VISA. Open all year.

Getting There: By car, take Interstate 5 to Roseburg, then drive 40 miles east on Highway 138. By air, major airlines have service to Eugene and Medford.

WALLOWA LAKE LODGE
Joseph

This comfortable, three-story rustic lodge at the south end of Oregon's Wallowa Lake is typical of the best old inns of the Northwest: unpretentious, roomy, informal, just enough modernization over the years to keep guests happy, and few frills. To be sure, certain local entrepreneurs have introduced such facilities in the neighborhood as a Go-Kart track, a roller-skating rink, miniature golf, and some alpine-type gift shops; but these are all easy to avoid.

Built more than half a century ago, the lodge has been owned and managed by the Wiggins family since 1945. Greg Wiggins has recently taken over active management from his grandmother, Irene. The lodge has a very large lobby with fireplace to scale, card tables and a make-yourself-at-home atmosphere. The Hole in the Ground (cocktail lounge) is on a lower level. The spacious dining room serves hearty breakfasts and smorgasbord-style dinners, but not lunch. Box lunches may be requested for outings.

The twenty rooms in the lodge are on the second and third floors. Most have connecting baths. They are adequately furnished with little effort to follow any particular decorating scheme. There are no easy chairs or antiques, but the beds are good. Besides the lodge rooms there are several kinds of cabins, all with private baths. Some are simply sleeping rooms; some are log cabins with kitchenettes, electric heat, fireplaces and two or three bedrooms; and others, larger and on the Wallowa River, will accommodate up to eight persons.

The lodge is next to Wallowa Lake State Park, with picnicking and camping, a children's play area, nature trails, and a marina and launching ramp. There are boats and motors for rent, also waterbikes, water sports equipment and canoes. There's good fishing in the lake for rainbow trout and Kokanee (landlocked sockeye salmon), from bank or boat. Licenses are available at the camp store across from the lodge. The cooks at the lodge will be glad to cook your catch for you.

Wallowa Lake is a jumping-off place for exploration of the 216,000-acre Eagle Cap Wilderness, one of the Northwest's more remote and unspoiled alpine areas, where rugged peaks reach ten thousand feet and there are more than sixty lakes, many abundantly stocked. There's an excellent trail system. All kinds of trips are possible, on your own or guided, on foot or horseback. Get in touch with Eagle Cap Pack Station (P.O. Box 416, Joseph, Oregon 97846) for guided horseback tours, from an hour to a week; guided hunts, fishing and camera tours as well as tours to Hell's Canyon.

If you want to fish farther afield than Wallowa Lake, try the Wallowa or Grande Ronde rivers, where enough steelhead and salmon come to make things interesting. If you pack into the lakes in the Wallowa Mountains you will find rainbow and eastern brook trout in plenty, though not large. The lakes are open year-round but are snow-free only from June to August. Check with the Oregon Game Commission, Box 226, La Grande, Oregon, for regulations and advice.

Less strenuous activities include a fifteen-minute gondola ride to the summit of eighty-two-hundred-foot Mount Howard. There's an easy one-hour loop trail around the mountaintop, through wild-flower-sprinkled meadows and with views of the jagged Wallowa Mountains, peaceful Wallowa Valley, Imnaha Canyon, and way off, Idaho's Seven Devils Mountains punctuating the skyline. Your walk may give you a glimpse of deer, maybe elk and bear. The Lichen restaurant on the summit serves lunch and snacks.

Or you could drive to Hell's Canyon, about thirty miles due east but 125 miles round trip by road—the last lap of which is steep, narrow and gravel. This takes you to Hat Point Lookout, where you have a breathtaking view of the deepest chasm in North America.

Wallowa Lake has historic as well as scenic interest. It is not far from the Oregon Trail, bits of which may still be recognized, especially if you have a good imagination. And this is Nez Perce country, site of the last great Indian war in the nation's westward push. The tribe's homeland in the Wallowa Valley was the point of origin for young Chief Joseph's amazing thousand-mile running battle with the United States Army. Old Chief Joseph's grave and monument are at the north end of Wallowa Lake.

WALLOWA LAKE LODGE, Joseph, Oregon 97846. Telephone: (503) 432-4082. Accommodations: twin and double beds; some baths in lodge with tub, some with shower, rooms without private bath have washbasins, baths in cabins have showers only; no telephones; no television. Rates: moderate, no meals included. Open to the public for breakfast and dinner; full bar service. Children welcome. No pets. No credit cards. Lodge open about June 10 to September 10; cabins, May 1 to October 1 (weather permitting).

Getting There: By car, from Portland, take Highway 80N to LaGrande, 82 to Enterprise, then take road south to Joseph and Wallowa Lake (15 miles from Enterprise). By bus, daily service from La Grande. By air, nearest commercial airport, Pendleton (130 miles west); bus service from Pendleton. Private planes may land at Joseph airfield.

COLUMBIA GORGE HOTEL
Hood River

It is heartening to see a grand old hotel come back and make a go of it. And that is precisely what the Columbia Gorge Hotel is doing.

During its first incarnation this expansive, tile-roofed, Mediterranean-style hotel was one of the West's most elegant inns, built in 1921 by timber-wealthy Simon Benson. For decades it was the haunt of the rich and famous, including Hollywood celebrities like Rudolf Valentino and Clara Bow. It became the goal of many motorists who braved the new and challenging Columbia Gorge Scenic Highway.

After the decline that befell so many fine country inns and resorts as the automobile age encouraged ambitious itineraries rather than leisurely stops, the old hotel became a nursing home. Then, several years ago, it was purchased by Boyd Graves who also owns Snoqualmie Falls Lodge (the renowned Northwest restaurant east of Seattle, near Snoqualmie Pass). Now the hotel on the Columbia is fully restored, a plush reminder that opulence is not dead.

The approach is via a curving drive through lawns and gardens. The spacious hotel lobby-lounge is much the same as half a century ago. Impressive and high-ceilinged but not cavernous, the room has tall velvet-draped windows and groupings of comfortable sofas, chairs and tables well placed for tea, cocktails or conversation. Benches are arranged around the fireplace. There are tables for cards and checkers, and a writing desk. The only jarring note is the piped music.

178

Outside, the country-house atmosphere is pronounced, and a brief walk before dinner or in the early morning induces a lord-of-the-manor feeling. The parklike grounds are semiwild on the river side, with mossy rocks and stone walls along the cliff's edge. From vantage points (well fenced) one may view the waterfall where Wah Gwin Gwin—the streamlet that has been meandering through the lawn—plunges two hundred feet down to the Columbia. Across the gorge rise the cliffs and hills of Washington.

It may take more than a slow stroll to work up enough appetite for the multicourse dinner. If you reserve in advance (a good idea), ask for a table in the long gallery on the river side. No matter where you're situated, all is elegant and the service is attentive. The Columbia River salmon is, as one would expect, superb; you may have it poached or broiled. Many of the recipes date back to the hotel's first and famous chef, Henry Thiele.

And then there's the Farm Breakfast, served on weekends, and for which reservations are essential. Anyone who has breakfasted at Snoqualmie Falls Lodge will know what to expect; others should be prepared for a meal of surpassing quantity and quality. It's served all year, 10 to 1 on Saturday and 9 to 1 on Sunday.

The guest rooms, on the second and third floors, are pleasantly furnished with antique reproductions. One of the finest rooms has a king-size bed with a canopy. There are televisions and telephones in the rooms. The tiled private baths are almost as big as the bedrooms. A morning paper is delivered to your door.

If you have come via freeway, you should certainly take time to explore some of the byroads in the area, and by all means the old Columbia Gorge Scenic Highway. It will take you to such outstanding attractions as Crown Point, with its celebrated view, and Multnomah Falls, the second highest waterfall in the country. There are golf courses nearby, hiking and climbing in the wild area around Mount Hood, and in winter, skiing. The hotel is only about fifty miles by good road from Timberline Lodge, on the slopes of the mountain. In the spring, the flowering orchards around Hood River are a sight to see.

COLUMBIA GORGE HOTEL, 4000 West Cliff Drive, Hood River, Oregon 97031. Telephone: (503) 386-5566. Accommodations, king-, queen-size and twin beds; private baths with tub/shower; telephones; television. Rates: moderate to expensive, no meals included. Open to the public for breakfast, lunch and dinner; full bar service. Children welcome. Pets welcome. Cards: AE, MC, VISA. Open all year.

Getting There: From Portland, drive east on Interstate 80N for 60 miles, take exit 62, and turn left on West Cliff Drive to hotel, which can be seen from the freeway.

FRENCHGLEN HOTEL
Frenchglen

Built in 1914, the Frenchglen Hotel was established to house the overflow of visitors to the nearby "P" Ranch. Since then, the hotel has added indoor plumbing and the ranch has ceased to operate, but not much else has changed in this out-of-the-way corner of southeast Oregon.

Frenchglen Hotel still concentrates on good food and simple lodgings and expects guests to entertain themselves, without benefit of mass media or built-in recreational facilities. There are a screened veranda with an excellent view of what little trafic passes through Frenchglen, a living room with books and magazines and a piano, a smallish dining room where meals are served family style, and that's about it.

The cooking is home style and hearty, featuring home-baked breads and old-fashioned treats like chicken and dumplings and Southern baked ham. Innkeeper Malena Konek is determined that no one will leave her table hungry.

The eight bedrooms are small, but comfortable, with good mattresses on the beds. There is no air conditioning, and summers in this part of Oregon can be hot. Baths are down the hall. Everything is very clean and neat, and quite adequate in view of the fact that guests spend most of their time elsewhere.

Once belonging to the Bureau of Sports Fisheries and Wildlife Department, the hotel is now owned by the Oregon Division of Parks and Recreation as a State Wayside. It was leased to Malena Konek and reopened to the public in 1976 after being closed for several years.

The name "Frenchglen" is a combination of the names of Peter French and Dr. Hugh Glenn. Peter French arrived in the Blitzen Valley in 1872 with a herd of cattle and six Mexican vacqueros. He acquired the squatter's rights of a man named Porter, got financial backing from his father-in-law, Dr. Hugh Glenn, and built an empire of 132,000 acres around his home base at the "P" Ranch. French raised cattle and horses, fought Indians and droughts and storms. His life came to a dramatic end in 1897 when he was shot from his horse by a neighbor.

In 1935, the "P" Ranch land became a part of the Malheur National Wildlife Refuge. The ranch house is gone, except for its chimney, but the old Round Barn still stands, with gnarled, solid juniper posts supporting it, and a weathered plank door on ninety-year-old iron hinges.

A primary attraction to visitors here is the wildlife refuge. The refuge museum, twenty-eight miles north of Frenchglen, has specimens of most of the 264 species of birds found in the area. This is one of the country's most important wildlife refuges, a much-frequented stop on the Pacific Flyway. Bird watchers should try to be here during the peak of the spring waterfowl migration (mid-March to early April) or in October. They may expect to see ducks, cranes, Canada geese, snow geese, whistling swans, sandhill cranes, herons, avocets—and maybe a white pelican. The songbird migration is at its peak in mid-May.

The Blitzen Valley runs through the refuge. From near the hotel, you can start a forty-two-mile auto tour of this fascinating valley. A fine interpretive guide, put out by the Malheur Refuge, tells you what to look for and where: the spot where Pete French was murdered, a recent volcanic crater, nesting sandhill cranes. Throughout the area, deer, antelope, muskrat, beaver, mink, raccoons and coyotes abound and can often be seen.

Another attraction for visitors to Frenchglen is Steens Mountain, directly to the east. This geologically interesting mountain (a true fault block peak) is thirty miles long and rises over 9,600 feet, falling a mile almost straight down to the Alvord Desert on its east side. This was Paiute Indian country, and those with patience to explore may find stories carved in rock and possibly arrowheads. However, artifacts are protected by Federal law and may not be collected or disturbed. Take pictures instead.

Hiking and backpacking into the Steens Mountain Recreation Lands will take you from the dry, treeless sagebrush-sprinkled plain through the juniper-clad rocky canyons, on to aspen groves and finally into the alpine high country with wild flowers and open meadows. Or you can drive, via a road that curls around and around and eventually deposits you on top of the world. Don't try to get to the top except between mid-July and October—there's likely to be too much snow other times.

182

Steens Mountain's lakes and rivers have been stocked with rainbow, brook and Lahontan cutthroat trout; anglers will also find plenty of the native redbow trout. As for hunting, there is an occasional season for big-horn sheep (recently re-established on the east side of Steens Mountain); pronghorn antelope and mule deer are also around, as well as game birds: sage grouse, mourning doves, quail and chukars.

Hunting and angling seasons and limits are under special regulation of the Oregon Fish and Wildlife Commission; check with the Portland office (1635 S.W. Alder Street) or local license agents.

FRENCHGLEN HOTEL STATE WAYSIDE, Frenchglen, Oregon 97736. Telephone: (503) 493-2565. Accommodations: twin, double and queen-size beds; community baths with showers; no telephones; no television. Rates: inexpensive, no meals included. Open to the public for breakfast, lunch and dinner; lunches packed on request; no bar service. Children welcome. No pets. No credit cards. Open March 15–December 1.

Getting There: By car, from Portland, 26 to John Day, 395 to Burns; from Burns take 205 south to Frenchglen (60 miles). From Bend, 20 then 395 to Burns; to Frenchglen as above. From Nevada, 95 then 78 to Burns; to Frenchglen as above. Nearest airport and bus station are at Burns.

CRATER LAKE LODGE
Crater Lake

Travelers to Crater Lake are mainly interested in the awesome sight of this collapsed volcano, which embraces one of the bluest and loveliest lakes in the world, at the crest of southern Oregon's Cascade Range.

All too many visitors come barreling up in cars or buses, stop to look and gasp and photograph, mill around in the souvenir shop, give a passing glance at the lodge and drive back down again.

Yet a stop at Crater Lake Lodge can make the experience truly memorable, affording time to see what is to be seen in a leisurely fashion, and even to get out of the tourist mob now and then.

Since this is a National Park, the lodge is much as you would expect: a long, rambling shingle and stone building, with a spacious lobby, a huge fireplace (the largest in Oregon, some say) and a cheerful red-carpeted dining room. All this is on the main floor, along with a rustic cocktail bar and a gift shop. On the upper three floors there are eighty bedrooms ranging from bare-essential to well-appointed. Not all rooms have private baths, but all those without have a basin in the room. You're advised to reserve well in advance, especially if you want to be on the lake side. And you should hold out for such a room; awakening to the expanse of intensely azure water, ringed by towering rock walls and rugged peaks, makes the whole trip come together.

For less money and less of a view, there are sleeping cottages above the cafeteria/gift shop building, with cold running water, electric heat and bunks or beds. Some of these have half-baths. A step up in facilities are the Ponderosa cottages with hot and cold water, thermostatically controlled heat, private baths with showers and a double bed plus bunks. No cottages have housekeeping facilities.

Things to do in the park range from those requiring very little energy, such as the thirty-five-mile limousine tour around the rim of the lake, or the nightly illustrated lectures in the lounge on the explosive history of Crater Lake, to more strenuous adventures such as hiking 1.1 miles down to the water's edge for a boat trip around the lake with perhaps a stop for exploration of Wizard Island. To the surprise of many, there is even fishing—a few determined rainbow trout and Kokanee salmon have persisted here since planting was discontinued in 1942.

For more information on the park and its many recreational opportunities write Crater Lake Natural History Association, P.O. Box 56, Crater Lake National Park, Oregon 97604.

CRATER LAKE LODGE, Crater Lake, Oregon 97604. Telephone: (503) 594-2511. Accommodations: double, single and bunk beds; some private baths with showers, some half-baths with showers; no telephones; no television. Rates: moderate, no meals included. Open to the public for breakfast and dinner (lodge), breakfast, lunch and dinner (cafeteria); full bar service. Children welcome. No pets in lodge, but permitted in cottages. No credit cards. Lodge open mid-June to mid-September; Rim Village cafeteria/coffee shop open weekends and holidays in winter; cottages available May to October, depending on snow conditions.

Getting There: By car, take Interstate 5 to Medford, then proceed 72 miles on Highway 62 to Crater Lake; or take Highway 97 north from Klamath Falls 50 miles to junction with Highway 62; or take Highway 97 south from Bend 75 miles to junction with Highway 138, then 36 miles to Crater Lake. By bus, from June 15 to September 10 buses are operated daily from Klamath Falls to the lodge; write or call lodge for schedule information.

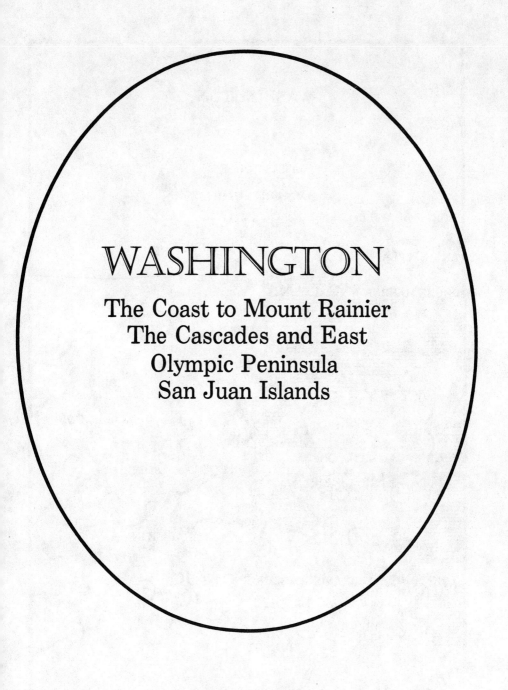

WASHINGTON

The Coast to Mount Rainier
The Cascades and East
Olympic Peninsula
San Juan Islands

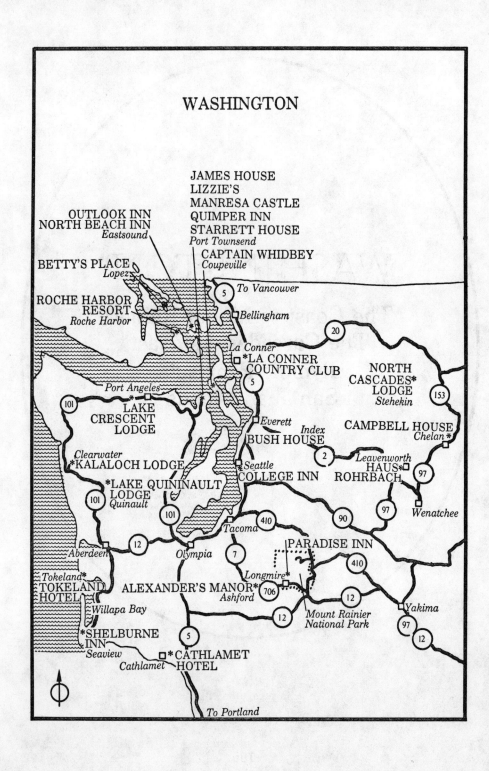

WASHINGTON

JAMES HOUSE
LIZZIE'S
MANRESA CASTLE
QUIMPER INN
STARRETT HOUSE
Port Townsend

OUTLOOK INN
NORTH BEACH INN
Eastsound

CAPTAIN WHIDBEY
Coupeville

BETTY'S PLACE
Lopez

To Vancouver

ROCHE HARBOR
RESORT
Roche Harbor

Bellingham

La Conner
*LA CONNER
COUNTRY CLUB

NORTH
CASCADES*
LODGE
Stehekin

Port Angeles

LAKE
CRESCENT
LODGE

Everett

CAMPBELL HOUSE
Chelan

BUSH HOUSE

Index

Clearwater
*KALALOCH LODGE

Seattle
COLLEGE INN

Leavenworth
HAUS*
ROHRBACH

*LAKE QUININAULT
LODGE
Quinault

Wenatchee

Tacoma

PARADISE INN

Aberdeen

Olympia

Longmire

ALEXANDER'S MANOR*
Ashford

Yakima

Tokeland*
TOKELAND
HOTEL

Mount Rainier
National Park

Willapa Bay

*SHELBURNE
INN
Seaview

*CATHLAMET
HOTEL
Cathlamet

To Portland

101
5
20
153
101
5
101
97
2
90
97
12
410
7
706
410
12
97
5
12

CATHLAMET HOTEL
Cathlamet

There are at least four good reasons to seek out the Cathlamet Hotel and its restaurant, Pierre's, in an out-of-the-way hamlet on the shores of the Columbia River: gastronomic, historical, scenic, and the satisfaction of discovering a little-known country inn.

First, gastronomy: Pierre's Restaurant has literally put Cathlamet on the touristic map. It's in a capacious house that Pierre and Claire Pype bought and joined to their hotel. The house is painted a cheerful red with white trim for the balconies, cupolas and gingerbread. It contains half a dozen little and not-so-little dining rooms, upstairs and down. The largest area upstairs is devoted, on Wednesday and Sunday during much of the year, to dinner theater-in-the-round, and to music, entertainment and dancing on weekends.

But the cuisine is what has brought fame to Pierre's. Chefs Ray Paul and Larry Dore serve up a consistently fine and varied menu. Daily fresh fish specialties (really fresh) may include Pacific sea scallops, grilled sand dabs, Pacific sole, ling cod Mornay. Then there are lamb, chicken, duck, lobster, a renowned beef Stroganoff and steaks respectfully prepared from properly aged beef. And—not least—there is shrimp De Jonghe, created by innkeeper Pierre Pype's great-uncle, Henri De Jonghe, a noted Chicago hotel owner.

Second, history buffs will learn from the wooden sign in front of the Wahkiakum County Courthouse, across from the hotel, that the first white man to visit the site was one of Vancouver's lieutenants in 1792, and that *cathlamet* is the Indian word for "rocky shores." For the full story, visit the historical museum, a block down the hill.

Third, the scenery is rural and unspoiled. The approach to Cathlamet from the east follows the curves of the majestic Columbia River, almost at water level, affording ever-changing views of the wooded Oregon highlands to the south. Opposite Cathlamet and reached by a bridge is Puget Island: a short ride on the only ferry still running on the lower Columbia connects it to the Oregon shore. The little island is a composite of farms, contented cattle and an extraordinary variety and number of boats, some of which appear to be moored in the fields. Thanks to the dikes and drainage that have been engineered to stop flooding, the whole island is laced with sloughs and canals—a boat-person's Eden.

Cathlamet itself is a microcosm of the small-town life we some-times fear is gone forever. It can get noisy on week-end evenings; after all, every true-blue western town has its well-patronized saloon. But by and large this is a peaceful little community, and likely to stay that way for a while.

The two-story yellow-brick hotel has operated continuously since it was built in 1927. In their herculean refurbishing since they bought it in 1974, Pierre and Claire Pype have firmly kept in mind their resolve to restore it as a nice, small-town hotel of the twenties, not as a grand turn-of-the-century hostelry. Most of the surprises are pleasant ones: the lobby, for example, is presentable but not especially inviting or distinguished, but up the red-carpeted stairs is a second lobby, also red-carpeted, with white wicker chairs and tables and much to occupy the eye, such as an intriguing stained-glass room divider and a mini-museum of old oddments in a couple of glass cases.

The twelve bedrooms are small and simply furnished with pieces that lean more toward Grand Rapids than Victoriana—which is how the Pypes planned it. Bedsteads are metal and inclined to creak, but mattresses are newer. The rooms are freshly painted and papered. Claire Pype, who has been in charge of decoration, obviously had a good time choosing the wallpapers, not only for the bedrooms but also for the two community baths and the shower room.

A Continental breakfast is served in your room at the time you designate when you check in. Service starts at 7 am, so there is no excuse for dawdling in your exploration of the area. Besides Puget Island, popular jaunts include Washington State's only remaining in-use covered bridge, at Grays River eighteen miles west of Cathlamet; and the Cathlamet marina, where Pierre Pype has moored the seventy-five-year-old lightship *Columbia*. He bought it in 1980 and intends to turn it into a floating restaurant. It is on the National Register of Historic Places.

CATHLAMET HOTEL and PIERRE'S RESTAURANT, 67-69 Main Street, Cathlamet, Washington 98612. Telephone: (206) 795-3997 or 795-8751. Accommodations: double beds, one room with double and single, some with baths with shower, some suites with connecting bath, two community baths and a shower room; no telephones; no television. Rates: inexpensive, Continental breakfast included. Open to the public for lunch and dinner; full bar service. Children welcome. Pets welcome. Cards: MC, VISA. Open all year.

Getting There: From the east, turn off Interstate 5 at Kelso and follow Highway 4 west to Cathlamet (27 miles). From the west, leave 101 at Megler (at north end of the bridge from Astoria), take 401 to its junction with 4 near Naselle (12 miles), then follow 4 east to Cathlamet (30 miles). There is moorage for private boats at the Cathlamet Marina, five short blocks from the hotel.

WILLAPA BAY AND LONG BEACH

This southwestern corner of Washington is unknown to freeway-hugging travelers, but is appreciated by those willing to make a little extra effort in search of unspoiled natural beauty and reminders of the area's colorful history.

Today's travelers may be comforted by the thought that getting there is easier now than it was in 1788. That was when explorer Lieutenant John Meares, while sailing along the northwest coast, discovered the bay—but dared not venture across the treacherous shoals at the mouth, and respectfully christened it Shoalwater Bay (later renamed Willapa Bay).

The area became somewhat more accessible a century later when vacationers could take a steamer down the Columbia from Portland to Ilwaco, then board a train that ran on a narrow-gauge track up North Beach as far as Nahcotta, which is about halfway up the Long Beach Peninsula.

This twenty-eight-mile-long, three-hundred-foot-wide peninsula serves as a slim protecting arm between Willapa Bay, Washington's largest bay, and the Pacific. Today there are several ways to get there, none very direct. The roads, though they are good, must climb hills and skirt irregular coastlines. And many destinations are harder to attain than they seem from a glance at the map or across the water. For example, Leadbetter Point, at the north tip of the Long Beach Peninsula, is visible from the Tokeland Peninsula, on the north shore of

Willapa Bay. But to get there you must go all the way around the bay (with a detour up the Willapa River in order to cross it at Raymond) and west to Seaview, where you are at last ready to take a straight shot northward to the end of the road. Then you must walk on through a wildlife refuge to the point itself. Nearly a hundred-mile journey from Tokeland—only eight miles away as the gull flies. But there are many rewards along the way. While in the Tokeland area, try to visit Landry's Smoke Signal Museum, about three miles north of Tokeland on Highway 105, on the Shoalwater Bay Indian Reservation. Built and operated by a Native American family, the striking wood building houses an amazing collection of artifacts and memorabilia. The high point for many is the superb collection of Indian baskets. Most Northwestern tribes' handiwork is represented, from Nez Perce to Klickitat to Queets. Look for the three-hundred-year-old Cowlitz basket that belonged to Mrs. Landry's great-great-grandmother, Cowlitz Mary. These, of course, are priceless, but Mr. Landry also has new baskets, which are for sale, made by the Makah Indians of Neah Bay.

After a stop at the Willapa Bay Lighthouse at North Cove (which in 1959 replaced one the sea had wiped out), this route takes you along the north edge of the bay and to Raymond, a lumber town on the Willapa River estuary. On to South Bend, the Oyster Capital of the West. As you proceed southward, you are never far from heavily timbered slopes and tidal flats. Sometimes the picturesque route passes by lush pastures reclaimed from the bay. Bruceport State Park is a good stop for a picnic among the trees. Then on around the southern end of the bay to Ilwaco, which competes with Westport for the title of Salmon Fishing Capital of the World. Hereabouts, thousands of sports fishermen go out every season on chartered boats for salmon. Others, shore-based, cast their lines for perch, flounder, sea bass and halibut from Fishing Rocks, a favorite cliff-fishing spot.

Seaview, two miles north of Ilwaco, is a good staging point for an investigation of the Long Beach Peninsula and a taste of what life was like here during the late 1800s and early 1900s, when the oyster was king and the incredibly long, smooth, sandy beaches brought throngs of holiday-makers.

The beaches still attract, and there are many reminders of those halcyon days. Today visitors come from near and far when tides are low to dig for razor, butter and littleneck clams and cockles. Unfortunately for oyster lovers, all the beds are now privately owned, but there's no lack of oyster bars and seafood restaurants. Surf fishing and crabbing are popular; so are swimming in the bay (it is dangerous in the ocean

190

surf), horseback riding or cycling on those twenty-eight miles of hard sandy beach, and hiking or strolling or sunbathing.

Farther north is Leadbetter Point, the newest addition to the Willapa Migratory Bird Refuge (which also includes Long Island at the south end of the bay—no public transportation from shore). At Leadbetter Point it is said that two hundred varieties of birds may be seen; and there are also wild strawberries, bears, driftwood and lonely sandy beaches where you may stand and gaze in a northeasterly direction at Tokeland, eight miles away as the gull flies.

Although in its heyday this area supported dozens of high-flying resorts and hotels, the only well-preserved and comfortable survivors are the Shelburne Inn at Seaview and the Tokeland Hotel. Another desirable headquarters in this area is the Cathlamet Hotel, forty-eight miles to the southeast from Seaview along Highways 101 and 4.

SHELBURNE INN
Seaview

The Shelburne was built in 1896 when Seaview was a young and muscle-flexing town, a gateway to the popular Long Beach Peninsula. The inn is a couple of blocks north of the town's main intersection. It is a rambling Victorian-style house, well weathered and with a stylish white picket fence made by owner David Campiche to the same design as a fence in historic Oysterville, farther up the peninsula.

After alternating periods of neglect and loving attention by a series of owners, the inn was purchased by David in 1977, and extensively restored and refurbished. Now he and his wife and co-innkeeper Laurie Anderson have apparently found the winning combination: Fill a charming old inn with English and American antiques that are not only functional and decorative, but are also for sale. Then establish a first-class restaurant under the same roof.

The Shelburne lobby is more of an antiques showroom than a tranquil retreat, but it does have a fireplace and rocking chairs. Just down the passage is the Shelburne Restaurant, also furnished with attractive antiques. Big oaken chests are used for silver, glassware and china. Tall windows with window seats are framed by drapes and graceful valances. A pot-bellied stove provides cheery warmth to supplement the fireplace and the electric heat. Since 1980, this has been the domain of owners-chefs Nanci Main and Jimella Lucas. The menu, not extensive, may offer steaks, Stroganoff and certainly seafood—the fresh sturgeon is superb. Delicious, melt-in-the-mouth

191

desserts include a Depravity Cake and a Brown Betty that belies its plain-jane name. Having eaten here, you will not wonder that James Beard keeps coming back.

Up an angled stairway are two floors of bedrooms. Here you may feel you've been transported to one of those English houses with such confusing hallways and so many turnings that you need an ancient servitor to guide you to your room, but it really doesn't take long to get your bearings. This was once a single home, built by Charles Beaver in 1896. Later he moved a similar home from across the street, joined the two together, and created the inn; hence the varying levels and many passages. The fifteen rooms are furnished with sturdy American pieces—even some of these are for sale. All rooms have electric heat and pleasant small-town views. Two have private half-baths, including the "honeymoon" or "anniversary" suite in the southwest corner; guests here are greeted with flowers and a bottle of champagne on ice. By arrangement, Laurie will serve a Continental breakfast in the hotel lobby, and on Sundays, brunch is served in the restaurant.

There are plenty of options for active and passive recreation in the area (see preceding section) but before you go too far afield, take the short walk to the ocean from the Shelburne, to get your bearings. You will pass through quiet residential streets, a restful contrast to summer-busy Highway 103, the main drag for tourists up and down the peninsula.

SHELBURNE INN, Pacific Highway 103 (P.O. Box 250), Seaview, Washington 98644. Telephone: (206) 642-2442; Shelburne Restaurant, P.O. Box 476, Seaview, Washington 98644. Telephone: (206) 642-4142. Accommodations: single and double beds; two private half-baths, community baths with shower or tub, sinks in rooms; no telephones; no television. Rates: inexpensive, Continental breakfast available but not included. Restaurant open to the public for lunch, dinner and Sunday brunch; wine and beer only. Children welcome. No pets. Cards: AE, MC, VISA. Open all year.

Getting There: From Portland take Interstate 5 to Longview, then turn west on Highway 4 to Johnson's Landing and take Highway 101 to Seaview (15 miles from Johnson's Landing). Or take Highway 30 to Astoria, cross the toll bridge over the Columbia River and take Highway 101 to Seaview (16 miles from Astoria). From Seattle, take Interstate 5 to Olympia, Highway 8 to Aberdeen and Highway 101 south to Johnson's Landing and Seaview. Nearest airport: Portland. Private planes may land at Chinook, five miles south on Highway 101. Boats may tie up at anchorages in Ilwaco, two miles south, or at Chinook.

TOKELAND HOTEL
Tokeland

On a secluded peninsula on Willapa Bay stands a venerable hotel, the renaissance of which is being hailed by well-wishers all over Washington and Oregon. After eight years of hard work by owners Al and Betty Smith, the hotel is now open again full-time. Fourteen rooms are furnished and ready for occupancy.

Since the hotel has been designated a State Historic Place, exterior remodeling is restricted. The faded barn-red, white-trimmed structure looks very like the pioneer Kindred farmhouse, built here in the late 1800s. The Kindreds' hospitality was so popular with friends and acquaintances that the owners enlarged it to create Kindred's Inn. The Tokeland Peninsula was drawing so many vacationers that many began to think of this as the future Coney Island of the West. As it turned out, development proceeded more sedately. But guests kept coming to the inn, even from Idaho, eastern Washington and California. By 1910 the building had been enlarged to its present dimensions. The inn continued under the Kindred family until the 1940s, then under several other ownerships until the Smiths bought it in 1974.

Betty Smith says she has been collecting antiques since she was six, and one suspects that she bought the hotel to have a place to put them. Her acquisitions overflow from the lobby, dining room, fireplace room and gift shop on the first floor and into the bedrooms. The lobby and sitting-room area are a cheerful yellow. On the well-waxed bare wood floors are rag rugs, with white wicker furniture. Ferns are everywhere, as is a richly varied assortment of Americana, from a rocking horse to a mannequin dressed in Gibson-girl costume keeping guard by the desk.

The dining room has windows all along the back wall, so everyone can see the lawns and the fruit trees and the wind-battered pines. Betty as hostess and her crew of waitresses all dress in period costumes, and service is quick and friendly. Back in the 1860s, one of the parents of the hotel's first proprietor and cook, Elizabeth Kindred, was reportedly the first to remark that "when the tide is out, the table is set." (About a dozen other historic figures are also credited with this familiar Northwest aphorism.) It's true that clams, crabs and oysters were staples on these shores long before white settlers arrived. So it is no surprise that the chef at the Tokeland is a seafood specialist, famous for his clam chowder, shrimp and scallops. But he's also versatile enough to turn out a baron of beef with Yorkshire pudding, a bounteous

Thanksgiving dinner or summertime favorites like strawberry-rhubarb pie. All soups, breads and dressings are homemade.

The low, sandy Tokeland Peninsula is small and quickly explored. You can drive to the end, past summer homes and pine-bordered lanes until you come to the Coast Guard station and marina. The sheltered harbor permits swimming and scuba diving.

TOKELAND HOTEL, P.O. Box 117, Tokeland, Washington 98590. Telephone: (206) 267-7700. Accommodations: double beds; community baths with shower; no telephones; no television. Rates: inexpensive, Continental breakfast included beginning spring 1982. Open to the public for lunch and dinner in summer, dinner in winter with Sunday dinner family-style; full bar service. Children not encouraged. No pets. Cards: MC, VISA. Open all year.

Getting There: From Seattle, take Interstate 5 to Olympia, 8 to Aberdeen and 101 or 105 to Tokeland. From Portland, take 26 or 30 to Astoria, bridge across Columbia, 101 to Raymond and 105 to Tokeland. There is moorage at a marina on the Tokeland Peninsula for private boats.

LAKE QUINAULT LODGE
Quinault

First there were the Quinault Indians. Then there were the homesteaders of the 1880s, who packed in through the Olympics or paddled up the Quinault River. Then came the loggers. Then a lodge was built on the south shore of Lake Quinault to put up the visitors to this developing country.

That was the genesis of Lake Quinault Lodge, one of the two distinguished historic lakeside lodges on Washington's Olympic Peninsula. Forty miles due south of Lake Crescent Lodge, Quinault was built in 1926 on the site of the 1890 building, which burned in 1922.

Lake Quinault Lodge is in the Olympic National Forest, and the park boundary is just across the lake. The lodge is, therefore, privately owned and operated and not within the purview of National Park Concessions. That may account for a number of features you might not expect in a rustic forest lodge, such as a sauna, bocce ball, a happy hour, and gas-log fires in the new "Fireside Annex" rooms. To say nothing of facilities for conventions and groups up to one hundred.

Lake Quinault Lodge

But in spite of its obviously successful efforts to keep up with changing tourist tastes, the lodge retains a high degree of cheery, comfortable prewar charm. The pleasant, spacious lobby invites leisure and fireside chatting. Wicker chairs and settees are grouped around the big brick fireplace, with its gleaming brass andirons, polished hearth and real logs. The view is across a sloping lawn to the lake, startlingly blue on a fine day but just as captivating when silvered by rain or mist. This is, after all, the edge of a rain forest, so you should expect an occasional shower or even downpour.

The lodge has a renowned dining room specializing in local seafoods and superb views. Accommodations in the main lodge are simple and maintain the original decor of the building, with cedar-plank walls and period furniture. In the new annex, rooms are downright luxurious, with wall-to-wall carpeting, big sofas, queen-size beds and full baths. All of these rooms have balconies or patios with lakeside view.

The lodge's facilities include a heated pool, a sauna, Ping-Pong tables, croquet and a private beach. You can fish from the dock or from a rowboat on the lake, which has rainbow, Dolly Varden and cutthroat trout. Silver and sockeye salmon pass through the lake on their way to spawn in the upper Quinault River. (Note: you'll need a license from the Quinault Indian Tribe, since the lake is part of their reservation; prices vary for weekdays, weekends and on- and off-season.) Upriver from the lake there is fishing in winter for steelhead.

Hiking trails into the park and the national forest take off almost from the lodge. Trailheads for others are a short drive away. People at the lodge will help you plot a course, and you'll get pointers from the Forest Service and Park Service illustrated talks, held in the lodge recreation room in summer. For example: there's a short loop trail to an exceptional grove of huge Douglas firs almost at the back door. There's a ten-mile drive, then a fifteen-minute walk, to the world's largest cedar, on the lake's north shore.

LAKE QUINAULT LODGE, P.O. Box 7, Quinault, Washington 98575. Telephone: (206) 288-2571. Accommodations: twin, double and queen-size beds; connecting baths in main lodge, private baths with showers in Lakeside Inn annex; fireplace units with private baths and queen-size beds; no telephones; no television. Rates: moderate, no meals included. Open to the public for breakfast, lunch and dinner; full bar service. Children welcome. Pets allowed, $4 fee. Credit cards: AE, MC, VISA. Open all year.

Getting There: By car, 40 miles north of Aberdeen or 124 miles south of Port Angeles via scenic Highway 101, take Lake Quinault South Shore Recreation Area exit; follow lakeshore road two miles to lodge. By bus, daily service from Aberdeen, by Grays Harbor Transit. By seaplane, to floating docks in front of lodge. Nearest commercial airport: Hoquiam.

KALALOCH LODGE
Kalaloch

Kalaloch Lodge is looking more and more like the "ocean village" it used to call itself, thanks to twenty-one new log cabins strung out to the south of the lodge. The new cabins all have partial ocean views, but the twelve older ones at the edge of the bluff have an unobstructed 180-degree prospect of driftwood-strewn beaches, giant rollers, the Kalaloch Rocks offshore, and the Pacific.

The lodge, of course, remains the most historic and most interesting building. This sprawling, gray-shingled, blue-trimmed structure still perches above the mouth of Kalaloch Creek, looking out across the breaking surf to the vast ocean.

There's been a lodge here since the 1920s, and for more than fifty years it was owned by the same family. Charles Becker saw the potentialities for a resort here when he was a young man and, starting small, built it up to a lodge with a gas station and several cabins by the 1930s. Then during World War II, when there was apprehension about possible Japanese attacks on the coast, Coast Guard patrollers were quartered at Kalaloch. During that era, the lodge burned down. After the war, the Beckers, who operated the lodge as concessionaires of the National Park Service, rebuilt it and added the cabins on the bluff.

In 1978 the Beckers retired and the lodge was acquired by Mr. and Mrs. Larry Lesley, who also own Lake Quinault Lodge and divide their time between the two. Besides adding the new cabins, they are also making changes in the lodge. Most noticeable, to the regret of many old friends of the lodge, is the transformation of the downstairs lobby to a gift shop. But a new sitting-and-reading-room directly above the old lobby has more privacy and an even better view. Both dining rooms are being expanded, the southern room acquiring a new semicircular bay. But the Indian heritage of Kalaloch is still evident. The totem pole still stands at the door, and the very name still reminds one that there was a native culture here long before the white man. *Kalaloch* may mean "easy living," "lots of clams," or "land of plenty"—take your pick.

Kalaloch Beach Ocean Village

Naturally, clams and other seafoods appear frequently on the menu. Stuffed prawns and baked salmon are specialties of the chef. Service is generally swift and attentive, though the dining rooms get quite crowded on summer weekends. It's wise to call ahead for reservations: the Washington coast is not plentifully endowed with good restaurants.

All the new cabins have one large room with a double brass bed and a double hideabed, and dividers between the living and sleeping areas. They have kitchenettes with tables and chairs, private baths with showers and wood stoves. There is also one new duplex; one of its units has one bedroom, wheelchair access and a Jacuzzi, the other has two bedrooms. The older cabins are also housekeeping. Some are two-bedroom, with fireplaces, and can expand to take nine people. All have private baths with showers.

Accommodations in the motel addition, Sea Crest House (nonhouse-keeping, no pets), are at the end of the village "street" in a grove of windswept trees, with large view windows and balconies or patio areas. Three units are three-room suites with fireplaces. All have private baths with showers.

There are eight rooms in the lodge, not large but cheerful and snug, especially during one of the roaring storms this coast can provide. All have private baths with showers and double beds with bright bedspreads. Four look out on the ocean, four across the highway to the dense fir forest.

Paths to the long stretch of flat, sandy beach are at your doorstep. There's beachcombing for driftwood, agates, jasper, and Japanese glass floats (for the lucky few). Clam shovels may be rented at the store for digging razor clams at low tide when in season (the lodge has a small grocery store as well as a gas station). You'll find many streams for fishing in the area (steelhead in winter, trout in spring), and in summer you may have a chance to dip ocean-run smelt.

Kalaloch is in the ocean strip of Olympic National Park, and within easy driving distance of the entrances to the Queets and Hoh rain forests, those world-famous natural areas where annual rainfall exceeds 140 inches.

If you've never investigated the other attractions of the park, Kalaloch would be one of several good places to start. Whether you're drawn to hiking, mountain climbing, nature observation, horseback riding, camping, fishing, beachcombing or beach hiking, you're close to it here. River float trips may be arranged with prior notification.

KALALOCH LODGE, Star Route 1, Box 1100, Kalaloch, Washington 98331. Telephone: (206) 962-2271. Accommodations: double beds, double hideabeds, single beds; private baths with showers; kitchenettes in cabins (no cooking or eating utensils provided); some with fireplaces; no telephones; no television. Rates: moderate, no meals included. Open to the public for breakfast, lunch and dinner; full bar service. Children welcome. Pets allowed in cabins only, $3 fee. Cards: MC, VISA. Open all year.

Getting There: By car, take Highway 101 north from Aberdeen (70 miles) or south from Port Angeles (90 miles).

LAKE CRESCENT LODGE
Port Angeles

This is one of the oldest and loveliest places to stay on the Olympic Peninsula, nestled in tall evergreens on the south shore of deeply blue, glacier-cut Lake Crescent. An old-fashioned lodge, it looks much as it did when it was built as Singer's Tavern in 1916. Early descriptions of the tavern pointed out features that still distinguish the lodge: a glassed-in sun porch on the lake side, a huge stone fireplace in the lobby, a dining room with a view of the lake, a row of small cabins and a long dock.

In those days the dock was for the two little ferries that plied Lake Crescent and were the only means of reaching the lodge. Today, the guest arrives after a scenic drive along the shore on a choice section of the Olympic Loop of Highway 101.

Meals are served in the sunny dining room, where the big windows look out on the garden and the lake. Specialties include salmon, steaks, Quilcene oysters and Dungeness crab Louis.

Accommodations include lodge rooms with polished wood floors and windows opening on the lake view. Lodge rooms have two baths with tubs down the hall. The comfortable cottages on the lakeshore, all in a row, are beginning to show their age but are well maintained. Each has its own little front porch. They are one or two bedroom, four with fireplaces and all with private baths. The new motel addition has a fiew and all possible creature comforts but less character. None of these accommodations is housekeeping, but there is one rustic cabin without a view but with a kitchen, which will take a family group up to eight.

The lodge is on a point formed by the delta of Barnes Creek, here calmed down considerably after its tumultuous descent from the

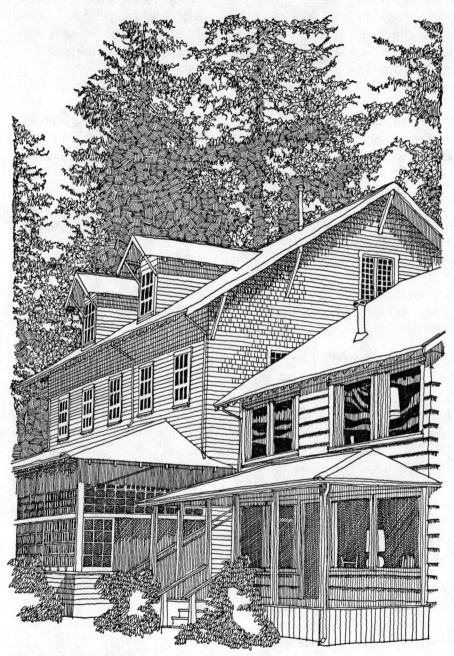

Lake Crescent Lodge

snowclad Olympics. A short nature trail leads from the nearby Storm King Ranger Station along the creek's lower reaches and to lovely Marymere Falls in its rain-forest setting. More ambitious hikes include a stiff climb up 4,500-foot Storm King Mountain, which rewards with breathtaking views of the lake, the inner Olympics and the Strait of Juan de Fuca.

Lake Crescent Lodge is approximately twenty road miles from Port Angeles, where charter boats are available for salmon fishing and the Black Ball ferry leaves for Victoria. From Port Angeles it is only a short drive over an excellent road to six-thousand-foot-high Hurricane Ridge, where the perpetually snowcapped Bailey Range—highest mountains in the Olympics—forms a backdrop for alpine meadows and grazing deer. Good walking trails lead you to closer views of wild flowers and snowfields and perhaps a mountain goat. For day trips like this, the cooks at the inn will pack you a box lunch. Also, there is a lodge at Hurricane Ridge (open days only) that serves food and has interpretive exhibits and telescopes to give you a good close look at peaks and glaciers.

Back at the lodge, there are tennis and badminton courts, and rowboats for rent. Fishermen come here in search of the Beardsley and Crescenti trout, unique to this lake.

LAKE CRESCENT LODGE, National Park Concessions, Inc., Star Route 1, Port Angeles, Washington 98362. Telephone: (206) 928-3211. Accommodations: single and double beds; community bath in lodge, private baths with tubs or showers in cottages and motel rooms; one cottage with kitchenette, some with fireplaces; no telephones; no television. Rates: inexpensive, no meals included. Open to the public for breakfast, lunch and dinner; full bar service. Children welcome. Pets allowed in cottages only. Credit cards: MC, VISA. Open Memorial Day weekend through Labor Day.

Getting There: Located on Highway 101 twenty miles west of Port Angeles or 137 miles north of Aberdeen on the scenic loop drive around the Olympic Peninsula, Lake Crescent Lodge is most easily reached by automobile. Port Angeles is served by San Juan Airlines from Sea-Tac International Airport and by Greyhound Bus Lines from Seattle. Ground transportation can be arranged through Gray Lines in Port Angeles or by local taxi service.

PORT TOWNSEND

Port Townsend, perhaps the most perfect Victorian town in the West and certainly so in Washington, is compact enough for the visitor to tour in a day. But a longer stay will prove rewarding. First, because there is much more to this town than lovely old homes and historic buildings. Second, because at last it has accommodations to match its historic and architectural distinction. Interesting and comfortable places to stay include Manresa Castle, which you can't miss as you come into town; several bed and breakfast establishments occupying historic mansions; and the old Palace Hotel.

A little knowledge of Port Townsend past will add to the appreciation of Port Townsend present. The protected bay was named in 1792 by Captain George Vancouver, that ubiquitous mariner, for an English marquis who never saw it. The first permanent settlers located here in 1851. The location was ideal for men of ambition and energy: on the main shipping route between the Strait of Juan de Fuca and Puget Sound, and next to the timber wealth of the Olympic Peninsula. The town's early promise was based on lumber and a nearby gold strike. Later, the prospect of a railroad link with the rest of the territory encouraged construction, but the link did not materialize.

During the 1880s the waterfront business district took shape. Its highly decorated brick and stone buildings, many with the dates of construction carved on the facades, lined Water Street. Most of them are still there. High on the bluff above, merchants and magnates built their imposing homes, which were embellished with gables, widow's walks, turrets, curlicues, rococo trim and bay windows, and filled with elegant furnishings. Nearly all of these homes still stand. Over two hundred houses in Port Townsend have signs with dates of construction and names of the first owners; many are on the National Historic Register.

But respectability was not universal in nineteenth-century Port Townsend. Down on the waterfront sailors from ships from all nations came ashore to play, and for a while Port Townsend had the reputation of being the wickedest city north of San Francisco. Then the boom collapsed around 1890 and calm ensued. The city of twenty thousand dwindled (the population is now around seven thousand) but stayed alive, thanks to its strategic location and the military activity at Forts Flagler and Worden and, in 1928, the establishment of Crown Zellerbach's pulp and paper mill.

Today much of Port Townsend's vitality derives from tourism. A primary attraction is the twice-yearly tour of historic homes held on the first weekend in May and the second weekend in September. Homes on the tour are privately owned and are opened only for the tour. But a few beautifully restored houses may be visited year-round. The Chamber of Commerce will provide a map and guide of sixty-five notable sights, including the historic homes.

Besides being a microcosm of late nineteenth-century architecture and a cultural center, Port Townsend has the advantage of being close to all the natural wonders of the Olympic Peninsula and Puget Sound.

The town has two marinas, seaside parks, golf courses and miles of beach. It is famous locally for its annual Rhododendron Festival honoring the state flower; for a series of fishing derbies (for king and silver salmon), the largest being in mid-August; for regattas on the breezy bay; and for the world's only Wooden Boat Festival.

Guests at bed and breakfast establishments can get the names of good restaurants from their hosts. Most people will recommend the Farmhouse, nationally famous and a short drive across the peninsula from town. It is open weekends only and is run by John and Dorothy Conway in a gracious home that really was an old farmhouse. The view is outstanding and so is the food, with a different menu every month. Reservations are essential. The Lido, in the heart of the marina and popular with boaters and fishermen, has consistently good Continental cuisine.

Getting There: By car, take ferry from Seattle to Winslow or Edmonds to Kingston, drive to Lofall and take the Hood Canal ferry to South Point, then drive on Highway 104 to the Quilcene–Port Townsend exit (26 miles from South Point to Port Townsend). Or take Keystone ferry from Whidbey Island directly to Port Townsend. Eastbound on Highway 101, take Port Townsend exit from Discovery Bay. By bus, take Greyhound from Seattle to Port Townsend. Nearest airport: Port Angeles. (The Hood Canal Floating Bridge, scheduled to be rebuilt by the fall of 1982, may then be taken instead of the Lofall–South Point ferry.)

JAMES HOUSE
Port Townsend

When Francis Wilcox James came to Port Townsend in 1853, the infant hamlet was considered the most promising seaport on Puget Sound. By the time he was ready to retire in 1891, the town had lived through its years of glory and was just beginning its long gentle decline. But James,

204

a canny businessman, had amassed his fortune and built an imposing Queen Anne–style house on the bluff. After James's death in 1920 it was sold, then much later became an apartment house during World War II. It was rescued by the William Eatons in 1965, who after extensive restoration opened it as a bed and breakfast house in 1973— the first such in the Northwest.

Next, in 1976, came Lowell and Barbara Bogart, who continued the good work, and in 1981, Rod and Deborah LaMontagne. Three of their four children help them run the inn and keep it in the apple-pie order to which its public has become accustomed. The parquet floors are polished, the cherrywood bannisters of the elegant stairway are agleam, miles of wood trim are freshly painted and the tiled hearths of the nine fireplaces are scrubbed and shining.

The LaMontagnes have made a few significant changes, such as returning the main-floor rooms to their original uses. The formal dining room (mostly for show, since breakfast is served in the kitchen) is now where the north parlor was, and both parlors are along the south side of the house. The organ is in one parlor, the piano in the dining room, and guests are encouraged to play. Ice and mixers are provided for those who wish to have drinks around the fireplace.

Rod LaMontagne has also discovered space to add two bedrooms. One is tucked away at the third-floor rear, and the other is in a separate cottage in the back yard and has a private bath.

All the rooms are furnished in exquisite taste, with much of the home's original furniture, and each has its special character. No. 2 (the James House doesn't go in for fanciful room names) has a fine view of Mount Rainier—and gaudy red wallpaper of which daughter Storey LaMontagne (resident innkeeper) says, "People either love it or they hate it." Room No. 1 has a little half-dormer window that artfully frames the view from the bed. The two garden suites, just below street level, are in the old brick-walled part of the house; one has a fireplace, one a parlor stove, and both have private baths and views of the pretty, sunken gardens.

The much-admired Bridal Suite is at the second-floor front. It has its own small tiled fireplace, an imposing walnut bedstead, a sitting room with a "fainting couch," and a small balcony with a superb view of town and bay. The suite, which was once the master bedroom, has a private bath.

The LaMontagnes serve breakfast around the oak table next to the big iron cookstove in the kitchen. The Continental breakfast, served from eight to nine-thirty, includes juice, coffee, a variety of teas and homemade bread with jam and preserves. Each of the five LaMontagnes cooks, and each has a group of specialties, so you never know which of some fifteen different breakfast breads—including cinnamon raisin, anadama, pumpkin walnut and apple-pie bread—will appear.

JAMES HOUSE, 1238 Walnut Street, Port Townsend, Washington 98368. Telephone: (206) 385-1238. Accommodations: double and twin beds; private baths with tubs; connecting and community baths, some with tubs, some with showers; no telephones; no television. Rates: moderate, Continental breakfast included. Children over 12 welcome. No pets. No credit cards. Open all year.

LIZZIE'S
Port Townsend

If Lizzie Grant ran her nineteenth-century home with the same verve and taste as it is operated today as a "Victorian inn," she must have been one of the most popular hostesses in Port Townsend.

Unfortunately we don't know much about the mysterious Lizzie, except that soon after she was married to Thomas Grant, a pilot boat captain, she purchased a plot of land on Port Townsend's fashionable bluff. Shortly thereafter, probably in 1887, the impressive two-story mansion was built. It was most unusual for a married woman to own property in those days—before Washington was even a state.

Thelma Scudi, who bought the house in 1980, has in her restoration captured the authentic spirit of Lizzie's day. She drew on her experience as an antique dealer and a professional historic-house renovator, in California and Washington.

For starters, she chose an exterior color scheme that is a refreshing change from the white used for so many Victorian restorations in this area. Lizzie's is a rich cream, accented by bright red trim. This calls attention at once to the splendid proportions of the tall windows of the bays that flank the entrance.

The two high-ceilinged connecting parlors on the first floor are furnished, but not crowded, with the kind of household effects that a discriminating wife of a seafaring husband might have acquired in Lizzie's day: Chinese hangings are draped alongside one of the fireplaces; a rosewood grand piano graces the rear parlor (which is also called the music room); leather chairs and sofas are set before the fireplace in this room. Ice is available if guests wish to have cocktails here.

At the back of the first floor is the bright, light-filled country kitchen, where guests will find fresh fruit, coffee and tea anytime, and where breakfast is served at 8:30. Both Thelma and resident innkeeper Diane Towne are likely to have a hand in preparing breakfast and joining in the breakfast-table conversation—always one of the attractions of a congenial B&B. Typical fare is juice, boiled eggs, fresh-baked scones, butter, homemade jams and copious refills of coffee or tea.

Each of the seven bedrooms has its own character and represents a distinct period, ranging from the 1840s to 1900. Lizzie's room, of course, is the grandest in the house, first-floor front, with a curtained bed, a fireplace, a private bath and a little round table in the bay window. The colors are vibrant—the carpet is red, wallpaper a dark green with rosy peacocks and peonies. There's a dazzling gilt and Chinese-red bureau. Charlie's, also on the first floor, is more restrained but it too has a private bath. And it has a splendid, well-polished armoire.

Upstairs are five more rooms. Sarah's has a breathtaking view of all that's worth seeing: the venerable town, the broad waters and the guardian mountains. This splendid room has two double beds, and easy chairs in the bay window. Hope's room, more modest and at the rear, is a small delight: With a view of Olympics from one window and a two-story-tall plum tree sheltering the other, it has quaint small-patterned wallpaper (and equally charming matching bedspread and curtains), a velvet upholstered rocking chair, marble-topped bureau, and brass coathooks on the wall—but no closet. The big walnut bedstead, like all those in the house, is high and comfortable. Thelma spared no expense in outfitting the beds. The two community baths are at the rear of the house. Both have old clawfoot tubs without showers and are provided with bubble bath and rosewater lotion.

Lizzie's is a ten- or fifteen-minute walk from downtown Port Townsend, and within easy strolling distance of a number of the town's architecturally interesting homes.

LIZZIE'S, 731 Pierce Street, Port Townsend, Washington 98368. Telephone: (206) 385-4168 or 385-9826. Accommodations: double, queen- and king-size beds; some private baths with tub; community baths with tub; one fireplace; no telephones; no television. Rates: moderate, breakfast included. Children welcome. Pets discouraged. Cards: MC, VISA. Open all year, but weekends and holidays only from October 1 to May 1 except by prior reservation.

MANRESA CASTLE
Port Townsend

It may have no portcullis, and you may spy a television antenna peeking out from behind a turret, but it's a very respectable castle all the same. Manresa Castle is a National Historic Site. And more important for the traveler, it is dedicated to a successful blending of gracious old-world atmosphere and modern comforts.

Manresa's history goes back to the end of the last century, its inspiration even further. Charles Eisenbeis, a native of Prussia, came to Port Townsend to make his fortune in the late 1800s. He started a brewery and a cracker factory and both prospered. He was the area's first big-time real estate promoter, and the town's first mayor. He built Manresa Castle for his young bride in 1892, in a style reminiscent of castles on the Rhine. Like them, Manresa is perched on an eminence, the highest point in Port Townsend. For years it was the pride of the flourishing young town. After the Eisenbeis family gave it up it was acquired and occupied by the Order of Jesuits (hence the cross on the main tower). Finally in 1970, it was opened as a guest house. Since 1973 it has been owned, managed and renovated by Mr. and Mrs. Ronald Smith.

The bedrooms, which open off the long halls that run the length of both floors, are neat and inviting, with fresh white curtains, very comfortable beds, period furniture such as oak dressers and gilt mirrors, and, in most, an unbeatable view of town, Sound, shipping lanes and Cascades. The Smith family (the two sons are important members of the team) has renovated thirty-seven bedrooms and added thirty-three bathrooms.

Manresa's restaurant is behind the lounge. Upstairs dining is more intimate, with alcoves for two. There is another small, elegant dining room at the right of the entry, where a Continental breakfast is served in winter, a full breakfast in summer.

MANRESA CASTLE, Seventh and Sheridan, Port Townsend, Washington 98368. Telephone (206) 385-5750. Toll-free number: 1-800-732-4281. Accommodations: double, queen-size and one king-size bed; suites (two doubles with bath), private baths with tub or shower, community baths with showers; no telephones; no television. Rates: moderate, breakfast included. Open to the public for dinner; full bar service. Children welcome. Small pets allowed, $5 charge. Cards: MC, VISA. Open all year.

Manresa Castle

QUIMPER INN
Port Townsend

A few blocks inland from Port Townsend's bluff is the Quimper Inn, already a veteran in this town's burgeoning bed and breakfast community. It takes its name from the Quimper Peninsula, which takes *its* name from Manuel Quimper, an early explorer.

The big square house was built in 1888 by Port Townsend druggist and shipping magnate Harry Barthrop, and stayed in the Barthrop family until 1941. It was a boardinghouse during the war and was then left empty for three decades.

Now, all is bright and clean and polished. Matthew and Mariii Jacobs are the third proprietors of the inn since its conversion to this role in 1976. They acquired it from Heidi and Tony Rodeghier, who had done much of the restoration. Matthew and Mariii have rebuilt the foundation, repainted, and infused the inn with their own personality. Mariii, an artist, has made the home a showcase of things she likes and things she has made. The latter include "soft sculpture" dolls and clowns, which recline on the beds (and look for the cheerful rooster doll in the dining room). The former run the gamut from original works of art on the walls to graceful, colorful parasols poised above the fine carved bedsteads. Though there are some choice antiques, this inn is an exception to the prevailing Port Townsend devotion to the Victorian period.

The inn has six bedrooms, with whimsical names like Gaff Schooner, Brasspyglass and Laughing Whale. Rooms are large and high ceilinged. Five have their original baths or half-baths. The one bath-down-the-hall has what Mariii describes as the "maid's tub": so small that you have to sit with your knees up. (It also has a shower.) All the rooms have great views. The Rose and Thistle, for instance, looks toward the mountains but as a bonus offers in the foreground the 1891 Jefferson County Courthouse with its illuminated tower clock. This room becomes a suite when opened up to the adjoining Windjammer. The other suite, the Gaff Schooner, has an antique tin tub with wood frame. Bay windows here frame vistas of Port Townsend and its bay, and distant mountains.

Breakfast is served at a long refectory table in the dining room. Here, another bay window looks out on a broad lawn and well-tended gardens. Besides fresh fruit and tea or French roast coffee, Matthew and Mariii serve croissants fresh from the oven. They're made with whole-wheat flour and honey and are served with butter and homemade jams. The Jacobs will proudly show off the country kitchen where the big wood stove performs so efficiently that it heats the whole house. There is, in fact, no heat in the bedrooms—"Staying here in the winter is a real adventure," say the Jacobs. That's when the thick down comforters on the beds prove their worth.

The Quimper Inn is in easy walking distance of downtown, and is in the heart of the historic-home district of Port Townsend.

QUIMPER INN, 1306 Franklin Street, Port Townsend, Washington 98368. Telephone: (206) 385-1086. Accommodations: double and queen-size beds; some private baths with tubs, some half-baths, one community bath with tub/shower; no telephones; no television. Rates: moderate, Continental breakfast included. Children over 12 welcome. No pets. No smoking within the inn. No credit cards. Open all year.

STARRETT HOUSE
Port Townsend

At the first sight of the Starrett House, towered and adorned with purple paint, you realize you are in for more Victorian opulence than you thought possible even in Port Townsend, which prides itself on living in the past with style. This is no modest mansion.

To get the full effect of the Starrett House's architectural exuberance, keep looking upward. From the entry hall a circular staircase swirls up through three stories to the peak of the turret. There, the ceiling displays frescoes of Graeco-Roman goddesses alternating with maidens representing the four seasons. (According to rumor, Winter was at first too unclothed for nineteenth-century sensibilities, and a few wispy draperies were painted on.) The ceilings of the downstairs parlors and dining rooms are also frescoed, mostly with floral or geometric motifs.

The frescoes' colors—pale roses, greens, blues and cream—are faded pastels, as though they might not have been touched since they were first painted by Otto Chapman, about 1890. That was shortly after the house was built by George Starrett as a wedding gift for his wife Anna. About fifteen years ago, somebody broke through the false ceilings that had been installed in the parlors when the house was converted into apartments during World War II. And lo and behold, there were the frescoes. This find led to more research in the tower, and when the peeling wallpaper was stripped off, the four seasons emerged. When Susan and Richard Thompson bought the house in 1980, most of

the restoration of the two main floors had been done by the two previous owners. The last had given it the startling purple exterior, after scraping through many old coats of paint and satisfying herself that purple must have been the original color.

The Thompsons offer dinners on summer weekends (as well as bed and breakfast the year around). Susan, a dedicated cook who constantly tests and introduces new masterpieces, is an inspired dessert and pastry chef. But she's also an advocate of the lightness and freshness of the nouvelle cuisine. So it is quite possible that even after a four-course meal that might include caviar, chilled green-pea soup, green salad and coquilles St.-Jacques, the guest may find room for Susan's chilled raspberry cream soup, or a Napoleon or tart from the pastry tray. Dinners are served in the imposing double dining rooms—one with a fireplace, one with a gleaming silver service on the sideboard, both with magnificent chandeliers.

Breakfasts—which are preceded by wake-up tea or coffee brought to your room on a silver tray—are almost as sensational as the dinners.

Susan dishes up scrambled eggs, fresh-from-the-oven doughnuts and biscuits, hash browns, homemade jams and jellies, fresh fruit and other treats.

All seven bedrooms are lavished with Victorian antiques. Some have parlor stoves. Some have alcoves or bay windows with fine views of the water or the mountains. There are puffy down comforters, bedside lamps, notepaper with Dürer reproductions, sweet-smelling potpourri—and a couple of chocolates, in the unlikely event of hunger pangs after one of Susan's meals. One room, the Bridal Chamber, has a lovely old-rose half-canopy on the brass bed, a French stove, a half-bath, and a shapely blue velvet sofa in the window. The largest room, with one of the finest views, is the Master's Quarters. Ann's Parlor (which can combine with the Master's Quarters to form a suite) has its own balcony. The community bathrooms are tidy, small and unadorned.

STARRETT HOUSE RESTAURANT AND INN, 744 Clay Street, Port Townsend, Washington 98368. Telephone: (206) 385-2976. Accommodations: double and twin beds, one room with half-bath; community baths with tub/shower; no television; no telephones. Rates: moderate, breakfast included. Open to the public for dinner by reservation April–September; group luncheons or dinners by special arrangement all year. No children. No pets. Cards: MC, VISA. Open all year except for brief winter closures.

THE CAPTAIN WHIDBEY
Coupeville

This venerable lodge on a cove on Whidbey Island's east shore has managed to preserve its character as an old-fashioned inn over nearly three-quarters of a century, with management by the same family since 1962.

The madrona-log lodge was built as a summer resort in 1907, when guests, coming by steamer from Seattle or Tacoma or elsewhere on Puget Sound, debarked at the private pier in front of the inn. The building has been in continuous use since then, though it lapsed from innhood into other functions three times, serving briefly as a general store, a post office and a girls' school.

Today most visitors come by ferry and then by car; this aside, the charm is as it was. It starts with the huge fieldstone fireplace that greets you as you step through the front door into the living room, with its easy chairs and a big low table covered with books and magazines.

213

Beyond the living room is the dining room, with a fireplace at one end and windows all along one wall. Here you have the best of both worlds: in the daytime, your view takes in the lawn, with a few picnic tables and benches under the trees and perhaps the ancient dog of the inn sunning himself; below the bluff, Penn Cove, where an occasional ship or pleasure boat skims by; and stately Mount Baker far off to the east. At night each table is a lamplit island in the firelit room. The food is good, too. The menu features native seafood such as salmon, crab, shrimp and oysters, as well as old-reliable "land foods" like steak and roast beef. Children are kept in mind: The lunch menu includes a peanut butter and jam sandwich. Next to the dining room is the Chart Room (cocktail lounge), brimming with nautical antiques and oddments.

Up a steep staircase from the living room is the library, remembered fondly by many a visitor. Its shelves bulge with everything from classic Greek drama to Book-of-the-Month Club selections. It also has a television, and games for children and adults.

The nine guest rooms on this floor are not large, but are quaint and comfortable. Beds, the only modern furnishings, are very good. Otherwise rooms are furnished with antiques, some dating from the inn's earliest days, such as marble-topped washbasins. There is one suite, the Honeymoon Suite, with a bedroom and a sitting room. All the lodge rooms share two baths. All overlook Penn Cove, so you are lulled to sleep by the lapping of waves.

Other accommodations include four cottages, nestled in the trees but with a marine view. Three have kitchenettes and all have private baths and fireplaces. Considerably more luxurious are the twelve lagoon rooms in two separate buildings, with verandas, private baths, many antique furnishings, and lovely views. They are not housekeeping. A recently added four-bedroom house across the cove can sleep eight and has a fireplace and a kitchen.

Small boats may tie up at the Captain Whidbey's own pier. There's clamming on the private beach (no season restrictions for hardshell clams here), also agate-hunting, and swimming in the lagoon.

Whidbey Island (second longest in the country) was discovered by Captain Vancouver nearly two centuries ago and named for one of his lieutenants. Just across the narrow neck of land from the inn on the island's west side is Fort Casey, with its historic lighthouse. Around the point from Fort Casey is the Keystone Ferry, which runs between Whidbey Island and Port Townsend, one of the gateways to the Olympic Peninsula. The whole island is still relatively rural and unspoiled. It's fine for bicycle touring. (Bikes may be rented through the inn.) Tennis and golf are close by. Salmon fishing hereabouts is also

214

a good pastime and can be sensational most of the year: humpback, Chinook, silver, king. You may moor your own boat at the inn dock and go out trolling, or charter a boat at Oak Harbor, seven miles away.

THE CAPTAIN WHIDBEY, Route 1, Box 32, Coupeville, Washington 98329. Telephone: (206) OR 8-4097. Accommodations: twin, double, twin double and queen-size beds; community baths with showers in lodge, private baths with tub/shower in cottages and lagoon rooms; some cottages with kitchenettes, all with fireplaces; no telephones; no television. Rates: moderate, no meals included. Open to the public for breakfast, lunch and dinner; full bar service. Children welcome. Cards: MC, VISA. Open all year.

Getting There: By car, car ferry from Mukilteo to Columbia Beach, then Highway 525 past Coupeville to Penn Cove. Or, Highway 20 south from Anacortes through Oak Harbor, then seven miles on Penn Cove Road. Or, car ferry from Port Townsend to Keystone east to Highway 525, north to Coupeville and as above. By boat, direct to Penn Cove. By air, daily commercial flights to Oak Harbor from Seattle (30 minutes) via Harbor Airlines.

LA CONNER COUNTRY INN
La Conner

Give this inn a few more years and it will look as rooted in its spot as La Conner itself, which has been on the banks of the Swinomish Channel since 1868. This channel gives La Conner good access to the fishing grounds of Puget Sound and the Strait of Juan de Fuca. Fishing, lumber and the rich farmland of the Skagit Valley have kept the area prosperous for more than a century. The town attracts a steady stream of tourists, intent on its colorful history, its well-preserved nineteenth-century architecture (it includes a National Historic District) and its fishing fleet and marinas, which are practically on the main street. La Conner has a near-monopoly on the adjective "picturesque" in north-west Washington. And now it has a proper inn.

Built only in 1977, the inn is fortunate in its trio of owners: Paul Thompson, his son Rick Thompson (who is resident innkeeper) and architect Glen Bartlett. Glen Bartlett designed the long, two-story structure, with cedar siding and shingles that quickly weathered to the same mellow, muted tones of the town's old houses and shops. At one end of the building is the reception area and the library-parlor; at the

215

other, the restaurant, clinging to the hill, its approach adorned with flourishing flower beds. The innkeeper's lodgings are on the lower floor of this shingled cottage, and the restaurant is on the upper floor, joined to the inn by a covered bridge. Only two tables overlook the waterfront, so reserve ahead if you want to watch marine activity. The back room, down a few steps, is kept aglow with a cheerful woodstove. The food is very good. Expect steak, prime rib, maybe chicken Kiev, and much fresh seafood. There is a daily seafood special and usually a pasta such as fettuccine. The cheesecake is fantastic, and some people come just for the Mud Pie.

After a satisfying meal and perhaps a stroll through town, the library-parlor is a warmly cozy room for a sit-down and a read. A big stone fireplace extends halfway across one wall, decked with milk cans holding dried flowers and grasses on hearth and ledge. On one wall there is an 1890 music box that will play "La Paloma" for a dime.

The rooms are large and comfortable, uncluttered and tasteful. Furnishings are good modern counterparts of traditional styles: brass bedsteads, oak and maple chairs and tables, bedside tables with reading lamps. Every room has a fireplace (gas). There is color television, but it is out of sight in the closet until called for. In the first-floor rooms, small windows frame vignettes of the town. Second-floor rooms have larger windows, are a bit more elegant and cost a bit more. They have beamed sloping ceilings and high-backed easy chairs. All bathrooms are roomy and almost as attractive as the bedrooms.

La Conner is full of things to do and see, and your hosts at the inn will be glad to advise. Ask about the Skagit County Historical Museum up on the hill, also the restored Gaches Mansion.

LA CONNER COUNTRY INN, Old Town, La Conner, Washington 98257. Telephone: (206) 466-3101. Accommodations: twin and queen-size beds; private baths with shower; television; telephones. Rates: moderate, Continental breakfast included. Children welcome. Pets permitted. Cards: AE, CB, DC, MC, VISA. Open all year.

Getting There: Take exit from Interstate 5 at Conway or Mount Vernon; follow signs west to La Conner. From Anacortes ferry dock, follow Highway 20, and watch for La Conner signs to turn south. The inn is at Second and Morris.

HOTEL DE HARO

Roche Harbor Resort

ROCHE HARBOR RESORT
Roche Harbor

Accessible by land, air or sea, Roche Harbor Resort is a pocket of turn-of-the-century charm and hospitality at the north end of San Juan Island (second largest in the San Juan archipelago).

The resort is a self-sufficient complex: hotel, restaurant, cottages and moorage for two hundred boats in one of the world's loveliest small-boat anchorages, and the most sheltered in the San Juans. There are also a laundromat, gas pumps, a grocery, a gift shop and a sportswear shop and a launching ramp. And, since this is a jumping-off place for waterborne travel into Canadian waters, Roche Harbor has a customs office.

The Hotel de Haro, still the center of activity, has been here since it was built in 1886 by John McMillin, pioneer business magnate. McMillin carved out his private empire at Roche Harbor in the 1890s and presided over it until the 1930s. His company town was based on the exploitation of an extraordinarily rich limestone deposit. Lime was much in demand all up and down the West Coast, and for a while McMillin had a monopoly on the business in the West. He built a hotel (naming it for an eighteenth-century Spanish explorer) because he enjoyed showing off his barony and wanted a proper place to lodge his visitors. President Theodore Roosevelt was here in 1906, hence the hotel's Presidential Suite. William Howard Taft was also a visitor.

The hotel was built around a Hudson's Bay post that had been on the site since 1845. Some of the post's massive original timbers can be seen, still holding it all together. The white-painted, cupola-crowned three-story building has a creaky but comfortable charm and has been scrupulously maintained. Most of the twenty rooms are small and simply furnished with period pieces such as wicker rocking chairs and marble-topped dressers. The four suites have private baths, and the Presidential Suite also has a fireplace and private veranda.

Nearby, McMillin built his own house, now the Roche Harbor Restaurant. Here as throughout the resort, the Tarte family (who have operated Roche Harbor since 1956) have preserved the past while introducing modern comforts. You approach the restaurant from the dock, or stroll from the hotel through a beautifully groomed semiformal garden. The varied menu includes excellent seafood from San Juan waters and beaches. The dining room looks out on all the boating activity of Spieden Channel, and the nightly ceremony of the retiring of the colors.

218

About a block from the hotel are the nine housekeeping "Company Town" cottages, which once housed McMillin's employees. They're completely furnished and just the thing for families. Higher rates and a six-day minimum stay during July and August apply to the cottages.

The resort complex has tennis courts and an Olympic-size heated pool and offers trail rides. Salmon fishing is almost always rewarding; Boston whalers and other boats and motors may be rented, for fishing or cruising. Rabbit hunting is a famous pastime on the island ever since the population explosion some years ago when a few bunnies were innocently introduced. There's no season, but be sure you're not trespassing. Farmers have become sensitive about nimrods who may aim at a rabbit and hit a cow.

ROCHE HARBOR RESORT, Roche Harbor, Washington 98250. Telephone: (206) 378-2155. Accommodations: twin, double and queen-size beds; four private full baths, community baths with tub or shower, private baths with tub or shower in housekeeping cottages; no telephones; no television. Rates: moderate, no meals included. Open to the public for breakfast, lunch and dinner every day in season, on weekends only in winter; coffee shop; full bar service. Children welcome. No pets. Cards: MC, VISA. Open May through October, weekends in winter.

Getting There: By car, take car ferry from Anacortes, Washington, or Sidney, British Columbia, to Friday Harbor on San Juan Island; thence, 11 miles by road to Roche Harbor. By boat, direct to Roche Harbor, or use docking facilities at Friday Harbor. By air, commercial flights daily to Friday Harbor from Bellingham and Seattle; at Roche Harbor, private and commercial charter planes can land.

OUTLOOK INN
Eastsound

Hundred-year-old Outlook Inn greets the visitor to Orcas Island's Eastsound at the beginning of the village street. It was first a hotel for produce and stock buyers who came to Orcas by steamer, docking at Eastsound. It has operated more or less continuously ever since, as a dance hall, a barber shop, a pharmacy, a jail—but mostly as an inn.

Throughout the two-story, white-painted structure you come upon interesting oddities. Like the three upright pianos lined up along one wall of the dining room; a well-polished cradle in a hall; and one room jammed with objects that various staff members have picked up here and there because they liked them, and which will sooner or later find a home in some bedroom or on a landing. This permissive approach to decorating extends to the rooms' color schemes too: some have wallpaper that is so gaudy it almost keeps you awake.

Aside from its oddball charm and historic significance, the inn claims fame nowadays for its food. The chefs take no shortcuts, respecting the importance of freshness in seafood and of permitting a soup stock to simmer for hours in the kettle. Meals are served in a pleasant room at the back of the inn, looking through French doors to the flower gardens, the orchards and an ancient greenhouse. Dinners include salad or soup; an entrée, which may be local salmon or beef from an island farm; a small compact loaf of homemade whole-grain bread; a dessert such as an exceptional apple pie; and Colombian coffee or a choice of teas.

Until recently the spacious room that stretches across the front of the building was the dining room. It is now the lobby-lounge, and a fine place to sit by the fire and look at the view. About all that remains of this room's former years as a country store and barber shop is the fireplace. Many of the additions are faithful reproductions of antiques, made locally: The staff made their own oaken tables, and the windows were done by etchers and stained-glass craftsmen from the island.

Rooms in the new wing look out on the back garden and a pond; the older rooms have a sea view, and one has a private bath and balcony.

Outlook Inn has been owned by the Louis Foundation since 1967. It's the main source of income for this nonprofit foundation, which has the hard-to-quarrel-with purpose of welcoming "people from all walks of life, from all religions, desirous of making the world a better place for mankind and, in turn, enriching their own lives." In an unaggressive way, the foundation is active in publications, education and study groups. Somehow Louis (he uses no last name) combines his role as a mystic and psychic with a superb mastery of innkeeping, and imparts to all the employees his dedication to pleasing the customers. The employees, incidentally, all donate their time to the foundation, and treat guests gently, considerately, efficiently.

Outlook Inn is equipped to take care of groups of up to forty people; inquire about meeting facilities and special rates. The inn has its own private saltwater beach. In Eastsound, at the heart of the island, you'll find a small historic museum, and several shops with curios, arts and crafts. It's just minutes by car from the island's justly famed Moran State Park, a five-thousand-acre, mostly wild area, with fishing, swimming and boating in two lakes; picnicking and camping; and even some mild mountain climbing. Mount Constitution, at twenty-four hundred feet the highest point in the islands, is easily reached by a good trail, and the view of the jewel-like archipelago and distant mountain ranges is worth every puff. Hiking and biking are popular activities all over the island. There's a golf course a couple of miles from Eastsound.

OUTLOOK INN, Eastsound, Washington 98245. Telephone: (206) 376-2581. Accommodations: double and twin beds; one private bath, all rooms have washbowls, community baths with tub or shower; no telephones; no television. Rates: inexpensive, no meals included. Open to the public for breakfast, lunch and dinner; wine and beer only. Children welcome. No pets. Cards: MC, VISA. Open all year.

Getting There: By car, take ferry from Anacortes, Washington, or Sidney, British Columbia, to Orcas, then eight miles by Eastsound Road to Outlook Inn, the first building you come to in Eastsound. By air, daily commercial flights from Seattle-Tacoma Airport via San Juan Airlines; Orcas Airport is a half-mile from Eastsound. Charter flights from Anacortes via Harbor Air. By prior arrangement, the inn will pick up guests at ferry dock or airport. By bus, Island Empire Bus Lines to ferry dock at Anacortes, by ferry to Orcas, arrange for pickup by inn. By private boat, moorage at Standard Oil dock at Eastsound.

NORTH BEACH INN
Eastsound

North Beach Inn, on the north shore of Orcas Island and just across the isthmus from tourist-happy Eastsound, is no johnny-come-lately. The beach cabins have been there since the 1920s and the lodge since 1932. Yet few off-islanders have discovered it, and those who have try to keep it to themselves.

The shingled lodge, set in lawns and gardens and approached by a gravel drive, looks like a comfortable summer home in the woods. Breakfast and dinner are served in the lodge dining room (summer only), where a stuffed elk head observes the scene benignly from the mantel. Home-cooked meals include only a couple of entrée choices per night, but the quality is excellent. The dining room is small and is a popular spot with knowledgeable islanders, so reservations are absolutely essential.

Guests stay in housekeeping cabins dotted along the beach. These are not architectural prizes, but they're efficient, comfortable and

surrounded by woodsy privacy. All have kitchens, fireplaces, electric heat, private baths—and sensational views across the water to more islands and gorgeous sunsets.

In the immediate vicinity, recreational opportunities include walking in the woods, sunning on the beach, swimming (there's a floating dock), tetherball, badminton and horseshoes. There are rowboats for rent, also "fishboats"—for which the guest must provide the outboard motor. Moorage floats are provided for guests' boats.

The inn, founded by the Gibson family, is still under family ownership. Reservations should be made well ahead of time; two years ahead would be advisable for July and August visits.

NORTH BEACH INN, P.O. Box 80, Eastsound, Washington 98245. Telephone: (206) 376-2660. Accommodations: one- or two-bedroom cabins; twin and double beds; private baths with tub/shower, some with shower only; no telephones; no television. Rates: moderate, no meals included. Open to the public for breakfast and dinner, summer only. Children welcome. Pets allowed. No credit cards. Open May to September; five cabins available year-round.

Getting There: By car, take car ferry from Anacortes, Washington, or Sidney, British Columbia, to Orcas Island; proceed nine miles on Eastsound Road, look for sign on left just before Eastsound. By air, daily commercial flights from Seattle-Tacoma Airport via San Juan Airlines to Orcas Airport, one-half mile from Eastsound. Charter flights from Anacortes via Harbor Air. By bus, Island Empire Bus Lines to ferry dock at Anacortes, by ferry to Orcas.

BETTY'S PLACE
Lopez

Betty and Smitty (Mr. and Mrs. B.A. Smith) have retired, after operating Betty's Place for eleven years and creating almost a cult among appreciators of unconventional inns and superlative food.

But all is not lost. Paul and Miloe Welshans have taken over and are carrying on in the manner to which guests at Betty's Place have become accustomed. Paul is a former electronics engineer from California and has for years been an accomplished chef by avocation. So running an inn was the logical objective when he decided to escape from the rat race. He is ably aided by Miloe, who is chief baker and pastry cook. Both are firm believers in honest home-style cookery, with plenty of fresh ingredients, loving attention, imagination and no microwaves.

The inn is so small that reservations well in advance are essential, even for meals, though the Welshans do their best to fit in drop-in dinner guests. There are three rooms in the inn and a cabin in back, which adds up to room for eight people, though the cabin can put up more than two if need be.

The dining room is small. Meals are served family-style; breakfast is whenever you get up and dinner is around 6:30. Guests may bring their own wine and liquor.

Lopez, smaller and less developed than San Juan or Orcas, is a self-sufficient little world with a village center at Lopez, a pleasure-boat moorage at Fisherman Bay, rural roads through quiet farmland and miles of beach to investigate, though much of the shoreline is privately owned. Odlin Park and Spencer Spit are two spots with easy access. Cyclists love the island for its flatness and its friendly folksiness, and have for years been among the best customers of Betty's Place.

If you stay on the island long enough to be willing to tear yourself away from Paul and Miloe's good food, an excellent meal may be had at Mackaye Harbor Inn, at the south end of the island.

BETTY'S PLACE, P.O. Box 86, Lopez, Washington 98261. Telephone: (206) 468-2470. Accommodations: king-size beds in main lodge; one private bath with tub/shower, one shared bath with tub/shower; cabin has twin beds, private bath with shower; no telephones; no television. Rates: inexpensive, no meals included. Meal service: breakfast; lunch and dinner by reservation. Children not encouraged. No pets. No credit cards. Open all year.

Getting There: Take Washington State Ferry from Anacortes, Washington, or Sidney, British Columbia, to Lopez Island; drive south from ferry landing two miles to Betty's Place, which will be straight ahead of you where the road makes a T.

THE COLLEGE INN
Seattle

Seattle is not yet blessed with a choice of bed and breakfast places, so the College Inn fills the gap almost single-handedly. It's in a good location: on the "Ave" (University Way), next door to the University of Washington and its many attractions and meetings, and only a few minutes from downtown theaters, restaurants, the waterfront and Seattle Center.

Built in 1909, when the Alaska-Yukon-Pacific Exposition brought hordes of visitors to Seattle, the tall, gabled, Tudor-style inn continued to take transient guests for some fifty years, then became an apartment house. Gladys Fred assumed management of the building in 1979, determined to reproduce its original style and function. Her extensive restoration and the acquisition of appropriate antique furnishings have produced a creditable semblance of an early-twentieth-century guest house. A canny as well as a hospitable innkeeper, Gladys realizes that many visitors to Seattle will appreciate economy along with quaintness; so she deliberately cuts down on the extras: there are no private baths,

no bottles of wine, and though the rooms are adequately furnished with good pieces, she has resisted the Victorian proclivity for fringes, velvet draperies, bric-a-brac and charming but useless little tables. All rooms have washstands, some antique. "We know a lot of our guests are looking for a place with character," she says. "And they're willing to go without some of the frills, if the price is right."

The inn's layout is upside-down compared with most others. Guest rooms are on the second and third floors, and the lounge and reception area is at the top of the house—up three flights of stairs. This long room with its dormer windows was once the attic. Here guests may have tea or coffee at any hour, read or write, play the piano, and visit with fellow-guests or ask Gladys where to go for dinner and how to get there. (Some of Seattle's most interesting ethnic restaurants are in the University District.) A Continental breakfast is served here, from seven to nine every morning. So many Europeans have discovered the College Inn that the atmosphere in the lounge is apt to seem more international than Northwest.

THE COLLEGE INN, 4000 University Way NE, Seattle, Washington 98105. Telephone: (206) 633-4441. Accommodations: single and double beds; washbasins in rooms; community baths with shower; no television; no telephones. Rates: moderate, Continental breakfast included. Children welcome. No pets. Cards: AE, MC, VISA. Open all year.

Getting There: Take University of Washington exit from Interstate 5, turn south on University Way to 40th. The inn is on the northeast corner.

MOUNT RAINIER

Mount Rainier is the number one scenic attraction in the Pacific Northwest. At 14,410 feet, it is the fifth-highest peak in the coterminous United States and has the most glaciers festooning its slopes: twenty-six. Winter snowpack at elevations you can reach by car may exceed thirty feet. A young mountain, it was formed by successive volcanic eruptions less than one million years ago. It dominates the landscape within a hundred-mile radius.

So much for the textbook superlatives. How to see Mount Rainier best? We recommend an approach from the southwest, which permits the traveler to establish a base camp near or at the Longmire park entrance. Within the park there are overnight accommodations year-round at Longmire and in summer at Paradise, none at the other visitor center, Sunrise. Recreational opportunities include climbing and hiking to some altitudes within and near the park practically year-round; there is skiing at Paradise from December to April.

Climbing: Everest conquerors practice regularly on this mountain. If you're an experienced mountaineer go on your own (but not alone) to the top, but be sure to schedule the climb with Paradise rangers. If you're more of a novice, climbing schools and guided climbs may be arranged, and equipment rented. Get information from Rainier Mountaineering at Paradise, or write them at 201 St. Helens, Tacoma, Washington 98402.

Skiing: The snow supply at Paradise is usually better than at other Northwest ski areas, though facilities are not so complete (no tows). Cross-country skiing is good but one must be alert to avalanche danger; be sure to check with rangers for routes and conditions. Snowshoeing is popular, as is inner-tube sliding.

Hiking: There are three hundred miles of trails in the park. Possible hikes range from easy one-day or less walks from the road or from visitor centers to nearby eminences or waterfalls, to two-week backpack trips all around the mountain. Guides and maps are available at visitor centers. Register at trailheads.

For picnic supplies, minimum groceries are for sale at stores at Longmire year-round and Sunrise (not Paradise) in summer. Nearest stores outside the park are at Ashford and Greenwater.

Horseback riding is permitted on some trails, but check with headquarters at Ashford or with rangers in advance. They can tell you where rental horses are available (there are none in the park).

Fishing: You may expect good luck with rainbow, Dolly Varden and other trout. No license is required within the park. The stream fishing season is late May to October 31, lake fishing July 4 to October 31. Check with rangers for detailed regulations.

Complete information on hiking, maps and weather is available from National Park Service, Tahoma Woods Star Route, Ashford, Washington 98304; or by calling (206) 569-2211.

Getting There: It is possible to start from Seattle and drive completely around Mount Rainier in one day, with brief forays to Paradise and to Sunrise, the visitor center on the east that gives you a spectacular view from the sixty-four-hundred-foot level. And if this is all the time you have it's better than nothing. If you don't care to drive it yourself, Gray Line runs one-day coach tours from Seattle. An alternative is to take the Gray Line coach from Seattle one morning, stop off at Paradise overnight or longer, and pick up the tour bus later. Contact Gray Line Tours, 415 Seneca Street, Seattle, Washington 98101.

If you drive from Seattle, take Interstate 5 south to Tacoma, then Highways 7 and 206 to Longmire; or leave Interstate 5 at Auburn exit and take Highway 410 to Sunrise. From Yakima, take Highway 12, then either 12 (to White Pass and access to south entrance) or 410 (to Chinook Pass and access to east entrance). All park roads except 706 to Paradise are closed in winter.

PARADISE INN
Mount Rainier

Mount Rainier's Paradise Inn has been sheltering mountain people for more than half a century. Like its counterpart, Timberline at Mount Hood, it's almost as beloved as the snowcapped peak that towers over it.

At fifty-four hundred feet, Paradise Inn gives you an unobstructed view of the massive mountain, and is well worth a visit, whether you're staying overnight or not. But remember, though the mountain is always there, Paradise Inn is open only in the summer.

The huge lobby, a mecca for day-trippers as well as overnight guests, is impressive, with its sturdy wooden columns and beams, stone fireplace and authentic Indian rugs. The dining room can take care of two hundred comfortably. The food is good, hearty and moderately priced. The most popular items are prime rib, steak, prawns and salmon.

There's a cocktail lounge, the Glacier Room—rather inappropriately named, in view of the warmth of its hospitality, but effectively reminding you that Mount Rainier is world famous for its twenty-six glaciers. There's a souvenir shop, and even a mezzanine with card tables, a happy solution for the rainy days that must be expected occasionally in the Pacific Northwest.

The rooms are simply furnished, comfortable and expandable. The management will provide extra cots, and there are a number of suites: two rooms with a connecting bath.

A short walk from the inn is the imposing Visitor Center. Though the inn is open only from June to September, the Visitor Center's snack bar is open on weekends all winter, for skiers and other hardy visitors. Winter snowfalls may reach twenty-five or thirty feet, but the Park Service keeps roads plowed and open for weekend travelers.

There are miles and miles of hiking trails branching out from Paradise, and if you're short on time or energy, a network of asphalt-paved walks will get you close to the high mountain meadows and stunted alpine firs. Wild flowers are at their most glorious in early August. Later in August and through September, the huckleberry, vine maple and mountain ash turn red. Keep a sharp eye out for mountain goats on distant cliffs and ridges if you have a camera with a zoom lens. Even if you don't, photographic temptations are irresistible. Deer and bear may approach, looking for a handout—but remember it's unlawful and dangerous to feed or touch any wild animal.

You may also take a short hike to the Nisqually Glacier; a steeper, three-mile one to the ice caves; and, if backpacking, join up with the famed Wonderland Trail that goes around the mountain.

PARADISE INN, Mount Rainier, Washington. Telephone: summer (206) 569-2706, winter 475-6260. For reservations: Paradise Inn, Mount Rainier National Park Hospitality Service, Guest Services, Inc., 4820 South Washington, Tacoma, Washington 98409. Accommodations: twin and double beds; most rooms with private bath with tub and/or shower; no telephones; no television. Rates: moderate, no meals included. Open to the public for breakfast, lunch and dinner; full bar service. Children welcome. No pets. Cards: MC, VISA. Open June through September; Visitor Center open May 21 to October 4; snack bar open weekends balance of year.

ALEXANDER'S MANOR
Ashford

Alexander's Manor, on the road to Mount Rainier, was built in 1912. And like many a grande dame, she makes no effort to hide her years. The glass-enclosed dining room that was added a few years ago already looks at home with the rest of the inn and is a nice balance to the octagonal four-story tower, the dominant architectural feature of the building for seventy years.

Gerry and Vicki Harnish, proprietors, are concentrating now on some main-floor remodeling and addition of bedrooms upstairs. They have already succeeded in their first goal: to make the inn, as it was sixty-five years ago when Elizabeth Mesler was the cook, "the best place to eat on the whole Mountain Highway."

Elizabeth was the wife of Alexander Mesler, for whom the Harnishes renamed the inn. This flamboyant New Yorker made his way westward in the nineteenth century. In the 1890s he landed at Ashford, near what is now Mount Rainier National Park. Here he built a lumber mill and opened an inn to feed and house the growing number of visitors to the mountain. After the Mesler family ownership ended, the inn was the well-known Papajohn's for some twenty-five years, and the Harnishes bought it in 1973.

The menu is changed frequently and is always a delight. It may offer steaks, shrimp, scallops, chicken Virginia and that Northwest delicacy, geoduck. A trout pond behind the inn provides the ultimate in fresh fish. Desserts include a chocolate cheesecake, a wild huckleberry strudel and a spectacular strawberry shortcake.

By the summer of 1982 the Harnishes expect to have accommodations year-round. So far they have been available only in winter, and are popular with skiers, hikers and bikers. Vicki Harnish has been acquiring a good collection of antique furnishings, mostly early twentieth-century American, for the twelve bedrooms, some of which are already in use. There is also a wing with more sparsely furnished rooms for guests willing to bring sleeping bags and rough it a bit.

ALEXANDER'S MANOR, Ashford, Washington 98304. Telephone: (206) 569-2300. Accommodations: twin and double beds; private baths with shower, community baths with shower; no telephones; no television. Rates: inexpensive, Continental breakfast included. Open to the public for lunch and dinner; wine and beer only. Children welcome. No pets. Cards: MC, VISA. Restaurant open year-round; rooms available year-round starting summer 1982, but generally only on weekends and holidays from January to May.

Getting There: From Tacoma, Highway 7 to Elbe, then 706 to Ashford. From Seattle, Interstate 5 to Tacoma, then as above; 55 miles from Tacoma, 85 miles from Seattle.

HAUS ROHRBACH
Leavenworth

Leavenworth is the picturesque village at the east end of the Stevens Pass Highway, where travelers often pause before or after the highly scenic trip through the Cascades. In the mid-sixties this somnolent little town set out to transform itself into a storybook Bavarian village. One of the best things to come out of that effort was the Haus Rohrbach. This European-style pension, tucked under Tumwater

Mountain and a mile and a half off the main highway, is said to be the only bed and breakfast inn in eastern Washington.

The first owner, William Rohrbach, built the pension in the mid-seventies, inspired by a trip to Switzerland. But despite his and his large family's best efforts, it became too much to keep up, as Mr. Rohrbach approached retirement age and his children left home. So he was happy to sell to a quintet of Seattleites who chanced on it while vacationing—and bravely took the plunge to give up good jobs in the city to become country innkeepers.

Three of the original plungers are still managing the inn. Well aware that most people come to these parts for the outdoor recreation, Bob and Kathy Harrild and Greg Lunz concentrate on seeing that their guests get a good night's sleep in homelike surroundings, and a bountiful breakfast before they start off on the day's adventures, which might include river rafting, downhill or cross-country skiing, sledding and snowshoeing in the inn's front yard, or a sleigh ride.

As for hiking, Icicle Creek and its trail country are world-famous for beauty and grandeur. Milder, shorter ventures are at hand on trails right behind the inn. Spring wild flowers and the spring and fall bird migrations attract many to the Leavenworth area. And fishing is another big attraction, for spring and fall steelhead in the Wenatchee River, and German brown trout, rainbow and perch in Fish Lake and other lakes nearby.

If all this sounds too strenuous, Leavenworth is also a shopper's and browser's and muncher's paradise. Several times a year, the entire town bursts into a frenzy of activity that attracts visitors from near and far: the Mai Fest, the Autumn Leaf Festival and the Christmas Lighting Ceremony. For the last, Haus Rohrbach decks its balconies with strings of lights, a cheerful twinkle under the mountain.

The year around, Haus Rohrbach is a snug refuge for the wayfarer. The twelve bedrooms are showcases of craftsmanship in wood: The polished bedsteads, bureaus and stools are products of the careful handiwork of William Rohrbach and his sons. The rather somber tone of the furniture and the fir wainscoting is relieved by white walls, crisp, brightly patterned curtains and bedspreads and pretty dried-flower arrangements, some of which are for sale. The third-floor rooms have had to adapt to the steep roof slope and have a variety of closet spaces and no abundance of headroom; only one room has a private bath. Most have access to the balconies that run all around the chalet, with views of far-off mountains, quaint Leavenworth in the middle distance and cattle in the field and ducks paddling in the Haus pond.

Breakfast is served at 8:30 in the common room. The innkeepers take turns at cooking in full view of the breakfasters. Their hearty fare includes omelets and scrambled eggs, pancakes, hot biscuits and breads, and scrumptious cinnamon rolls. On fine summer mornings breakfast is served on the balcony, and a strolling accordion player entertains on weekends.

HAUS ROHRBACH, Route 1, Box I-E, Leavenworth, Washington 98826. Telephone: (509) 548-7024. Accommodations: twins, doubles and one king-size bed; community baths with tub/shower or shower only; one room with private bath; no telephones; no television. Rates: moderate, breakfast included. Children welcome. No pets. No credit cards. Open all year.

Getting There: From Highway 2 through Stevens Pass, take Ski Hill Drive from downtown Leavenworth, turn on Ranger Road to inn (1-1/2 miles). Leavenworth is 125 miles from Seattle, 23 miles from Wenatchee. Greyhound serves Leavenworth; arrange with inn for pickup at bus depot. Amtrak and Cascade Airways serve Wenatchee.

CAMPBELL HOUSE
Chelan

Lake Chelan is an outstanding beauty spot with much to pause for: swimming, boating, and exploring by car as far as you can along both sides of this deep mountain-girt lake. As for lodging, the town of Chelan, at the southern tip of the lake, has plenty of motels, but only the Campbell House approaches what the setting deserves.

231

This hostelry has been on the spot since 1901, and still stands squarely on its downtown corner, dominating the little town and giving focus to the spreading annexes and cottages that accommodate its guests.

The present owners, Dan and Arthur Campbell, are grandsons of the original owner, Clinton Campbell. Two great-grandsons, Clinton and Arthur, are also now involved. This continuity explains why so much of the early flavor persists in the inn. Much of the heavy, well-polished furniture survives from Clinton Campbell's day, and what has been added is in character. This is especially true in the "parlor," where you may have cocktails in a lush red-velvet setting that evokes San Francisco's palmy era. On fine days, you may sit on the veranda that runs around three sides of the building and watch the world go by. The dining room does not make much effort to appear old-timey, but serves good steaks, chicken and seafood.

Lodging is in one of the motel-like annexes or in the beach cottages. The former are air-conditioned and have televisions; the latter are cozy and immaculate and have housekeeping facilities. All have private baths, and most have sweeping views of the lake. There are also five remodeled cottages from the auto court that flourished here in the thirties, when guests parked the flivver next to the cold-water cabin, used the central washroom and laundry, and repaired to the Campbell House for a good meal. These cottages have been completely modernized and are now very comfortable, but they do not have a lake view.

Along with many innkeepers, the Campbells have had to adjust their operations to attract meetings and conventions. A former apartment house across the street has been turned into a conference center.

There are two outdoor swimming pools, and you may also swim in the lake. Boat stalls may be reserved, a feature much appreciated by visitors who bring their own boats in order to cruise Lake Chelan.

The town of Chelan dates from the building of Fort Chelan here in 1879. It has always been a convenient stopping place for cross-state travelers. During the summer it is very busy indeed, clogged with motorists en route to or from eastern Washington, Grand Coulee Dam, the Okanogan country. It's a lively center for boaters, water skiers and fishermen, and it is the departure point for up-lake trips on the little steamer, *Lady of the Lake.* (For schedule information, see the entry for North Cascades Lodge.)

CAMPBELL HOUSE, P.O. Box 278, Chelan, Washington 98816. Telephone: (509) 682-2561. Accommodations: twin, double and queen-size beds, some king-size beds in motel units; some suites in motel accommodating up to six people; private baths with tub/shower; telephones; television. Rates: moderate to expensive, no meals included. Open to the public for breakfast, lunch and dinner; full bar service. Children welcome. No pets. Credit cards: AE, MC, VISA. Open all year, restaurant open early March to late December.

Getting There: By car, take Interstate 90 from Seattle to Cle Elum, then Highway 97 north to Chelan. From Spokane, take Highway 2 west to Orondo, then north on 151, and cross the Columbia River via bridge at Chelan. Greyhound has daily bus service on Highway 97, north from Wenatchee or south from Canada.

NORTH CASCADES LODGE
Stehekin

This isn't the easiest place to reach in Washington State. You either take the spectacular four-hour boat trip up Lake Chelan, or charter a float plane; there's no road access. Or you could hike in across any of several mountain passes. Once at the lodge, you're in Stehekin country: one of the most beautiful and peaceful mountain valleys in all America.

The North Cascades Lodge has been a National Park Service facility since 1972. But for years, until the creation of the North Cascades National Park, it was the privately owned Stehekin Landing Lodge. Wisely, concessionaire and innkeeper Gary Gibson has not changed it much. The focal point is still the boat landing, where the *Lady of the Lake* docks daily. (She and her predecessors have been bringing visitors uplake from Chelan since the 1890s.) The rustic dining room, with a coffee shop at one end and an outdoor terrace for snacks and sunning, is just up from the boat landing. Food is hearty and well cooked, planned for people who are working up big appetites.

Single and multiple sleeping and housekeeping units are available, some in single cabins and others in the two-story alpine lodge buildings. Most can be stretched to accommodate large groups or families. All are strictly national-park-rustic, with natural-finish wood the dominant material for construction and furniture. Beds have bright plaid spreads, there are plenty of extra warm, woolly blankets, and there's ample storage and floor space for bulky gear. Some units have a balcony, with a view of the lake and the mountains.

The first thing you'll want to do is explore Stehekin Valley. Take the shuttle bus twenty-three miles up the bumpy dirt road that goes from the head of Lake Chelan along the rushing Stehekin River. The

233

driver is nice about stopping so you can photograph a waterfall or a deer or maybe even a mountain lion. The road ends at a remote alpine paradise with camping and picnic sites and the trailhead for the stiff hike across Cascade Pass.

Or, you may climb and hike. The famous Cascade Crest Trail cuts right across Stehekin Valley, and fine trails go up all the main side valleys. There are also shorter hikes from the lodge that you can do in a day or less, and guided nature walks. Package hiking tours are managed by the Courtneys of Stehekin, with pack animals carrying the heavy gear. They will also arrange extended horseback trips through the North Cascades Park.

Take a rubber-raft trip for a day on the Stehekin River (river conditions permitting). Or do your own boating from the lodge dock; boats and motors may be rented. Fish for rainbow, eastern brook and cutthroat trout and Kokanee salmon. You'll need a fishing license, available at the lodge. Swim, if you're hardy; Lake Chelan is always cold, even in summer.

In winter there's cross-country skiing. The lodge, with the Courtneys, offers good weekend and weekday ski packages, and gives lessons.

Take advantage of evening programs by the Park Service, and inspect the Pioneer Interpretive Farm. Or just sit in the sun and gawk at jagged snowcapped peaks, forest-clad slopes and blue lake water. This is the kind of place where you can do as much or as little as you like. For more information on the park, write National Park Service, Sedro Woolley, Washington 98284.

NORTH CASCADES LODGE, Stehekin, Washington 98852. Radiophone: (509) 682-3822. Reservations telephone: (509) 682-4711. Accommodations: twin and double beds, hideabeds, rollaways, cots available for large groups; private baths with tub and/or shower; no telephones; no television; kitchenettes. Rates: moderate, no meals included. Open to the public for breakfast, lunch and dinner. Cards: MC, VISA. Children welcome. No pets. Open all year.

Getting There: From Seattle take Highway 90 (Snoqualmie Pass) or 2 (Stevens Pass) to Wenatchee, then 97 to Chelan. Or take 20 to Twisp, then 153 to Chelan. All these routes are very rewarding scenically. At Chelan, park your car at boat dock. *Lady of the Lake* leaves 8:30 am, arrives Stehekin 12:30 pm summer and 12 noon winter. Boat runs daily May 15 through October 15; Monday, Wednesday, Friday and Sunday, rest of year; no Sunday service January 1 to February 15. By air, float plane service from Chelan via Chelan Airways, near City Marina.

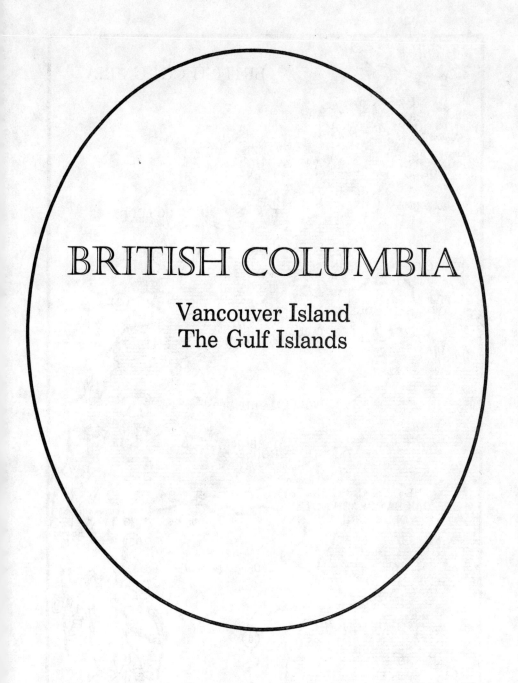

BRITISH COLUMBIA

Vancouver Island
The Gulf Islands

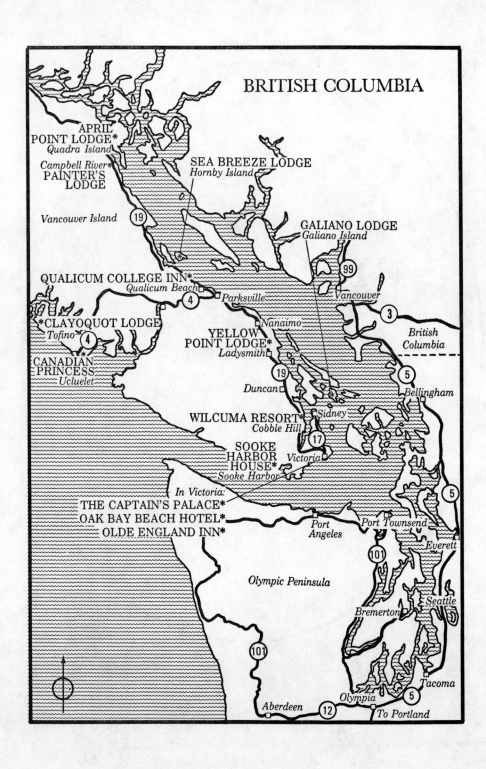

BRITISH COLUMBIA

APRIL
POINT LODGE*
Quadra Island

Campbell River*
PAINTER'S
LODGE

SEA BREEZE LODGE
Hornby Island

GALIANO LODGE
Galiano Island

Vancouver Island

19

99

QUALICUM COLLEGE INN*
Qualicum Beach

4

Parksville

Vancouver

3

British
Columbia

*CLAYOQUOT LODGE

Tofino

4

Nanaimo

YELLOW
POINT LODGE*
Ladysmith

19

5

CANADIAN
PRINCESS
Ucluelet

Duncan

Bellingham

WILCUMA RESORT*
Cobble Hill

Sidney

SOOKE
HARBOR
HOUSE*
Sooke Harbor

17

Victoria

In Victoria:

THE CAPTAIN'S PALACE*
OAK BAY BEACH HOTEL*
OLDE ENGLAND INN*

*Port
Angeles*

Port Townsend

5

Everett

Olympic Peninsula

101

Seattle

Bremerton

101

Tacoma

Olympia

5

Aberdeen

12

To Portland

VICTORIA

British Columbia, of which Victoria is the provincial capital, joined the Dominion of Canada only in 1871, but a great deal of history is concentrated here: not only the exciting adventures of exploring and settling a new land, but also the inherited traditions brought from the mother country. The result is as English a place as you'll find on this side of the Atlantic, with a strong sense of the frontier.

Downtown Victoria is fairly compact, and though there is a great deal to see, it is probably best to do your initial exploring on foot. Suppose you arrive by ferry at the inner harbor. At once stop to ask the polite, well-informed staff at the Tourist Bureau for maps and guides. Then off you go. To the stately Parliament Buildings, so like London's that you half expect to hear Big Ben. To the venerable Empress Hotel, where, even if you don't stop for tea, a stroll through the splendid lobby is worth the trip. To Beacon Hill Park, containing the world's tallest totem pole, a deer park and a cricket field—a nice melding of the Northwest Indian culture, never far off in this part of the country, and the English tradition.

In the other direction you'll find most of the shops Victoria is famous for. The temptations to take advantage of them will be irresistible, so it's good to have Christmas and birthday lists in mind when you come. There are antiques, woollens, needlepoint, china, tartans, tea, and—representing the indigenous culture—sealskin moccasins, baskets, carvings and Cowichan Indian sweaters. You should visit Bastion Square, a careful restoration of a bit of old Victoria, less crassly commercial than some such projects. You'll find the excellent Maritime Museum here. By now you will have realized why this is called the City of Gardens; even on the busy downtown streets, hanging baskets of lobelia and geraniums delight the eye.

A visit to the Provincial Museum, between Parliament and the Empress, is a must—no matter how many times you may have been

there. The new Indian wing augments the museum's reputation for brilliant design and imaginative display. And don't neglect Thunderbird Park behind the museum; the awe-inspiring totem poles there, together with those inside, make up the finest collection anywhere of this art form unique to coastal tribes of British Columbia and southern Alaska.

Farther afield, by car or bus, you will want to see world-famed Butchart Gardens, a twenty-five-acre fairyland north of the city. Try to go before June or after Labor Day if you want to avoid the crowds.

Getting There: By car and ferry, take Highway 101 to Port Angeles, Washington, then ferry to Victoria; or Highway 5 and Highway 20 to Anacortes, Washington and ferry to Sidney, B.C., then 20 miles or 32 km south on Highway 17 to Victoria; or Highway 17 from Vancouver, B.C. to Tsawwassen, then ferry to Swartz Bay, then 22 miles or 35 km south on Highway 17 to Victoria. The Canadian Pacific ferry, *Princess Marguerite,* runs from Seattle to Victoria every day (summer only). All car ferries also take foot passengers and bicycles. Victoria ferry docks are within walking distances of downtown points of interest and bus tour operators. By air, daily commercial service from Seattle-Tacoma or from Vancouver to Victoria. By bus, Trailways from Seattle or Vancouver. Both Victoria and Vancouver have central listings for bed and breakfast places; call the Victoria Visitors' Bureau, (604) 382-2127, or the Vancouver Visitors' Bureau, (604) 682-2222.

OAK BAY BEACH HOTEL
Victoria

Inns may come and inns may go, but Oak Bay Beach Hotel goes on forever. Despite its name, it meets all criteria for a good country inn. Victoria's only seaside hotel, it is just far enough out of town to make you feel well away from the madding crowd.

The present owner, with due respect for a fifty-year tradition of elegance, has adapted smoothly to the tastes of a more easy-going less-formal clientele. Afternoon high tea is still served in the dignified main lounge or on the veranda, but nowadays one comes just for the pleasure of it, not to be seen by the "best people." Instead of an elaborate Sunday dinner, you now partake of a family smorgasbord buffet. Pomp and circumstance have given way to an emphasis on friendly relaxation.

As the management says, "We must establish a few traditions of our own." One of these is the taking of after-dinner coffee and liqueurs in the lobby, around the fireplace. The lobby is well supplied with groups of big, comfortable upholstered chairs and sofas and small tables for tea or cocktails. Soft light comes from brass table lamps, the six-foot-tall clock ticks gently, and there are always fresh flowers.

Another tradition is a cup of cheer in the cozy Snug, modeled on the lounge of an English pub. Like much of the hotel interior, it repeats the half-timbered theme of the exterior. It has a fireplace, well-polished round tables, and ever so much atmosphere. It also offers good English pub fare such as Scotch eggs, ploughman's lunch, fish and chips.

The dining room offers smorgasbord lunches Sunday through Friday. Dinner specialties include excellent prime ribs and Yorkshire pudding, and lamb from Vancouver Island's own farms.

The Tudor-style hotel was built in 1931, after the original (1928) building burned. It is decorated in good taste throughout, and fine English antiques will greet you at every turn. The dining room, for instance, has two buffets dating from the 1600s. Rooms on the second floor are large and comfortable, and include some suites of two or three rooms. But it is on the third floor that wonders have been wrought. The management has just completely renovated these bedrooms and suites to reflect different periods of English history. They include the Prince Albert Room, the regal King Henry VIII Suite, the Georgian Suite, the Samuel Pepys Room and the Elizabethan Room—twelve in all, lavished with antiques acquired in England.

The scrupulously tended gardens, which run from the terrace to the private beach, are right out of an English novel, and are a panoply of changing colors from spring until fall. There are sea views from the dining room, seventeen of the guest rooms, and of course from the terrace and patio. You'll see passing fishing boats, freighters and yachts, to say nothing of killer whales, seals and ducks. You may even hope for a glimpse of Cadborosaurus, the legendary sea serpent of Cadboro Bay.

OAK BAY BEACH HOTEL, 1175 Beach Drive, Victoria, British Columbia V8S 2N2. Telephone: (604) 598-4556. Accommodations: single, double, queen- and king-size beds; all rooms with private bath with tub/shower, some two-room suites with connecting bath; some rooms with balconies, some with sea view; telephones; television. Rates: moderate to expensive, no meals included; room service available. Open to the public for breakfast, lunch and dinner; full bar service. Children welcome. No pets. Cards: AE, MC, VISA. Open all year.

Oak Bay Beach Hotel

OLDE ENGLAND INN
Victoria

As the name indicates, this inn is a bit of old England transplanted to Victoria. Since Victoria, at the south end of Vancouver Island, is, in itself, the most English city in Canada, the setting is appropriate. Situated in a secluded wooded spot with vistas of the sea and mountains, the inn is within easy reach of town (five minutes by car or taxi, fifteen by bus).

Built as a private mansion for a homesick Yorkshireman, T. H. Slater, by the noted Victoria architect Samuel McClure in 1909, it was acquired in 1946 by the present owner, Mrs. R. Lane, and her late husband, Squadron Leader S. Lane of Yorkshire, England. It opened as an inn in that year and remains a family business today with the assistance of daughter Dorothy and her husband, and son Cyril and his wife. Cyril Lane is now co-owner and manager.

After thirty years of devoted labor and research by the Lanes, the inn is now set in an English village, complete with replicas of Shakespeare's birthplace and Anne Hathaway's cottage. There is also a conglomerate of small shops known as Chaucer Lane where reproductions of Harvard House, Garrick Inn and the Olde Curiosity Shop jostle purveyors of genuine English toffee, fine bone china and postcards.

Clearly, this is no place to come unless you are completely enamored of everything English. But if you are not put off by the tourist-attraction atmosphere and the crowds, you may find the Olde England Inn rather fun. You will certainly find it plush and convenient.

You have your choice of rooms in the main inn or behind the facade of the English Village. All rooms have private baths and television; many have canopied and four-poster beds. The intricately carved oak four-poster with a heavy silk canopy in the Elizabethan Room dates from the reign of the first Elizabeth. The King Edward VII Room is in Louis Quatorze style and has a graceful bed draped with purple velvet and the gold-gilt canopy from the bed where Edward VII slept in Warwick Castle. Gilt clocks, gleaming wall sconces and fine china vases and bowls add to the elegance. Fortunately, the management has equipped all the antique beds with modern mattresses. Seven rooms have fireplaces and one has a balcony.

Meals served in the antique-laden dining room include such items as roast baron of beef, Prince Philip's kidney "pyes" and a "real English sherry trifle."

Olde England Inn

The inn is open all year, as are the village and other attractions. There are daily guided tours of Anne Hathaway's Thatched Cottage and Gardens. An Anglophile could easily spend a day immersed in the almost overpowering English atmosphere found here. The inn is a museum in itself, with an outstanding collection of lovingly gathered antiques.

OLDE ENGLAND INN, 429 Lampson Street, Victoria, British Columbia V9A 5Y9. Telephone: (604) 388-4353. Accommodations: double, single and twin single beds, many canopied; private baths with tub, shower or tub and shower; no telephones; television. Rates: moderate to expensive, no meals included. Open to the public for breakfast, lunch, tea and dinner; full bar service. Children welcome (babysitters available). Pets allowed. Cards: AE, DC, VISA. Open all year.

THE CAPTAIN'S PALACE
Victoria

Where but in Victoria, that bastion of Empire, could you find a beautifully preserved nineteenth-century mansion billing itself as "the world's smallest hotel"? And where but the Captain's Palace could you wine, dine and sleep in the heart of downtown Victoria, surrounded by the elegance of antique furniture and rugs, stained glass, frescoes, tapestries and carved paneling?

The Captain's Palace has stood on Belleville Street since 1897, looking out on the ships in the inner harbor as sails gave way to steam and diesel. The lovely *Princess Marguerite* ferry (Seattle-Victoria run) regularly slips up to her dock practically at the Palace's front door.

The building was erected for a noted early British Columbia industrialist, W. J. Pendray, who came to the area seeking gold. He made, lost, and made again a couple of fortunes. He built what still looks like a gentleman's spacious but restrained nineteenth-century London town house in a quiet Mayfair close, with a quaint pepper-shaker tower and wide verandas. The delightful topiaries in the gardens (tidily pruned birds and animals) still charm children and passing tourists.

When the Pendrays left the mansion, it was taken over by the Sisters of Our Lady of the Angels, who ran it as a girls' boarding home. Shortly after the nuns departed in 1966 it was bought by Florence and Bill Prior, who opened an elegant eatery in the house in 1970. Mrs.

The Captain's Palace

Prior, who has carried on since her husband's death, still presides over the inn with charm and efficiency.

The restaurant soon became famous, with seven intimate candlelit dining rooms seating a total of 150. The staff wears period clothes, and one of the dining rooms, the Library, is equipped with that Victorian fancy, a hidden door camouflaged by paneling and shelves. The menu specializes in seafood. For dessert it's hard to resist the Palace's secret-formula Venetian Cream, a confection of creams, brandy and liqueurs. Top your evening with a "Tree Climber," a mélange of spirits whipped into a snowy confection and served in a huge cut-glass cranberry-rimmed champagne goblet.

When the Priors took over the mansion they brought with them their own collection of priceless Old World antiques that they had been acquiring for twenty years; the result is a fascinating museum wherever you look. Walls and ceilings are richly carved, mostly in polished oak and mahogany paneling, with some wall areas covered in brocade. Mirrors are throughout: gold-framed round convex mirrors, mirror paneling, and mirrors in baroque antique frames. Rooms are lit by chandeliers and candles, the light reflected in fine cut glass, silver and brass. Marine themes dominate the numerous paintings. Many windows are stained glass, framed in heavily valanced, looped and tasseled velvet or brocade drapes. Small sculptures surprise and charm the eye. Clocks abound, tinkling, chiming and booming the hours.

Overnight guests reach the second floor by curved and carpeted stairs. Each of the two suites has a sitting room separated from the bedroom by a tiny serving foyer where a bottle from the Palace's wine cellar awaits. The Priors restored the unusual hand-painted frescoes on the walls and high curved ceilings. It took months of painstaking work, delicately scraping off layers of paint and paper with razor blades, until the seventy-five-year-old originals emerged. Now the rooms, decorated with both frescoes and framed pictures, resemble a Victorian art gallery.

Some of the ornate furniture is heavy, such as the big, solid, carved oak double bed and a great matching chest of drawers with a wide beveled mirror. Some is delicate, such as the slender, curved-back settees and needlepoint-covered chairs. Each unit has its own little balcony overlooking the gardens and the harbor. The double beds are deep and comfortable, with lavishly flowered linens matching the spreads and curtains; carpets are thick and soothing, and each suite has a modern tiled bathroom with tub, shower and, bless Mrs. Prior, excellent lighting.

Breakfast is served downstairs in a cheerful yellow and white glass-enclosed veranda.

THE CAPTAIN'S PALACE, 309 Belleville Street, Victoria, British Columbia V8V 1X2. Telephone: (604) 388-9191. Accommodations: two two-room suites with double beds; private baths with tub and shower; no telephones; no television. Rates: expensive, breakfast included. Open to the public for breakfast, lunch, afternoon tea and dinner; full bar service. Children welcome. No pets. Cards: AE, MC, VISA. Open all year.

SOOKE HARBOUR HOUSE
Sooke, British Columbia

This tiny seaside inn twenty-three miles southwest of Victoria has for some years been one of the area's best-kept secrets. But under new owners Sinclair and Fredrica Philip, the word is getting around that here is a place worth a journey—for adventurous cuisine, excellent accommodations and a refreshing approach to innkeeping.

The neat white house with black trim looks like some country-loving old-timer's private home. But it was built as an inn in the early thirties by a Dutch gentleman-farmer called Kohout. Subsequently it sheltered students of the Lavertu Conservatory of Music—members of the Lavertu family still come to visit the restaurant. The Philip era began when this young couple came back to the west in 1979, looking for a business to buy. Fredrica is French and Sinclair, a Canadian, had lived in France for twelve years during which time he acquired a Ph.D. in economics, and a good knowledge of wine. When they chanced on Sooke Harbour House and discovered it was for sale, everything fell miraculously in place.

Today, after the usual crises and trials that seem to befall all new owners of old inns (painting, plumbing, wiring, reroofing, etc.), they are embarking on the construction of two new terraces, one at sea level and one next to the dining room. And they are adding a second-story suite, with two rooms, a private bath and a large sundeck. That will bring the total number of sleeping units to five, which Sinclair thinks is a good place to stop.

The inn is on a low headland overlooking Sooke Harbour and Whiffen Spit. To the south is the Strait of Juan de Fuca, with Washington's Olympic Mountains stretching across the horizon. The front yard is unassuming, except for a huge maple tree that the Philips have just had declared a Provincial Heritage Tree. Now it can't be cut down, no matter who owns the property.

The glass-paned front door opens directly onto the dining room, the focal point of Sooke Harbour House's fame. A small auxiliary dining room is to the right.

There is no lounge or lobby, but the fireplace side of the dining room serves as such. This area may be used as a cocktail and conversation corner, reading room or after-dinner sitting and sipping room.

The whole first floor, including the restrooms and dining rooms, has been adapted for wheelchair access. The Philips have just added a smaller dining room beyond the main room, paneled with pine planking and offering the best view in the house. All tables are inviting, with candles, delicate dried-flower arrangements (by Fredrica), coral napkins and graceful stemware. This room is also a gallery of artifacts and works of art. The Philips have a whole basement full of things to show off, from their own and their parents' years of collecting, and plan to change the "gallery" frequently.

The food is superb. The inn prides itself, with justification, on the freshness and variety of its fish and local produce. Chef Joseph Sanladerer trained under French chefs and has worked on several continents. The menu may include poached salmon with sorrel sauce; rabbit with Dijon mustard sauce; vegetable crêpes with zucchini, mushrooms, chives and some mystery ingredients (probably herbs from the inn garden). His desserts are irresistible: walnut torte, chocolate mousse, South Sea sherbet with Demerara rum. All fruit sherbets are made on the premises. Dining is taken seriously here, and the waitresses, who are multilingual, are glad to discuss your choice of food and wine with you. The menu, like the decor, is changed every few months. Once a week or so, there is likely to be a musical evening, with guitar or piano or violin or even a bit of drama.

Bedrooms are up a narrow stairway, along a passage, down more steps, around a corner—as in many an English country inn. The rooms are in that tradition too: simply furnished, flowers on the dresser, everything tidy, birds singing in the trees just outside the window. The community bath is down the hall. Breakfast will be served in your room if you leave your order on your doorknob before retiring.

The Philips can suggest excursions to explore this out-of-the-way corner of Vancouver Island. Nearest would be a walk to the end of Whiffen Spit, a mile-long finger of sand and rock that zigzags its way almost across the bay, with a lighthouse as goal and seals and otters and perhaps whales to observe en route. Toward the end it broadens, and there are wind-bent firs and grassy areas level enough for a picnic. A more ambitious excursion would be to the end of the road at Port Renfrew, start of the notoriously difficult West Coast Life Saving Trail.

Botany Bay, near Port Renfrew, is fascinating for the variety of its sea life in a unique geologic formation of rocks and pools that is exposed at low tide. Surfing at River Jordan is world famous, thanks to the huge rollers that come speeding down the strait to crash ashore here. Summertime swimming in the "potholes" of the Sooke River is popular, especially for families with children. A park there offers fishing and picnicking.

SOOKE HARBOUR HOUSE, 1528 Whiffen Spit Road, Sooke, British Columbia V0S IN0. Telephone: (604) 642-3421. Accommodations: double and queen-size beds; one suite with private bath with tub/shower; community baths with tub/shower; no telephones; no television. Rates: inexpensive to moderate, no meals included. Meal service: breakfast, lunch and dinner; full bar service. Children welcome. Pets allowed. Credit cards: AE, MC, VISA. Open all year, subject to brief annual closures.

Getting There: From Victoria, follow Highway 14 (Sooke Road) 23 miles to Sooke; one mile or 1.6 km beyond village look for Whiffen Spit Road on left, follow it to inn.

WILCUMA RESORT
Cobble Hill

Wilcuma (which, the convenient legend has it, is Indian for "You'll like it here") is one of those resorts that Canada does so well: unpretentious, civilized yet easygoing, with service that is so good you hardly notice it. Alas, it would not be possible to duplicate such a lodge today—only the gentle passage of years can produce this ambience of assured charm.

Wilcuma was built in 1902 as a country estate for a seagoing Englishman, one Captain Lanes, and remained a private home until it was converted to an inn in the 1930s.

It's at the end of a winding country road that departs from Vancouver Island's Highway 1 south of Duncan. Just when it seems the road is going over the bank and into the bay, there's Wilcuma Resort. The cottages on the hillside that you have passed are part of it, and the centerpiece is the Tudor-style lodge itself. It is two stories, combining wood shingles and half-timbering with neat white trim. It's set among tall trees: cedars, dogwood, firs, maples and arbutus (the last known in the United States as madrones or madronas). Above and below the lodge sloping lawns are dotted with shrubbery, English flower beds and

249

deck chairs for sea watchers. Their watch may reward them with glimpses of bobbing ducks, flotillas of swans looking warily for a handout, otters, killer whales, freighters en route to the log port at the head of Cowichan Bay, and Cowichan Indians practicing and racing in their canoes.

There is lodging in the main house and in cottages. A few cottages that had been lodging for the staff became the first guest houses, and others were added to make today's total of ten. They are all housekeeping, with private baths, and range from one to three rooms.

Three cottages are right on the beach. Some have fireplaces, some Franklin stoves. There's also electric heat. Furnishings are comfortable but not quaint. Because of the wide spacing and surrounding trees, there's ample privacy.

In the lodge itself, Barbara and Ralph Wiesner, who own and run the lodge today, have preserved the original country-house atmosphere. There are three pleasantly proportioned upstairs rooms with views, fireplaces and private baths. Some furnishings are antiques. Commodious easy chairs, soft carpeting underfoot and a fire in the grate make your room a snug retreat if weather or ennui keeps you indoors.

The lobby is tastefully and comfortably furnished. Here you may sit by the fire, play backgammon, sip a drink or converse (or all four). Or you may step down the hall to another lounge area: the Nook and Granny. Here there are well-filled bookshelves and the same pervading sense of peace and ease.

The dining room is small and elegant and has windows on three sides. The menu often features local seafoods. For overflow, or for private parties, there is another room beyond the lounge, especially pleasant in summer when all the windows are opened.

Outside, there is a heated pool, but the brave (especially European visitors) go right into the chilly bay and survive. Fishing can be most rewarding, and Ralph Wiesner will rent you a boat and engage a guide. The world's record coho is said to have been caught here. Salmon fishing draws many people, so do cod and sea bass. Crab may be caught from Wilcuma's private wharf. Ashore, there are golf and tennis. Cowichan Bay's grass tennis court is said to be older than Wimbledon. Court connoisseurs from far and near have standing reservations to come annually to Wilcuma for this alone.

WILCUMA RESORT, R.R. 3, Cobble Hill, British Columbia V0R 1L0. Telephone: (604) 748-8737. Accommodations: double and twin beds; private baths with tub or shower; no telephones; television in some rooms and some cottages. Rates: moderate, no meals included. Open to the public for breakfast, lunch and dinner April through Labor Day; dinner only on weekends in winter; full bar service. Children welcome. Pets in cottages only. Cards: AE, Chargex, VISA. Open all year.

Getting There: Take Highway 1 (Island Highway) north from Victoria, watch for Wilcuma Bay signs near Cowichan Bay, and take either Cowichan Bay Road or Old Koksilah Road; watch for more signs leading you to Lanes Road and the resort.

GALIANO LODGE
Galiano Island

Canada's Gulf Islands share with their neighbors south of the invisible border, the San Juans, a sunny clime, the charm of being a bit hard to get to, and the enticement of hidden inns and restaurants.

Galiano Lodge on Galiano Island, one of the five major Gulf Islands, is not exactly hidden, being visible from the ferry as you glide into Sturdies Bay. Then it's a two-minute walk to the lodge. But it could serve as a cozy base for further exploration of the secrets of this long, green, cliff-girt island.

Galiano's history goes back to its sighting in 1792 by a Spaniard, Captain Dionisio Alcala Galiano. Yet more than a century after its settlement, the island still seems rural and remote, though it is less than an hour by ferry from the mainland. Sailors and seafarers have known it best and have sheltered in its marinas and coves. One of the pleasure-boat people's favorite havens is Galiano Lodge, with its moorage for two dozen vessels.

The lodge, built after the old one burned in 1952, is an inviting low white building with a neat lawn stretching down to the shore. Meals are served in the lodge dining rooms. There is also a comfortable lounge and bar, complete with fireplace and player piano. Except for four rooms in the main building, accommodations are in three separate one-story annexes. The lodge itself takes pride in its antique charm (with furnishings to match), but the sleeping units are less quaint. They are attached, as in a motel, and have fine views of the gardens, lawns and bay.

The lodge has gone through several ownerships in the past few years. Werner Aellen, who bought it in 1981, plans to keep the flavor but quadruple the accommodations by 1982.

The lodge's reputation for good food and good company appears secure under this new management. And fortunately, it has one asset that few inns can boast: It is possible to come without a car and still taste the charms of this lovely island. That's a persuasive fact for visitors who have experienced summertime and holiday weekend ferry lines. Two notable view points are within easy walking distance of the lodge. Bellhouse Park, somewhat developed but not too much, has benches and picnic areas and superb views of the eastern approach to Active Pass.

Another good destination is Bluff Park, which may be reached in about an hour by a walk along rural roads (fringed with Himalaya black-berry bushes, fruit ripe for the plucking in season), and up through some of the tall timber that still clothes most of the island. For more extensive exploring guests may bring their bicycles on the ferry, or rent bikes at the lodge, or take advantage of the Galiano limousine, which may be engaged for touring the island. There are tennis and swimming at the lodge.

GALIANO LODGE, Box 187, Galiano Island, British Columbia V09 1P0. Telephone: (604) 539-2233 or 539-2315. Accommodations: four rooms in lodge with single beds, private baths with tub and shower; twelve rooms in annexes with double and single beds, private baths with tub and shower; no telephones; no television. Rates: moderate, no meals included. Open to the public for breakfast, lunch and dinner; picnic lunches available; full bar service. Children welcome. Pets welcome. Cards: AE, MC, VISA. Open all year.

Getting There: By car or on foot, take B.C. ferry from Tsawwassen on the mainland to Sturdies Bay, walk to lodge or drive (300 yards); or take B.C. ferry from Swartz Bay, Vancouver Island, to Montague Harbour, where by arrangement a lodge car will meet you. By boat or air: moorage available at the lodge ramp; reserve ahead.

YELLOW POINT LODGE
Ladysmith

What an ideal location for a resort, thought M. G. (Gerry) Hill when he first saw Yellow Point, back before World War I. This rocky point juts out into the Strait of Georgia, about seventy-five miles north of Victoria on Vancouver Island's east coast. Mr. Hill built a small lodge and cookhouse, then added cottages along the beach, and eventually opened the present, larger lodge in 1939. Today he runs the inn along with his son Richard and manager-partner Ron Friend.

Yellow Point Lodge is made of native logs and surrounded by nature that has been only slightly modified by man. One can easily imagine arriving in a 1929 Pierce-Arrow touring car to enjoy a vacation in this serene, secluded setting. And a vacation or weekend here is still a chance to experience an otherwise vanished style of life. Here guests are encouraged to be self-motivated in their choice of recreation. And they like it. About 80 percent of the clientele are repeat guests of many years' standing, who often reserve their accommodations a year or more in advance. One woman, now 81, has been coming from Wichita every year since the inn opened.

Yellow Point is set in 180 acres of private parkland with a network of trails through the forest and more than a mile of waterfront with secluded coves and beaches. It sits on a massive outcrop of bedrock, leveled and smoothed by ancient glaciers to form naturally sculpted patios. There's easy access to the two-hundred-foot saltwater swimming pool, carved by nature out of the rock, and to the nearby open-air beach sauna and hot tub. From almost everywhere there is a magnificent panoramic view of sea, sky and shore line, backed by fir-clad hills and mountains.

The main lounge of the lodge is as relaxed as your own living room, with a piano, a Ping-Pong table, writing desks, games and cards. Morning coffee and afternoon tea are served here. The room's focal point is a huge stone fireplace. A couple of tree trunks poke up through the floor—Gerry simply built the room around them. They look perfectly at home.

The nine lodge rooms, most with private baths, are tucked into the corners and under the eaves, adapting to the shape of the inn with its two peaked-roof wings. Room 5, for instance, has a tiny bath fitted in a niche in the corner, and an outdoor balcony that looks through a giant oak tree toward the rock-bound pool. Most rooms are rather small and simply but comfortably furnished with sturdy, old-fashioned chests and bedsteads.

Besides lodge accommodations there are some two dozen cottages and cabins scattered through the woods and along the shore. Biggest are the Parsonage and Three Oaks, which are like family homes.

Then there are several smaller cottages with private baths, and some small cabins for two, actually sleeping rooms, with wood stoves and without private bath. From most of these it's about a hundred feet along the trail to the community shower in the trees.

Dining is informal, at long tables. Breakfast is self-service on the sun porch in summer and is served in the dining room in winter. Old-timers are glad that chef Millie Hogg has returned, after a few years off—with her dry Scottish humor and her genius at the cookstove intact. Meals are hearty and home style. Guests may bring their own liquor.

Besides swimming, fishing, beachcombing, and walking, there are jogging trails and tennis, badminton and volleyball courts hidden among the trees. The lodge also provides canoes, rowboats and sailboats. You may have driftwood fires, oyster feasts and clambakes on the beach. Impromptu parties often take place in the lodge, which has a sprung floor for dancing.

Reservations should be made well in advance, and in July and August preference is given to bookings of a week or more.

YELLOW POINT LODGE, R.R. 1, Ladysmith, British Columbia V0R 2E0. Telephone: (604) 245-7422. Accommodations: twin and double beds; most lodge rooms have private baths with tub or shower, those without baths have washbasins, cottages have private baths with shower, cabins and barracks have community showers; no telephones; no television. Rates: inexpensive, all meals included. Meal Service: breakfast, lunch and dinner, for guests only. No children under 16. No pets. No credit cards. Open all year.

Getting There: By car, car ferry from Port Angeles or Seattle, Washington, to Victoria, British Columbia, then north on 1 to Ladysmith; look for right turn with sign to Yellow Point. Or, car ferry from Horseshoe Bay, British Columbia, to Nanaimo, south on Island Highway 3 miles or 4.5 km, turn left to Cedar and Yellow Point Road. By air, flights may be chartered from the Bayshore Inn in Vancouver to floats directly in front of lodge (summer only).

QUALICUM COLLEGE INN
Qualicum Beach

An exclusive boys' boarding school might seem an unlikely spot for an inn. But there it is, on the shores of Qualicum Bay: the Qualicum College Inn, a school from 1935 until 1970 and an inn ever since.

The owners have carefully kept most of the flavor of the boys' school. You see it everywhere: the Old Boys' Dining Room is the main restaurant; the Prefects' Lounge serves cocktails; the Headmasters' Lounge and the Masters' Common Room serve as banquet and convention facilities.

The original building housing forty students now accommodates only twenty guests, so the rooms are much more commodious. A new

254

Qualicum College Inn

annex has thirty additional rooms. A similar wing is planned for the other side of the main building, with twenty-five more rooms. All rooms have a private bath, and every room has a splendid view of either mountain or forest or sea. In both main inn and annex, rooms' decor combines comfortable modern beds and thick wall-to-wall carpeting with English inn-style furnishings: reproductions of substantial dark dressers and chests, cushioned window seats. Two of the rooms have fireplaces; one choice large room has a balcony.

The inn is approached by a drive that deposits the guest at massive oak doors. On the other side the view is of a grassy field, a charming little gazebo and a square squat structure that houses the swimming pool. At the right a trail down the bluff leads to a sandy beach and the broad expanse of the Strait of Georgia.

Qualicum College Inn offers some irresistible package vacations. Nearby are hiking, fishing, swimming and golfing. Just a few miles down the road, Highway 4 takes off for the island's west coast. The inn makes a good staging point for a trip to Ucluelet, Long Beach and Tofino (see entries for Canadian Princess and Clayoquot Lodge). For day trips from the inn, the kitchens will pack a wicker basket for two loaded with fine picnic fare and a bottle of wine.

QUALICUM COLLEGE INN, Box 99, Qualicum Beach, British Columbia V0R 2T0. Telephone: (604) 752-9262. Accommodations: twin, double and queen-size beds; private baths with tub and shower; telephones; no television. Rates: moderate, no meals included. Open to the public for breakfast, lunch and dinner; full bar service. Children welcome. Pets allowed. Cards: AE, VISA. Open all year except for a ten-day closing in January.

Getting There: By car, B.C. car ferry from Horseshoe Bay on mainland British Columbia to Nanaimo, then 29 miles or 46 km north on 19; or 92 miles or 148 km from Victoria on 1 and 19.

SEA BREEZE LODGE
Hornby Island

Hornby Island, a four-mile-square dot of land off the east coast of Vancouver Island, is an astonishing mixture of old-fashioned homely charm, natural beauty and prehistoric riches. Placid hedgerowed farmlands slumber cheek by jowl with beaches, Indian petroglyphs and towering Douglas firs.

Sea Breeze Lodge, on the north shore of the island, was built in 1930 as a farmhouse, just one of the handful of comfortable homesteads that housed the population of the little island, but blessed with an enviable site: a panoramic view of water and woods, private sandstone and pebbly beaches, and tide pools down the bluff, where the sea is surprisingly warm.

The island has only a couple of commercial establishments, a restaurant near the ferry dock and the co-op grocery with its one gas pump. Like all Hornby, Sea Breeze is very much a family place. Taking the children there is like treating them to an old-fashioned stay on a country farm, and they love it.

Sea Breeze remained a farmhouse until 1940 when it was opened to the public, with the addition of cabins. In 1972 it was bought by Brian and Gail Bishop, who have added other amenities for guests' comfort. But never, they say, will there be television, phones, noise, discos, bright lights. The one-story, dark-stained lodge still looks like an unpretentious private residence, and the family-style meals add to the friendly informality.

The Bishops cling to the old idea of innkeeping. All meals are included in the rates and are served family-style in the main lodge's dining room. Menus combine farm style with sophistication: from hearty beef stew and Gail's fresh-baked bread and apple cobbler to imaginative smorgasbord spreads. Local seafood is offered: barbecued salmon, butter clams, scallops and occasionally abalone. The oysters are superb. Salads come fresh from the Bishops' garden. Lunches are served on the patio. Non-residents are welcome for dinner, but should reserve at least a day ahead.

The eight rustic cottages can accommodate up to thirty-five persons. They're set rather haphazardly and quite far apart on the meadows around the lodge, and all have splendid views. Like the lodge, they don't pretend to be anything they're not: Little more than sleeping rooms, they are well maintained and the beds are good. Private baths with showers have been added to eight of the cottages; the remaining three still share a bath. Cottages with baths are available as housekeeping cottages in off-season.

Guests can choose from a variety of peaceful activities, such as a bonfire on the beach, or a game of tennis on the grass. Walks on the beach turn up fossils, Indian petroglyphs, odd rocks, an incredible array of marine life and perhaps a glimpse of a wary mink. Walks inland are an adventure in flora and fauna and a delight for birdwatchers. There's a pony for the children to ride; there are Ping-Pong and boating, and swimming in the warm waters of a provincial beach a couple of miles away. Fishing is excellent here (spring salmon, and coho in the summer) and the Bishops' sons are available to guide guests to choice fishing waters.

Reservations should be made well in advance, since many regular guests book a year ahead, especially for July and August.

SEA BREEZE LODGE, Hornby Island, British Columbia V04 1Z0. Telephone: (604) 335-2321. Accommodations: twin and double beds; private baths with shower, community bath with showers; no telephones; no television. Rates: inexpensive, all meals included. Meal service: breakfast, lunch and dinner; full bar service. Children welcome. Pets tolerated. No credit cards. Open April 15 to September 15 (except for housekeeping cottages, which may be rented off season).

Getting There: By car, car ferry from Horseshoe Bay to Nanaimo, then north on 19, 53 miles or 85 km to Buckley Bay (which is 13 miles or 21 km south of Courtenay). Car ferry to Denman Island, drive across Denman and take car ferry to Hornby Island. Ferry schedules are synchronized to make this work, but do vary according to season and day of the week, so ask for schedules.

PAINTER'S LODGE
Campbell River

Discovery Passage, near the mouth of the Campbell River on the east coast of Vancouver Island, is one of the world's best salmon-fishing areas, as E. P. Painter knew when he came here in the 1920s. He launched a successful business of building rowboats and renting them to fishermen. Soon he built cabins to house his customers. Next came a dining room and, in 1938, the big lodge that still stands.

Mrs. Painter continues to live nearby, but Mr. Painter has died and the lodge is now owned by T.A.T. Properties, which also owns the Campbell River Lodge, across the river and closer to town.

In the last fifty years the lodge's guest roster has been studded with such names as Bob Hope, Joe E. Brown, Vincent Price, Irene Dunne, former Prime Minister Diefenbaker and John Wayne. Some celebrities and many less noteworthy guests have caught fish respectable enough (thirty pounds or over) to warrant a photograph for display in the lodge.

There are several reasons to stay here even if one is not in search of fish. For one thing, it's midway on the main and only road that runs the length of Vancouver Island, from Victoria to Port Hardy. It's also a way point for Strathcona Provincial Park to the west and Quadra Island to the east, a short ferry ride away.

The lodge, much like an old-fashioned hotel, is comfortable and without any concessions to modern mass-produced tastes. (There is, however, an occasional strain of piped music in the public rooms.) The bedrooms are on the upper two floors: quiet, not commodious but with all the necessities, furnished pretty much the way they must have been for years. (Test your mattress.) All rooms have private baths. Many have views of the water. Otherwise the prospect is of the lodge's nicely landscaped lawns and gardens, and the swimming pool.

The twenty-two cabins are rustic and far from elegant, and most are showing their age. They come in various sizes; four are housekeeping. The Chalet, with three bedrooms, bath, dining room and living room with fireplace, can shelter six persons.

Seafood is prominent on the dining room menu. Recently enlarged, this room has not lost its old-time charm and one can hardly tell where the new wood-paneled walls start and the old ones leave off.

Next to the dining room is a lounge-bar with big puffy chintz-covered chairs and sofas. Your companion here is a moose head over the fireplace. There's also a pub-style lounge downstairs, the Sandbar.

The lodge has boats, motors and tackle and can provide guides. In April and May, there is steelhead and trout fishing in fresh water, blueback and spring salmon in the ocean; in summer, saltwater salmon fishing is at its peak, with Tyee salmon runs until September, coho August to October; in winter, there is steelhead fishing in the rivers.

PAINTER'S LODGE, Box 460, Campbell River, British Columbia V9W 5C1. Telephone: (604) 286-6201. Accommodations: single, double and queen-size beds; all private baths with tub and shower in lodge, shower in cabins; telephones; television in lobby. Rates: moderate, no meals included. Open to the public for breakfast, lunch and dinner; lunches packed for boats; full bar service. Children welcome. No pets. Credit cards: AE, MC, VISA. Open all year.

Getting There: By car, 165 miles (266 km) from Victoria on Highway 1 to Campbell River. Drive north through town and across bridge; look for lodge sign on right. Or take B.C. ferry from Powell River on mainland to Courtenay; drive north on 1 to Campbell River (29 miles or 47 km from Courtenay). By bus, Vancouver Coach Lines from Victoria. By air, Pacific Western Air from Vancouver.

APRIL POINT LODGE
Quadra Island

The inn at April Point is a vigorously surviving example of the hospitable Northwest fishing lodge.

Its story began when Phil Peterson, who was with McGraw-Hill in San Francisco, used to come to Vancouver Island with his family for fishing vacations in the forties. They would stay in Campbell River but fish off Quadra Island, directly across Discovery Passage. They fell in love with April Point, a promontory just north of the ferry landing at Quathiaski Cove. The intricate tidal currents off the point have always attracted salmon and in turn salmon fishermen. And the woodsy peninsula, with its cove and tiny satellite island, attracted the Petersons as much as the fish did. So they bought it, or two hundred acres of it.

There were a few cabins and boathouses along the shore that had been built by reclusive fishermen and other shunners of civilization. From that small start grew April Point Lodge: first a dining room, then a swimming pool, then in 1948 the main lodge. That year the Petersons moved here permanently.

The Enterprise has been growing and changing ever since; in fact it gives the impression of being in a chronic state of transition. For example, the long deck along the front of the lodge was recently converted into a beautiful cedar-and-glass dining room. A year or so later, they got around to putting on the last bits of siding at the corner of the addition. This is very much a family-run operation, and the approach to maintenance is something like that of the homeowner who does as much as he can as he can get at it.

Since Phil Peterson's death eight years ago, his wife Phyllis has continued as guiding spirit in the kitchen. She is deservedly famous for her pastries, breads and sticky buns. Three of the younger Petersons are in partnership with her as owners-managers: Eric, Warren and Joy.

New accommodations to replace the long-gone original cabins have been added steadily, getting grander as the years go by. Now the lodge can put up one hundred guests. Their choices include housekeeping cottages back in the trees; five guest houses by the water with kitchenettes and a common deck; a pair of two-bedroom boathouse suites with big living rooms; ultradeluxe guest lodges; two lodge suites with kitchens, sundecks, two bedrooms and huge living rooms, one with a grand piano; four pool annex rooms; and five sleeping rooms in the lodge. All accommodations have private baths, and most have fireplaces.

The dining room is elegant. Entertainment is guaranteed, what with all the activity in Discovery Passage. There is no dinner menu. The waitress announces the two or three entrée choices (for example, Dungeness crab, Porterhouse steak, rack of lamb) and except for dessert, there are no more decisions to make. All is laid on in high style, with prices to match. This is no place for the faint of wallet.

The extremely pleasant little bar-lounge off the dining room is still as it was before the latest additions, and is a cozy retreat for cocktails, reading, and sipping port by the fire.

Coddled in such luxury, why should any one leave to go fishing? But that, after all, is April Point's forte. Guides, fuel, tackle and boats (all Boston whalers) are available. Minimum boat rental is four hours. The high season for salmon is June into September, but fishermen also go for perch and cod. Wilderness trips in search of steelhead and trout may be arranged.

Guests are encouraged to bring their own boats. There is moorage at the lodge, and more is being added at the nearby cannery, part of the far-flung April Point enterprise. This also incorporates three miles of waterfront, Phyllis Island just offshore (named for Mrs. Peterson), and two hundred acres of largely undeveloped woodland, with hiking trails. Between or instead of fishing forays, there's all the island to explore—or at least all that can be reached by trail, water or secondary (and some tertiary) roads. On the east side of Quadra is Heriot Bay, terminus for the little ferry to Cortes Island and home of the 65-year-old Heriot Bay Inn, beloved by islanders.

APRIL POINT LODGE, P.O. Box 1, Campbell River, British Columbia V9W 4Z9. Telephone: (604) 285-3329. Accommodations: twin, double and queen-size beds; private baths with shower or tub/shower; no telephones; no television. Rates: inexpensive to expensive, no meals included. Meal Service: breakfast, lunch and dinner; full bar service. Children welcome; children under 12 free. Pets welcome. Cards: AE, MC, VISA. Open April 15–October 15; groups up to 20 accommodated off-season.

Getting There: By car, drive north from Victoria on Highway 1 to Campbell River (165 miles or 266 km), take ferry to Quadra Island; the lodge is five minutes away via Pidcock Road. By air, charter flights to Campbell River or April Point from Seattle (two hours) or Vancouver (one hour); or Pacific Western Air from Vancouver to Campbell River, arrange with lodge for pickup. Moorage for private boats available.

CANADIAN PRINCESS
Ucluelet

This fine 235-foot vessel provides nearly all the pleasures of a sea voyage with no danger of mal-de-mer, shipwreck or collision with an iceberg. It's permanently moored off the town of Ucluelet, on Vancouver Island's west coast. It may seem strange to classify a ship as a country inn, but the *Canadian Princess* meets all the qualifications: comfort, personal attention, good food, a pleasant location and an interesting past.

Its story began in 1932, when the *C.S.S. William J. Stewart* was launched at the Collingwood Shipyards in Ontario. For nearly half a century the *Stewart* did yeoman duty as a hydrographic survey ship in British Columbia. Every summer she transported a crew of five dozen or so on survey trips along the seventeen-thousand-mile coastline with its myriad twists and turns and uncounted islands. In 1944 the ship was damaged seriously and had to be beached. But after repairs in Victoria she went back for thirty-one more years of surveying and charting.

The *Stewart* was retired in 1975 and mothballed. After a couple of years, the still-seaworthy vessel was purchased by Bob Wright, owner of Oak Bay Marina in Victoria. He recognized a good ship when he saw one, and resolved to give her a new lease on life, as a floating hotel—or a stationary cruise ship. The remodeling was really more of a restoration. Cabins have double-decker single berths (though a few have double beds); compact, well-organized storage; and washbowls.

The cocktail lounge on the Promenade Deck is called the Chart Room because that's what it used to be: the area below the bridge where surveyors would spread out their big charts. It's now the ship's snug and hospitable lounge, with a portrait of the great man himself on the wall. (Stewart was a longtime head of the Hydrographic Service.)

One level down on the main deck is the former crew dining room, now enlarged by incorporation of a couple of staterooms and called the William J. Stewart Room. The menu features the freshest of seafoods, with salmon the star. Oysters in casserole, grilled cod with Parmesan cheese, and broiled salmon with dill sauce are among the specialties. The *Canadian Princess* welcomes mealtime guests who are not staying on board, but reservations are advised.

While on the ship, see if you can wangle a tour of the engine room, all agleam with brass, polished woodwork and fresh paint. The steam engines look ready to spring into service at the captain's command—which indeed they are. "If the channel were dredged, we could go out to sea tomorrow," says First Officer Rick Crosby.

262

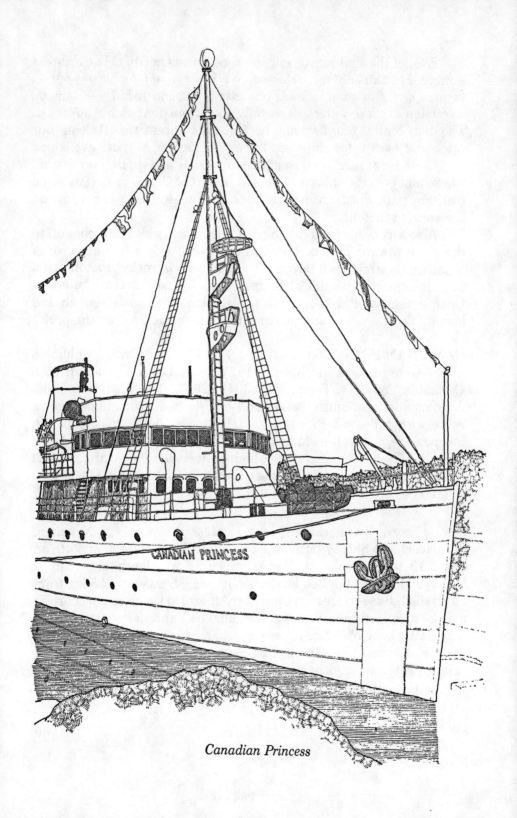

Canadian Princess

Even if the ship remains in one spot, guests needn't. The *Princess* is mother to a fleet of forty-three-foot cruisers that take parties out on various kinds of excursions. Foremost is salmon fishing—a famous attraction of these waters, especially good from June through August. The daily limit is four fish, and back at the *Princess,* they'll clean your catch and pack it for shipment home. Tackle and bait are available.

Or, there are cruises through the Broken Islands in Barkley Sound. These ninety-eight untamed islets form part of Canada's first national maritime park, Pacific Rim Park. Special whale-watching cruises are on the spring schedule.

Also accessible from the ship is Long Beach, which stretches off to the north toward Tofino. This is a relatively people-free expanse of broad sandy stretches interrupted occasionally by rocky promontories. Late, lamented Wickaninnish Lodge overlooks one of the rock outcrops. Once a remote and hospitable private inn, it's now a remote and hospitable restaurant and interpretive center operated by the park.

CANADIAN PRINCESS, P.O. Box 939, Ucluelet, British Columbia V0R 3A0 or c/o Oak Bay Marina, 1327 Beach Drive, Victoria, British Columbia V86 2N4. Telephone: (604) 726-7771 or (604) 598-3366. Accommodations: single berths and double beds; community baths, some with tubs and showers; no telephones; no television. Rates: inexpensive, no meals included. Open to the public for breakfast, lunch and dinner; full bar service. Children welcome; special rates for children on nature cruises. No pets. Cards: AE, MC, VISA. Open April to October.

Getting There: By car, car ferry from Horseshoe Bay, B.C., to Nanaimo, or Anacortes to Sidney, or Seattle or Port Angeles to Victoria; north on 1 and 19 to Parksville, then west on 4 to Port Alberni and then to Ucluelet (177 miles or 285 km from Victoria, 86 miles or 138 km from Parksville). Bus service runs from Port Alberni to Ucluelet. Air charters may be arranged from Victoria, Nanaimo or Vancouver to the Tofino Airport. By boat, *M/V Lady Rose* (mail, passenger and cargo boat) sails, in season, from Port Alberni to Ucluelet. Check for schedules with Alberni Marine Transportation Ltd., P.O. Box 188, Port Alberni, British Columbia.

CLAYOQUOT LODGE
Tofino

The mellowed turn-of-the-century serenity of Clayoquot (pronounced Clack-wot) Lodge is in contrast to its rugged surroundings off Vancouver Island's stormy Pacific shores. Built in 1905, the lodge is situated on its own 140-acre private island. Stubbs Island (originally Clayoquot Island and still named as such on old maps) is in Clayoquot Sound, three-fourths of a mile across the bay from Tofino.

Clayoquot Lodge is on the site of the first white settlement on Vancouver Island's western coastal area, where the British merchant navy had set up a ship's chandlery in 1875 to refit ships carrying on a brisk but hazardous fur trade with the coastal Indians. Sailors found the old trading post, now a barn near the present lodge, a welcome haven after braving the rough seas and the snarling surf (the area's waters are littered with shipwrecks).

Frequently remodeled over the years, the historic lodge retains its air of homey comfort. It's under group ownership now, and is managed by Gordon and Pat Robertson. Gordon sometimes skippers the little launch that transports guests to and from the Tofino dock.

There are eight rooms upstairs in the lodge, one a two-room suite, plus a separate self-contained cottage, charmingly decorated in the style of its period, just a few yards across the lawn from the lodge. With two bedrooms, it can sleep up to six and is equipped for light housekeeping.

The dining room, managed by European-trained John Sandner, offers Continental cuisine with a West Coast flavor.

However strong the temptation to dream and drowse sybaritically by the lounge's crackling fire, the guest who ventures out to explore the spectacular beauty can. stroll the nearby beach with its lupine-covered sand dunes and dense populations of gulls and other seabirds; circumambulate the whole island in two or three hours, along stretches of sandy or surf-pounded rocky beaches, through groves of ancient cedars; take one of the short hikes through a primeval rain forest; charter the lodge's Boston whaler for fishing or exploring nearby shores; play croquet, horseshoes or badminton; admire the well-tended gardens.

Determined indoor people can relax in one of the two sitting rooms on the main floor, conveniently joined by a well-stocked bar and furnished with deep sofas and settees, ample fireplace, books, and a discreet television in a corner.

An old wall clock ticks away behind the bar but no one takes any notice. Time is a state of mind on the island and schedules mean little. Slow-paced relaxation is the lodge's heritage, and that isn't likely to change.

CLAYOQUOT LODGE, P.O. Box 188, Tofino, British Columbia V0R 2Z0. Telephone: (604) 725-3284. Accommodations: twin or double beds; private baths with tub/shower; no telephones; no television. Rates: expensive, transportation to and from Tofino included, no meals included. Open to the public for lunch and dinner (nonresidents should make reservations); full bar service. Children welcome. Pets discouraged. Cards: VISA. Open April to October.

Getting There: By car, take the car ferry from Horseshoe Bay to Nanaimo, or Anacortes to Sidney, or Seattle or Port Angeles to Victoria; drive north on Highway 19 to Parksville, then west on Highway 4 to Tofino (86 miles or 138 km from Parksville). By air, scheduled flights from Vancouver to Tofino. By boat and bus, take the mail boat *Lady Rose,* in season, three times a week from Port Alberni to Ucluelet, then a bus 26 miles from Ucluelet to Tofino; check sailing schedules with Alberni Marine Transportation Ltd., P.O. Box 188, Port Alberni, British Columbia. The lodge's boat meets guests at Tofino Harbor and transports them the short distance across Clayoquot Sound to Stubbs Island (call ahead for pickup). Private boats may tie up at the lodge dock.

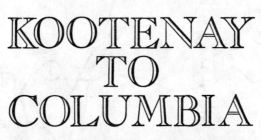

KOOTENAY TO COLUMBIA

The Idaho Panhandle
Eastern British Columbia
Eastern Washington

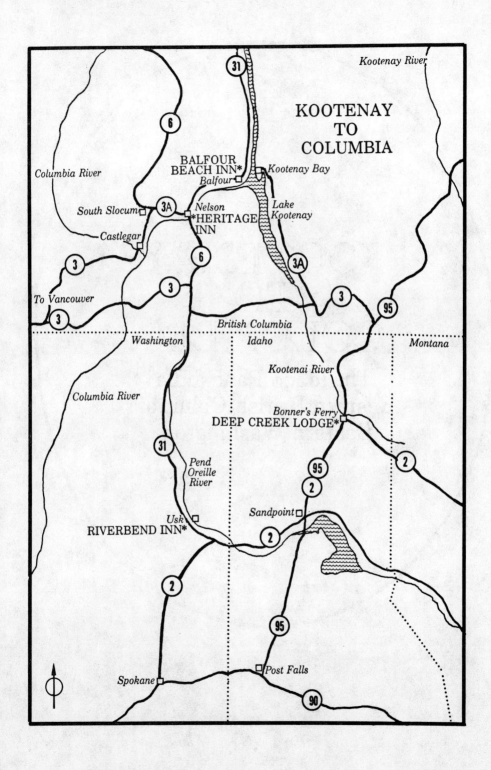

KOOTENAY
TO
COLUMBIA

Kootenay River

31

6

Columbia River

BALFOUR
BEACH INN*
Balfour
Kootenay Bay

South Slocum
3A
Nelson
*HERITAGE
INN
Lake
Kootenay

Castlegar

3

6

3

3A

To Vancouver

3

3

95

British Columbia

Washington   Idaho   Montana

Kootenai River

Columbia River

Bonner's Ferry
DEEP CREEK LODGE*

31

Pend
Oreille
River

95

2

2

Usk
RIVERBEND INN*

Sandpoint

2

2

95

Spokane
Post Falls

90

KOOTENAY TO COLUMBIA

The north Idaho Panhandle, the northeast corner of Washington and the southeast corner of British Columbia do not show on any map as a defined geographic area. But for the tourist and traveler, this rather remote segment of the far West has its own character, a heritage from the rough-and-ready, simpler days of the first settlers.

Three river systems that run back and forth across the U.S.-Canada border—the Columbia, the Pend Oreille and the Kootenai (Kootenay in Canada)—determine the location of the few north-south highways in this area.

A few refuges provide comfort for the traveler along these routes: the Balfour Beach Resort and Heritage Inn in British Columbia, Riverbend in Washington. In Idaho there's Deep Creek Lodge, on the old highway between Sandpoint and Bonner's Ferry.

DEEP CREEK LODGE
Bonner's Ferry, Idaho

Deep Creek's grounds are bisected by the road, which is unfortunate, though there's little traffic. On the east side is the old lodge, looking like the resurrected roadhouse that it is. Half the cabins are on this side, half on the west; all front on the creek. The lawns around the lodge and cabins are beautifully maintained, and shaded by tall pines, cottonwoods and firs. The small heated pool is also on the west side. On *all* sides are forested hills, except the north where Deep Creek flows through a pleasant farming valley toward the Kootenai River. Two railroads run through this valley, and the sound of the occasional freight train is a nostalgic footnote to the pervading sense of yesterday.

Deep Creek Lodge was built in the twenties, as a combination gas station-tavern-restaurant. In the thirties and forties cabins were added. With gambling, slot machines and a dance hall, Deep Creek became one of the most popular roadhouses in this neck of the woods. Today its bar and restaurant are still favorite hangouts for oldtimers of the Kootenai Valley, but the raucous rowdy days are gone. Present managers Dave and Marce Bauermeister (her parents ran the lodge from 1973 to 1979) joined owner Jeanie Leek in 1981. The fare is of the country steakhouse variety, with an occasional treat like fresh-caught trout. A much-admired breakfast item is Alaska Gold—hash browns with cheese and onions.

Most of the thirteen cabin units are housekeeping. Nothing is fancy; cabins have the essentials—table, bureau, rocking chair, two double beds (Beautyrest mattresses). Overflow guests can sleep on cots on the porch.

Fish are rare in the gurgling creek that runs through the resort, but brown and rainbow trout and silver salmon abound in nearby streams and lakes, and sturgeon are often caught in the Kootenai. There's a noted swimming hole down the road near Naples, at Trestle Creek. For winter visitors, there is snowmobiling, and Schweitzer Basin is just thirty miles away. A few miles north, in the broad valley of the Kootenai, is a little-known wildlife refuge, the haunt of herons, ducks and birdwatchers. Lake Pend Oreille with its many recreational offerings is thirty miles to the south.

DEEP CREEK LODGE, Bonner's Ferry, Idaho 83805. Telephone: (208) 267-2373. Accommodations: double beds; private baths with shower; some units with kitchenette; some family units with two rooms; telephones; television. Rates: moderate, no meals included. Open to the public for breakfast, lunch and dinner; full bar service. Children welcome. Small pets welcome. Cards: MC, VISA. Open all year.

Getting There: From Highway 95, from the north, look for sign on the right for turnoff just south of Bonner's Ferry; from the south, the turnoff is just north of Alpine Tavern (about 25 miles north of Sandpoint).

BALFOUR BEACH INN
Balfour, British Columbia

This lakeside enclave may be more of a resort than a country inn, and it is not on a main-traveled road. Nevertheless, travelers and vacationers in southeastern British Columbia will appreciate this stop on the incredibly blue and beautiful Kootenay Lake. Many will want to rent a houseboat for an extended voyage around these lovely waters.

The approach from the south is along the east shore of the lake. This journey culminates in what is touted as the longest free ferry ride in British Columbia (some say the world), a forty-minute cruise from Kootenay Bay to Balfour on the west shore. The other approach, from the west, follows a riverside highway up the West Arm of the lake until it deposits you at Balfour, which consists of not much more than the ferry landing and its commercial adjuncts. Balfour Beach Inn is two minutes north of the landing. It is a sprawling conglomeration of one old lodge, two newish motel-like annexes, one aging marina and a thriving houseboat-rental business. The rooms are what you would expect in a well-maintained country motel; many are housekeeping. The lodge itself, which has been here in one form or another for eighty years, incorporates the original log cabin that was its forerunner. There are two dining rooms. The Dolly Varden Bar, which has been added across the front of the building, has the best view of the lake and is the liveliest spot—especially on weekends when there is entertainment. So lively, in fact, that the management no longer rents rooms in the lodge. (Too noisy.)

But nobody comes here merely to stay inside and eat, drink, sleep, or to swim in the pool. Many come to make this their base for a houseboat trip, which permits exploration of the entire eighty-mile-long lake during the summer. Proprietor Ernie Shauer recommends reserving weeks or months in advance. Lake fishing promises Kokanee salmon, Rocky Mountain whitefish, Kamloops and Dolly Varden trout and ling cod. The lodge will freeze your catch.

There are also boat and motor rental, a little beach for the children, outdoor lounging areas and more sunshine than you would expect in these mountains. That is because the range to the west acts as a barrier to rain-laden clouds.

BALFOUR BEACH INN, Box 5, Balfour, British Columbia V0G 1C0. Telephone: (604) 229-4235. Accommodations: one- and two-room units, double beds, some with kitchenette, some suites; private baths with tub and shower; no telephones; television. Rates: inexpensive to moderate, no meals included. Open to the public for breakfast, lunch and dinner; full bar service. Children welcome. Pets welcome. Cards: MC, Shell, VISA. Open all year.

Getting There: From Vancouver, take Highway 3 to Castlegar (613 km or 381 miles), then 3A to Balfour (78 km or 49 miles). From Spokane, take Interstate 90 to Post Falls, then 95, Washington 1 and B.C. 21 and 3A to Kootenay Bay (314 km or 205 miles from Spokane). Free auto ferry leaves Kootenay Bay for Balfour every hour, 20 hours a day. There is moorage for seaplanes at the inn.

HERITAGE INN
Nelson, British Columbia

Nelson, a lively little city in southeastern British Columbia, has a riverside chockablock with mills and humming factories. It's at a cross-roads of well-traveled tourist and commercial routes, in the heart of some of the province's most spectacular scenery and near popular recreation areas.

Yet a few square blocks of downtown Nelson are so perfectly preserved that you'd swear you were back in the early 1900s when rich, important men were building edifices that would show the world just how rich and important they were. Many of these structures are in the B.C. Registry of Special Heritage Sites. In the midst of this concentration of well-preserved but museumlike architecture is the Heritage Inn, a reconstructed relic that bridges the gap between then and now, while combining the charm of a country inn with the convenience of a city hotel.

In 1898, J. Fred Hume (who founded Nelson) and his brother Horace felt the bustling little mining town on the west arm of Kootenay Lake was ready for a first-class hotel. So they built one—with a hexagonal turret, a variety of rooftop dormered chambers, and wooden balconies so guests could keep on top of the town's doings. The original stones of the lower part of the exterior walls are still there, and so is much of the exterior woodwork: sills, doors, railings of the entry porch.

The restoration, which seems to be geared as much to the wild Old West as to Victorian elegance, is still under way, guided by innkeeper Dave Martin. The coffee shop would make a cowboy feel right at home. The restaurant is the General Store. But the lounge recognizes the importance of higher things and is called the Library. There is another

272

room, well removed from guests' quarters and dedicated to dancing and night life.

Thirty of the rooms have already been renovated. Some of the corner rooms are so generously proportioned as to be almost like suites. Many rooms have fine views of the hotel's neighbors in the historic area, such as the courthouse across Vernon Street, which was designed by the architect of Victoria's Empress Hotel and Parliament buildings. The rooms all have private baths, most with the original deep tubs. All have color television and telephones. Dave Martin plans to renovate thirty-four more rooms as soon as possible.

Nelson is only about an hour, along the scenically rewarding West Arm of the Kootenay, from Balfour Beach and the ferry across Kootenay Lake. (See Balfour Beach Inn entry.)

HERITAGE INN, 422 Vernon Street, Nelson, British Columbia VIL 4E5. Telephone: (604) 352-5331. Accommodations: double and single beds; all rooms with private baths, most with tub and shower, some with tub only; television; telephones. Rates: moderate, no meals included. Open to the public for breakfast, lunch and dinner; full bar service. Children welcome. No pets. Cards: AE, MC, VISA. Open all year.

Getting There: By car, Highway 3 from Vancouver to Castlegar and South Slocum, then 3A to Nelson (420 miles or 676 km from Vancouver); or 23 miles or 34 km from Balfour on Kootenay Lake (see entry for Balfour Beach Inn). By air: Pacific Western to Castlegar.

RIVERBEND INN
Usk, Washington

Riverbend Inn is in a corner of Washington that few tourists know. It is not even on the main highway, so it goes unnoticed by motorists speeding between British Columbia and Washington. But if your travels take you to these parts, it is worth seeking out.

A couple of unused metal barns loom when you turn onto the dirt drive that leads to the inn's plain back-porch entrance, and there's little attempt to pretty up the approach. But when you look to the left you see long lush meadows where half a dozen horses may be grazing and where a small herd of private planes may be tethered. As backdrop, the lazy Pend Oreille River slides around the bend below the inn, with dark wooded hills on the far side.

273

The inn, a big remodeled house, is unpretentious. However, as soon as you step inside and are greeted by your hosts, Harold and Florence Dilling, you will feel you have found a home. The Dillings bought the ranch in 1951, when the house at the bend of the river was already forty years old. The original homesteaders were the three Le Clerc brothers, of whom Napoleon was the most memorable. He was captain of the sternwheeler *Metaline,* which plied the river in the early days of the century. The Le Clercs had a log cabin here before 1900. Then in 1912 a realtor, Walter Merryweather, built the big house, situated to afford a fine view of the river and as much as possible of his 965 acres. Merryweather was succeeded by several other owners who raised beef cattle, grew hay and sold timber. Finally the Dillings bought the place in 1951. They ran it as a beef cattle ranch for six years, then switched to dairy cattle. But by the 1970s the Dillings began to take seriously the many suggestions from admiring neighbors and visitors that they turn the old place into an inn.

In 1974 they began the major job of gutting the entire house, saving as much usable lumber as they could, and rebuilding close to the original style. The result, opening in August 1974 as Merryweather Inn, was a comfortable guest house with seven bedrooms on the second floor, each with its own bath, and a roomy dining room on the ground floor, which also serves as sitting room, lounge and reading room. It has a fireplace and a piano, both much in use. Later the Dillings added a wing to house a game room and a 115-year-old oak bar.

Florence Dilling made all the quilts that perk up the bedrooms, and she usually has a quilt-in-progress on a table in the dining room. She and her husband bought the furniture for the bedrooms at auctions and on antique-hunting expeditions: iron and brass bedsteads, massive carved dressers, washstands with china pitchers, rocking chairs—sturdy old pieces, typical of the periods the house has lived through. Besides the colorful quilts, Florence has placed cheery rag rugs in most of the rooms.

Downstairs in the dining room, the Dillings have permitted themselves to stray from the functionalism of the bedroom decor, with displays of family china, decorative plates, kerosene lamps and Mason jars. There are several small tables, and half a dozen long tables with bright print cloths, where meals are sometimes served family style. The big bay windows look down a grassy field toward the river.

Dinner, served farmers' hours—six to nine at the latest—offers good plain American cooking. Vegetables are fresh off the farm. Desserts (Florence's creations) include fruit pies and a famous Washington Nut Pie. Riverbend offers a few wines, and guests are permitted to bring their own.

Like so many Northwest inns, this one is as much a place to start from or come back to as a place to be, though there are boating and fishing practically in the front yard. A quaint hand-painted map at the entrance gives a good picture of available recreation hereabouts: fishing, hunting, boating, skiing, hiking, golf, camping and snowmobiling. Calispell Lake, southeast of Usk, is sought by bird watchers who come to see bobolinks, veeries, catbirds and ospreys.

RIVERBEND INN, Route 2, Usk, Washington 99180. Telephone: (509) 445-1476. Accommodations: queen, double and one twin, private baths with tub or shower; no telephones; no television. Rates: moderate. Open to the public for breakfast, lunch and dinner; wine and beer only. Children welcome. Pets permitted. Cards: MC, VISA. Open all year.

Getting There: From Spokane, take Highway 2 north for 35 miles, turn off on 211 and proceed to Usk (15 miles). At Usk, take bridge across the Pend Oreille and follow the road on the east side of the river to Riverbend (about five miles). If in doubt, ask for directions at the tavern in Usk. By air, private planes may land at the Riverbend landing strip. Call ahead to arrange to be met by buggy or sleigh.

INDEX

278

BIOGRAPHICAL NOTES

Jacqueline Killeen and Charles Miller collaborate on the restaurant guide, *Best Restaurants of San Francisco and Northern California.* Ms. Killeen, a fourth-generation Californian, is also the author of *101 Nights in California* (a guide) and *101 Secrets of California Chefs* (a cookbook). Miller, also a native Californian, is the author of the travel guide, *Skiing Western America.*

Rachel Bard has a master's degree in history from the University of Washington. A native Washingtonian teacher and free-lance writer, she is also the author of *Squash* (a cookbook); *The Successful Wood Book: How to Choose, Use and Finish Every Kind of Wood;* and *Newswriting Guide: A Handbook for Student Reporters.* Her history, *Navarra: The Durable Kingdom,* is being published by the University of Nevada Press.

Roy Killeen, whose drawings illustrate this book, is an architect, formerly with Anshen and Allen of San Francisco. He also has designed 101 Productions' "Mini-Mansion" series of historical architectural models and illustrated a number of other 101 books.

All of the contributors to *Country Inns of the Far West* share an avid interest in history, food and spending their rare leisure moments in country inns.